Praise for earlier editions of

Hiking South Carolina Trails

"Describes more than 500 miles of trails through wilderness and historic areas along the coast. Includes trail lengths, interconnections, access, degree of difficulty, and campsites."
—*Backpacker* magazine

"Whether you hunt, fish, enjoy birdwatching, photography, or simply communing with nature, *South Carolina Trails* will broaden your horizons."
—*The Herald,* Rock Hill, South Carolina

"Gives explicit detailed information on hiking trails . . . especially for those who wish to camp overnight or enjoy getting into really remote areas. . . ."
—*South Carolina Game & Fish*

"Comprehensive, excellent format, clear, concise . . . a great asset to hikers."
—Donald W. Eng, U.S. Forestry Service, Columbia, South Carolina

"Offers a trail for everyone from beginner to experienced hiker."
—*Living in South Carolina*

Help Us Keep This Guide Up to Date

Every effort has been made by the author and editors to make this guide as accurate and useful as possible. However, many things can change after a guide is published—establishments close, phone numbers change, hiking trails are rerouted, facilities come under new management, etc.

We would love to hear from you concerning your experiences with this guide and how you feel it could be made better and be kept up to date. While we may not be able to respond to all comments and suggestions, we'll take them to heart and we'll also make certain to share them with the author. Please send your comments and suggestions to the following address:

The Globe Pequot Press
Reader Response/Editorial Department
P.O. Box 833
Old Saybrook, CT 06475

Or you may e-mail us at:

editorial@globe-pequot.com

Thanks for your input, and happy travels!

Hiking South Carolina Trails

Fourth Edition

by
Allen de Hart

The
Globe
Pequot
Press

Old Saybrook, Connecticut

To the volunteers who design, construct,
and maintain the trails in South Carolina.

Copyright © 1984, 1989, 1994, 1998 by The Globe Pequot Press

Library of Congress Cataloging-in-Publication Data

De Hart, Allen.
    Hiking South Carolina trails / by Allen de Hart. —4th ed.
        p.   cm.
    Includes indexes.
    ISBN 0–7627–0223–0
    1. Hiking—South Carolina—Guidebooks.   2. Trails—South
    Carolina—Guidebooks.   3. South Carolina—Guidebooks.   I. Title.
GV 199.42.S58D4   1998
796.51'09757—dc21   98–24364
                                                                CIP

Manufactured in the United States of America
Fourth Edition, First Printing

Contents

List of Illustrations vi
List of Maps vii
Acknowledgments viii
Preface xi
Introduction 1

I. NATIONAL FORESTS **11**
  Sumter National Forest **17**
    Section 1. Andrew Pickens Ranger District 17
    Section 2. Long Cane Ranger District 67
    Section 3. Enoree Ranger District 83
  Francis Marion National Forest **93**
    Section 4. Witherbee and Wambaw Ranger Districts 93
II. NATIONAL PARKS, REFUGES, AND U.S. ARMY
  CORPS OF ENGINEERS PROJECTS **117**
    Section 1. National Parks 117
    Section 2. Wildlife Refuges 127
    Section 3. U.S. Army Corps of Engineers Projects 139
III. STATE PARKS, FORESTS, HISTORIC SITES,
  AND WILDLIFE MANAGEMENT AREAS **143**
    Section 1. Upcountry and Mountains 146
    Section 2. Upper Midlands 182
    Section 3. Lower Midlands 196
    Section 4. Lowcountry and Coast 211
    Section 5. Other State Properties 224
IV. COUNTY AND MUNICIPAL TRAILS **237**
    Section 1. Counties 237
    Section 2. Municipalities 245
V. PRIVATE AND COLLEGE TRAILS **283**
    Section 1. Private Trails 283
    Section 2. College Trails 311
VI. THE PALMETTO TRAILS **317**

Appendix 323
General Index 330
Trail Index 335

List of Illustrations

Photos by author unless otherwise indicated.

Page 10: Foothills Trail, Sassafras Mountain Area, from South Carolina Parks, Recreation and Tourism.

Page 16: Pickens Ranger District, Sumter National Forest, by Danny Outlaw.

Page 36: Foothills Trail, Upper Whitewater Falls.

Page 40: Toxaway River Footbridge.

Page 55: Foothills Trail.

Page 66: Edisto River Canoe and Kayak Trail, from South Carolina Parks, Recreation and Tourism.

Page 85: Buncombe Trail, Enoree Ranger District, Sumter National Forest.

Page 96: Swamp Fox Trail boardwalk, near Turkey Creek.

Page 116: Guillard Lake Trail, Francis Marion National Forest.

Page 130: Bull's Island, Cape Romain National Wildlife Refuge.

Page 144: Raven Cliff Falls, Mountain Bridge State Natural Area.

Page 173: Cleveland Cliff from Rim of the Gap Trail.

Page 190: Hickory Knob State Park, by George Lee.

Page 200: Lee State Park, from South Carolina Parks, Recreation and Tourism.

Page 210: Pelicans at Charles Towne State Park.

Page 238: Typical South Carolina Marsh, from South Carolina Parks, Recreation and Tourism.

Page 247: Braille Trail, Hopeland Gardens, Aiken.

Page 264: Reedy River Falls Historic Park, Greenville.

Page 282: Asbury Trail, Asbury Hills United Methodist Camp.

Page 296: Magnolia Gardens.

Page 316: Lake Moultric sunset from Palmetto Trails.

List of Maps

Foothills Trail 49–54, 56–65
Turkey Creek Trail 72–74
Long Cane Trail 80–82
Buncombe Trail 88–90
Swamp Fox Trail 98–105
Jericho Trail 110–13
Kings Mountain Hiking Trail 156–57
Palmetto Trail 320–21

IMPORTANT NOTICE

Map pages for each trail are *numbered* in the order that the trails are described. Please observe the map number on each map page.

DISCLAIMER

The Globe Pequot Press and the author assume no liability for accidents happening to, or injuries sustained by, readers who engage in the activities described in this book.

Acknowledgments

During the research for all the editions of this book, I have depended primarily on assistance from the South Carolina Department of Parks, Recreation and Tourism; the National Forest Service; and the officials in county and municipal government. In addition, I have had counsel from directors and managers of private properties who offer recreational programs to the public.

In the state-park central operations of the Department of Parks, Recreation and Tourism, Joe Watson, chief naturalist, was my major resource person for the first, second, and third editions. Jim Schmid, state trails coordinator, was my chief source of assistance for the fourth edition. Others who assisted in the first two editions were Raymond M. Sisk, former director; John E. Ransom, architect in engineering and planning; Charles Harrison, park operations; Kenneth O. Kolb, assistant director; and Mike Foley, chief historian.

Donald W. Eng, former U.S. Forest Service supervisor, provided essential information in the first and second editions, and William S. Craig, director of recreation, public affairs, and cultural resources, assisted in the second and third editions. In the Sumter National Forest, I received assistance from district rangers Larry Cope, Enoree District, for the first and second editions; R. Joel Gardner, Edgefield District, for the second and third editions; Horace Jarrett, Andrew Pickens District, for the third edition; Michael C. Vinson, Tyger District; and John E. Cathey and supervisory forester Carl Arnold, Long Cane District. In the Francis Marion National Forest, I received assistance from district ranger Carl D. Minehart, Wambaw District, for the first edition, and James Brotherton, district ranger, Witherbee District, for the third edition.

Foothills Trail information was provided by Glenn Hilliard, chairman of the Foothills Trail Conference, and Charles Borawa, supervisor of project recreation, Duke Power Company, for all editions; and Walt Schrader, outdoor recreation activist, and George Kessler, forester of the College of Forest and Recreation at Clemson University, for the first edition.

Those who gave me material assistance for the fourth edition were Ken Diggers and Thomas Dawson of Palmetto Trail; Virginia Hawkins, Foothills Trail Conference; Alice Riddle, Enoree Ranger District, SNF; Russell Davis, Asbury Hills UM Camp; Christopher Revels, Kings Mountain NMP; Tim Ivey, Wildlife Management Section of DNR; Jim Lawracy, City of Columbia Parks and Recreation; Janet Robinson, Magnolia Plantation and Gardens; Dennis Hart, Woods Bay SP; Todd Ward, Barnwell SP; Al James, Landsford Canal SP; Scott Stegenga, Table Rock SP; Kirk Johnson, Rose Hill Plantation SP; P.B. Ellis, Greenville Park and Recreation Service; Tom Jewell, Westvaco; Carol Camp, Sumter and Francis Marion NF Headquarters; George Sawyer, Jr., Kalmia Gardens of Coker College; Henri Watson, Old Santee Canal SP, and Hurley Badders, Pendleton District Commission. Hurley Badders, Scott Stegenga, and Thomas Jewell also assisted in the second edition.

Traveling, hiking, and researching across the state required long days and nights of work. I am grateful for those who gave me food, shelter, and general hospitality. They included Mr. and Mrs. Danny Outlaw, Camden; Mr. and Mrs. Mike Clarey, Greenville; Captain and Mrs. Roger Tucker, Charleston; Mr. and Mrs. David Phillips, West Columbia; and Duncan Hutchinson, Columbia.

Trail assistants from colleges, universities, and hiking clubs were essential in enabling me to measure and describe the trails, to locate places to camp, to meet the officials, and to have shuttle service. For their companionship in both adverse and pleasant weather, in time of fatigue and rest, the following hikers deserve recognition: Jeff Brewer, Bob Brueckner, Kevin Clarey, David Colclough, Debbie Cooper, Steve Cosby, Ginny, Gary, and Robert (Jr.) Dillon, Jan Ewing, Jeff Fleming, Richard Galway, Sammy Gooding, Steve Harris, John Hayes, Tate Hayman, Greg Hippert, Steven Hughes, Dick Hunt, Bob Johnson, Robert Kistler, Lee Little, John

Matthews, Ray Matthews, Walter May, Danny Outlaw, Les Parks, Dennis Parrish, Linda Pressman, Scott Smith, Nile Spiegel, Eric Tang, Ryan Watts, Taylor Watts, Buster White, Darrell Williams, Travis Winn, and Mark and Kevin Zoltek.

Additionally, special gratitude goes to Sally Hill McMillan, who, as former director of The East Woods Press, nurtured and promoted the first edition and gave her strong support to the second edition when The East Woods Press merged with The Globe Pequot Press. Bruce A. Markot of The Globe Pequot Press provided guidance and assistance for the third edition, and Paula Brisco in the fourth edition.

Preface

May the countryside and the gliding valley streams content me . . .
let me love river and woodland.

Virgil, Georgics II

I have been walking and hiking and exploring the trails of South
Carolina since 1943. Each year I learn of new trails with new views
and mystery; and each year I visit some of the old trails that have
familiarity and classic charm. In preparation for updating this edition, a number of trails have been rehiked and new trails have
been measured. Hurricane Hugo destroyed some trails in 1989, and
they are not described in this edition. Major changes in this edition are the increase in trails in the Mountain Bridge State Natural
Area, the extension of the Swamp Fox Trail, and the progress of
the Palmetto Trail.

From the upcountry where editor Jim Clark invited us to "vistas of unforgettable discovery," to the beaches where poet Hervey
Allen described the sound of the sea as being "like a train among
the hills, always passing but never gone," my adventurous expeditions have taken me to the heart of the state's natural beauty and
the hospitality of its people.

Among the state's poplars, pines, and palmettos, I backpacked
and camped in the national forests; walked among historic places
in the Old Walled City of Charleston and Magnolia Gardens; sank
my boots in the swamps of the Congaree, Salkehatchie, and Hell
Hole Bay; fished and hunted in the "Santee-Cooper Country"; rode
horses in Hitchcock Woods; canoed on the Edisto and the Saluda
Rivers; rafted the wild Chattooga River; and bicycled on James Island. To share these many outdoor activities with others has been
an unforgettable experience, and it is the purpose of this guidebook to invite you to share it with us.

When I started serious research in 1980 to update information about the foot trails and to hike each mile of them, I felt like Euell Gibbons stalking wild asparagus in a salt marsh. My most encouraging source of information was the Recreation Division of the Department of Parks, Recreation, and Tourism (PRT) in Columbia, which was then planning a comprehensive study of state trails. Meanwhile, I contacted all county and city recreation departments, chambers of commerce, national forest offices, and a long list of outdoor sports enthusiasts. I followed the obscure Indian trails, fishing trails, old wagon trails, Boy and Girl Scouts trails, and the trails through the woods to Grandma's house.

Two years later it was of great assistance in my double-checking the trails inventory when the *Comprehensive Trail System Study* (of pedestrian, equestrian, bicycle, and ORV trails) was published for PRT by the Carter-Goble Associates, Inc., and Edward Pinckney Associates, Ltd., research teams. The state's primary study neither provided information on whom to contact for specific locations nor gave any trail descriptions; however, a corroborating study, *Trail Opportunities in South Carolina,* gave detailed map locations, addresses, and telephone numbers for about 50 percent of the land trails. (River trails had already been listed in *South Carolina River Trails,* published by PRT in early 1978.)

Introduction

Types of Trails

South Carolina has classified its trails in five categories: pedestrian, equestrian, bicycle, river, and vehicular. They are usually described as scenic, historical, recreational, and nature—the latter emphasizing the flora and fauna. Among a few vehicular trails are the Florence Beauty Trail and the Laurel Hill Wildlife Drive. The Cherokee Foothills Scenic Highway, SC 11, is a 115-mile route of outstanding natural beauty, which also passes by historic and recreational sites. Free information material is available from the South Carolina Council of Governments, P.O. Drawer 6668, Greenville, SC 29606; e-mail, dean@scacog.org; (864) 242–9733. Among the multiple-use hiking and equestrian trails in the national forests are the Long Cane Horse and Hiking Trail (25.1 miles), the Buncombe Trail (27.8 miles), and the Jericho Trail (19.8 miles). The latter also includes hiking and mountain biking. The majority of the 500 miles of equestrian trails are on private property and therefore are not described in this book. For information on stables, ranches, clubs, and equestrian events, consult the South Carolina Horsemen's Council at (803) 734–2349 or 662–6568. A 40-mile motorcycle trail is in the Francis Marion National Forest.

The state already has six major bicycle-touring trails that are routed to include natural and historic areas with stopovers at state or commercial campgrounds. Routings are on designated roads with low traffic volume as much as possible. The north–south Carolina Connector Route (221.6 miles) is from McColl at the North Carolina state line to the Savannah River at the Georgia state line, near Garnett. The route goes through Sumter, Santee, and Branchville. Another route from North Carolina to Georgia is the Coastal Route (227.2 miles). It goes from Cherry Grove Beach on state roads through Conway, Andrews, the Francis Marion National Forest, and Walterboro, and joins the Carolina Connector at Varnville. The other north–south route is the Central Route (169.5 miles), which begins at Kings Mountain State Park and goes through York, Chester, Batesburg, and Aiken to the Georgia state line near Augusta. Among the three mainly east–west routes, the Northern Crescent (334.9 miles) is the longest. Its west trailhead is at Fairplay near I-95 at the Georgia state line and follows the Cherokee Foothills Scenic Highway (SC 11) to Gaffney. From here it goes to Kings Mountain State Park, Rock Hill, and Lancaster, where it follows SC 9 all the way to the coast at Cherry Grove Beach. The Walter Ezell Route (288.8 miles) (named in honor of the leader who promoted the concept of state bicycle routes) is a northwest–southeast route between Keowee Toxaway State Park in the foothills that runs through Clemson, Saluda, Santee, and the Francis Marion National Forest to end at McClellanville. From the Chattooga National Wild and Scenic River near Mountain Rest, the Savannah River Run Route (303.7 miles) generally parallels the course of the Savannah River. It passes through Walhalla, Calhoun Falls, Sumter National Forest, Aiken, Barnwell, Yemassee, and Beaufort and ends at Hunting Island State Park. Bicyclists are subject to highway traffic laws; they must ride on the right side of the road with traffic flow and avoid all controlled-access highways. The state provides a free bicycle-touring guide/map available from PRT and the South Carolina Department of Highways and Public Transportation. It is an essential source, with a list of bicycle clubs, resource addresses, color-coded highway routes, information on distance between road intersections, safety statistics, and a year-round climate chart. Write or call Recreation Division, PRT, 1205 Pendleton St., Columbia, SC 29201, (803) 734–0142; or Traffic Engineering, Department of Highways, P.O. Box 191, Columbia, SC 29202, (803) 737–1052. In addition, it is advisable to request from PRT a free copy of "South Carolina State Parks Camping and Other Facilities." Bicycle trails within the cities are most common in the urban greenways of Anderson, Charleston, Columbia, Florence, Hilton Head Island, and Rock Hill. Bicycling is also popular on the wide beaches of Kiawah Island, Sullivan's Island, and Isle of Palms. County parks with bicycle trails are described in Chapter IV.

For river trails the state has designated segments of the Ashepoo, Black, Congaree and Cooper, Edisto, Enoree, Little Pee Dee, Saluda, Santee and Wambaw, Savannah, and Tyger Rivers for canoeists and boaters. Detailed descriptions and maps of these and seventeen other river trails are in Gene Able's and Jack Horan's *Paddling South Carolina: A Guide to Palmetto State River Trails,* Sandlapper Publishing, 1281 Amedia St. (P.O. Box 730), Orangeburg, SC 25116, (803) 531–1658. Also, the Walterboro-Colleton Chamber of Commerce, 213 Jefferies Boulevard, Walterboro, SC 29488, (843) 549–9595, has a free map of the 56-mile Edisto River Canoe and Kayak Trail. A wild, untamed river with abundant wildlife, it is reported to be the "world's longest free flowing blackwater stream."

Some of the land trails are in need of maintenance; others are manicured like formal gardens. They may be of asphalt, cement, gravel, sawdust, wood chips, pine straw, board, sand, or combinations. Some are eroded dirt, but most are of natural duff. Bridges are just as varied: relocated rocks, logs, steel, laminated or creosoted wood. The longest trail bridge is the nearly 200-foot suspension bridge at the Toxaway River/Lake Jocassee access. The longest trail is the Foothills Trail (85.2 miles); by 2000 the longest will be the Palmetto Trail.

How to Use the Book

Hiking trails are grouped in sections in six chapters: national forests; national parks, refuges, and U.S. Corps of Engineers projects; state parks, forests, historic sites, and wildlife management areas; county and municipal parks; private and college trails; and the Palmetto Trail. Because the majority of the trails are in the national forests and the state parks, an introduction opens those chapters. For each recreational area the name of the county is provided in parentheses to give you highway map orientation. At the end of each area description, but before the trails found in it, I have listed an address and telephone number for additional information. You will also find resource information in the appendix for government agencies, citizens' groups, trail suppliers, and a trail and general index. On the first line of each trail description is its length, level of difficulty, topographic map, and main trailhead.

Abbreviations

To save space and minimize repetition, the following (and similar) abbreviations are often used.

N, S, E, W, NE, SW, etc. (north, south, east, west, northeast, southwest, etc.)

PRT (South Carolina Parks, Recreation and Tourism)

NFS (National Forest Service)

NPS (National Parks System)

FR (National Forest road)

USGS (United States Geological Survey)

I-26 (Interstate 26)

US 301 (United States highway 301)

SC 6 (South Carolina primary highway 6)

SR 857 (South Carolina secondary road 857)

mi (mile, miles)

km (kilometers)

yd (yards)

ft (feet)

in (inches)

jct (junction or intersection)

svc (service)

rec (recreation)

hq (headquarters)

fac (facilities)

Maps

Trail guidelines are overlaid on U.S. Geological Survey (USGS) contoured topographic maps for the state's longest trails in areas where backpacking and camping are more likely. To conserve book space, they have been reduced. Because it is impossible to include a map for every trail, many of which are short, the descriptions provide sufficient detail for you to locate the trailhead with a state or county map.

Following each trail heading is the standard USGS map title. It is a quadrangle map survey bounded by parallels of latitude and meridians of longitude covering 7.5 minutes at a scale of 1:24,000 (1 inch = 2,000 feet). You can purchase these maps from a dealer in the state (see Appendix) or order them from the Branch of Distribution, U.S. Geological Survey, Box 25286, Federal Center, Denver, CO 80225; (888) 627–3325. As you must pay in advance for these maps, you may wish to request (free of charge) an Index Map of South Carolina and a price list. Expect to wait two to four weeks for delivery. Topographical maps can be exceptionally useful, with a compass, in unfamiliar mountain and swamp backcountry.

A state-highway map is free from the Silas N. Pearman Bldg., Room 536, 955 Park St., Columbia, SC 29202, or write to S.C. Dept. of Highways, P.O. Box 191, Columbia, SC 29202. From this address you can order county, city, outline, and traffic-flow maps. State-park maps are available (free) at the state parks, or you can write to PRT, 1205 Pendleton St., P.O. Box 113, Columbia, SC 29202; (800) 872–6277. Maps of national forests are available (free) from the Public Affairs Office, U.S. Forest Service, 4931 River Rd., Columbia, SC 29210; (803) 561–4000; and from ranger district offices. The NFS also has more detailed maps (for a small fee), such as the "Chattooga National Wild and Scenic River," and the "Trail Guide" from the Andrew Pickens Ranger District, Sumter National Forest. For catalogs of nautical charts and intracoastal waterway routes, write to Distribution Division (C-44), National Ocean Survey, Riverdale, MD 20840. For maps of the Santee-Cooper, Lake Marion, and Lake Moultrie area, write to Santee-Cooper Country, P.O. Box 12, Santee, SC 29142. For maps of Lake Moultrie, Lake Marion, and Cooper River, write to S.C. Public Service Authority, Project Land Division, Santee-Cooper, 223 North Live Oak Dr., Moncks Corner, SC 29461. For Lake Murray information contact Lake Murray Rec Association, P.O. Box 67, Silverstreet, SC 29145.

Contact Duke Power Company, Corporate Communications Dept., P.O. Box 33189, Charlotte, NC 28242, for information on Jocassee, Keowee, and Waterlee Lakes. Request maps for Lake Hartwell and Thurmond Lake from Savannah Engineer District, Public Affairs Office, U.S. Army Corps of Engineers, P.O. Box 889, Savannah, GA 31402.

Trail Length, Time, and Difficulty

Each trail was measured with a Rolatape model 400 measuring wheel, known to my students as the "clicker," "unicycle," "wheel barrow," "walking wheel," "running cane," "wheel of fortune," and "weed catcher." I have measured the trails to within the nearest 0.1 mile. If you hike one way on a trail, and use a vehicle shuttle at the other end, only the mileage (*mi*) is given in the **Length** section following every trail name. If *round-trip* follows *mi,* it means that you will need to backtrack, use a road, or hike farther once you have completed the basic trail in order to return to your starting point. If a trail has *mi,* one or more and *combined,* it means that the trail connects with other trails for a combined length.

No hiking time is listed, because walks on a trail vary. Saunterers may stop to consult a wildflower book. Photographers may be using stealth, and athletes may be jogging for a soccer team. The average hiker with a backpack could plan for 2 miles per hour on gradual contours. With a day pack and flat land, a hiker could easily average 3 miles per hour.

I have rated trails *easy, moderate,* and *strenuous* for difficulty. This is based on an average, healthy hiker, not a toddler or ridge runner. *Easy* means that you can hike the trail without fatigue or exertion, as on the Edisto Nature Trail. *Moderate* means that you may tire from the exertion and take an occasional rest. An example is the Buncombe Trail. *Strenuous* trails have steep or longer climbs, necessitating more frequent or longer rest stops, as on the Pinnacle Mountain Trail.

Animal and Plant Life

Space limitations make description of geological formations and plant and animal life impossible for every trail, but noteworthy details are included. For the best wildlife observation, leave your dog at home and go early in the morning or late in the afternoon to known watering holes. I have listed where and when you may see waterfowl and animals. Some plants are listed with both genus and species, which indicates the plant is rare, infrequent, or easily confused with a similar species. Oaks are often listed in the plural because a variety of species is present.

South Carolina has more pines than palmetto *(Sabal palmetto),* the state tree, so it is fitting that writers have accorded the pines more attention. Dr. Archibald H. Rutledge, naturalist, sportsman, and the state's first poet laureate, wrote about the pines as "parish pinelands sweet and old," or "splendor-coronetted pine" and about forest that "glimmers mystic, mute—veiled enchantress" in *Deep River* (The R.L. Bryan Company). Paul Hamilton Hayne in "Voice of the Pines" and "Aspects of the Pines" saw them as tall, "with dark green tresses," solemn, somber, tranquil, and luminous; and Henry Timrod, a lifelong friend of Hayne, wrote about the pines in *Ethnogenesis,* a moving reaction to the First Southern Congress at Montgomery in 1861: "And in our stiffened sinews we shall blend the strength of pine and palm!" Of the ten pine species in the state, the loblolly *(Pinus taeda)* and the short leaf *(Pinus echinata)* are the most common.

The following books are recommended as botanical and zoological references: *Manual of the Vascular Flora of the Carolinas* by Albert Radford, Harry E. Ahles, and C. Ritchie Bell (University of North Carolina Press); *Wild Flowers in South Carolina,* by Wade T. Batson (University of South Carolina Press); *Birds of the Carolinas,* by Eloise F. Potter, James F. Parnell, and Robert P. Teulings (University of North Carolina Press); *Amphibians and Reptiles of the Carolinas and Virginia,* by Bernard Martof, William Palmer, Joseph R. Bailey, Julian Harrison III, and Jack Dermid (University of North

Carolina Press); and *South Carolina Mammals* by Frank B. Golley (Charleston Museum).

Support Facilities and Information

The excellent camping areas in the state include thirty-three state parks and more than sixty-five commercial campgrounds. For trails where camping is not allowed, I have listed the nearest (or most desirable) campground under **Support Facilities.**

A good book for the walker or hiker is *The Complete Walker* by Colin Fletcher (Knopf, Inc.); and for campground locations *Woodall's Campground Directory,* published annually by Simon and Schuster, is helpful.

For information about hiking supplies, visit a trail shop (some addresses are in the Appendix) and subscribe to a hiking magazine such as *Backpacker,* Rodale Press, Inc., 33 East Minor St., Emmaus, PA 18098, (800) 666–3434 or (610) 967–5171.

Health and Safety

Concern for health and safety is always important on the trails. Fatalities and injury are most frequently the result of poor or risky judgment. Hypothermia, caused by the lowering of body heat, can be fatal even in temperatures of up to 45 or 50 degrees Fahrenheit. Sweaty or wet clothes are a common cause of hypothermia, and the victim often is not able to detect the problem. If someone shivers uncontrollably or speaks incoherently, take immediate action to warm the person.

Drowning, falling, and misuse of firearms are other dangers. Deaths from poisonous snakes or electrical storms are rare, but watch where you walk, and do not lean against trees in storms. It has been said that, to stay safe in the woods, you must "use your head first, and if things go wrong, remember to keep it."

Be sure to carry a first-aid kit. Carry pure drinking water. If this is not practical, purchase a dependable water filter from a sports store. Although springs, wells, and running streams are listed, this does not mean that any of them are safe for drinking. Use only

8

water that is designated as safe by a sign or brochure in national, state, and other parks and forests. *Wilderness Survival,* by Bernard Shanks (Universe Publishers), is a good source of health and safety information.

Time to Go Hiking

We "never know when an adventure is going to happen," Christopher Morley told us, and John Burroughs advised us to "take the path you took yesterday to find new things." Whether you walk or hike for adventure or discovery, you'll find that walking is "true magic, a psychological alchemy," "a muscular symphony," an aid to digestion, and a preventive to circulatory and respiratory disorders, as various authorities have claimed. It can transform the body and the mind. Sierra Club member Patricia Bagwell said that hiking allowed her to hear herself think. Many years ago Fiona Macleod wrote in *Where the Forest Murmurs* that nature was so beautiful and complex "that the imagination is stilled into an aching hush." Brad Ketchum, editor-in-chief of *The Walking Magazine,* wrote in 1993 that walking is a physical act and a metaphor. As a metaphor, "walking is synonymous with challenge, triumph, introspection, perspective, and enrichment."

Trails are like life—always changing, always offering surprises or new challenges. They are also like friends—there when you need their comfort and solace from the stresses of life. You will find many trails in this book that give you a sense of peace, of kinship with nature, and of belonging to nature. I have described their locations and some of their secrets, but other secrets and inspiration await your visit. From the rugged and wild Chattooga River Gorge to the smooth sands of the Atlantic Ocean, there is a trail for everyone: long backpacking trails, short nature trails, urban greenway trails. They are yours, ready to be explored and enjoyed.

Welcome to the trails of South Carolina.

Chapter I
National Forests

There comes a quiet to the wood,
As if it uttered solitude.
Archibald Rutledge,
"In a Forest," *Deep River*

South Carolina has two national forests, the Sumter and the Francis Marion. Both were established in 1936 and named after South Carolina heroes of the Revolutionary War. Sumter, with 360,386 acres, has five districts: Andrew Pickens, Edgefield, Long Cane, Enoree, and Tyger. Francis Marion, with 251,703 acres, has two districts, Wambaw and Witherbee. The national forests represent 3 percent of the state's land area. They are part of a 191-million-acre National Forest system in 44 states and are administered by the National Forest Service, an agency of the U.S. Department of Agriculture.

At one time all 612,089 acres of national forest in the state were privately owned. Almost all had been heavily timbered, and sections had been wasted from erosion and poor agricultural practices. Wildlife had disappeared or been severely reduced in these once magnificent forests and rich soils. As a result, state and local governments petitioned Congress to purchase land to support the sagging economy in the 1930s.

Congress directed that the forests be managed so that the five renewable forest resources—water, timber, forage, wildlife, and recreation—would be controlled for the maximum benefit and multiple use of the public. Multiple use objectives vary from district to district, depending on needs for timber harvesting, reforestation, recreational facilities, and wildlife habitats.

Each national forest is required to develop and follow a forest-management plan—the Land and Resources Management Plan (usually called the Forest Plan). The Forest Plan is a product of forest personnel recommendations and public requests in planning and updating projects every 10 years. In addition, the Environmental Impact Statement (EIS) has to be prepared in detail.

During the 1990s some of the management projects have been designed to allow natural processes to continue in the five wilderness areas; to inspect, repair, or replace bridges, including trail bridges; to maintain and rehabilitate existing facilities and trail mileage; and to have archaeologists survey approximately 13,000 acres to locate, evaluate, and protect significant prehistoric and historic sites.

The Forest Plan also requires the protection of selected wildlife species, such as the red-cockaded woodpecker and the swallow-tailed kite. Many streams, lakes, and former borrow-pits are managed to produce trout, bass, bream, and catfish. All of these forest projects are in the Wildlife Management Area program and are managed cooperatively with the South Carolina Department of Natural Resources (DNR). Sensitive plant species are protected, in an agreement between the Nature Conservancy and the NFS, by identification and management plans.

In 1992 visitors spent nearly a million visitor days using the resources of the Francis Marion and Sumter National Forests. (A visitor day is any combination of uses that totals 12 hours.) Estimates based on registration forms, traffic counts, and rangers' reports show a wide range of activities. Visitor days totaled more than 219,800 for those who enjoyed "just riding around"; hunting, 208,700; fishing, 52,200; canoeing and motor boating, 70,900; tenting and camping, 193,300; hiking, 41,900; and berry picking and wood cutting, 18,800. There were more than 150,000 visitor days for other categories such as picnicking, motor boating, rafting, kayaking, horseback riding, swimming, and water skiing.

Assistance in maintaining the trails and other recreational projects had been the work of the Youth Conservation Corps (YCC) and the Young Adults Conservation Corps (YACC) until the 1980s, when the budgets were almost totally cut. Since that time Senior Community Service Employment Program (SCSEP) crews have expanded and, together with volunteers, assist in a number of project areas. One of those projects has been that of locating, surveying, and protecting prehistoric and historic sites on 120,000 acres.

Timber management is a major responsibility of the National Forest Service, but private timber companies contract and harvest the timber for the National Forest Service because the National Forest Service does not have harvesting equipment. Private contractors pay about $7 million in revenue annually for the timber they harvest. Following the harvest, the National Forest Service reforests by planting, seeding, or using natural methods. Where does the revenue go from the timber sales? The law requires that 25 percent of the funds collected go to the counties in which there is national forest in lieu of taxes to help pay for public schools and roads. A portion is retained to ensure reforestation, and the rest goes to the U.S. Treasury. A staff of about 215 manage the state's national forests.

Before you go hiking and camping in the national forests, know the following guidelines from the National Forest Service:

1. Most of the developed recreation areas are open from late spring to early fall, and a few are open all year. Trails are open all year. Contact the appropriate ranger district to be sure of open dates.

2. Off-road vehicles (ORVs) and all-terrain vehicles (ATVs) are not allowed on hiking and horse trails. However, they are allowed on most forest roads unless posted otherwise. Traffic laws in the forests are the same as elsewhere in the state. Trailers and other RVs are permitted, and electric hook-ups are available at Buck Hall Recreation Area in the Wambaw Ranger District near McClellanville.

3. Primitive camping is allowed only at designated campsites, and permits are required for camping elsewhere. Hikers may select their own sites within the Chattooga Wild and Scenic River corridor and the Ellicott Rock Wilderness, providing the site is at least 0.25 mi from a road and 50 ft from a stream. Free per-

mits are available from ranger district offices and will usually be issued unless conflicts are anticipated.

4. Permits are not needed for campfires, but care should be used for fire prevention and only "dead and down wood" should be used.
5. Hunting and fishing in the forests require state licenses. Hunting on Sundays is prohibited. Hikers are advised to avoid the first few days of hunting season—during either-sex deer hunts—and to wear bright clothing when using the forests during big-game hunting season. Seasons change slightly each year. Their dates are announced in a publication by the South Carolina Department of Natural Resources that is available wherever licenses are sold.
6. "Pack it in—pack it out" is basic forest courtesy.
7. Be considerate. All of us have equal rights to the forest. If you see a violation of forest, local, state, or federal law, report it.
8. Park vehicles so they do not block gates, roads, or parking areas.
9. Numerous tracts of private land dot the forests like a crazy quilt. Avoid trespass; ask permission.
10. Horses are allowed on some of the multiple-use trails. Tie horses away from campsites to avoid damage to camp-area vegetation.
11. Protect water supplies from contamination.
12. Do not climb the waterfalls. The dangers are obvious.
13. Vandalism has increased, so lock your car and hide valuables.
14. Request free brochures and maps from the supervisor's or district offices, or purchase one of the detailed "Forest Visitor Maps."

Francis Marion and Sumter include segments of all the state's major areas of topography and natural resources, from the mountains to the seacoast, and they offer extraordinary opportunities for recreation. There are more than 400 campsites; more than 150 picnic sites; wilderness, scenic, and swimming areas; thousands of acres of lakes and miles of streams; and more than 186 mi of hiking trails. In addition, there are 88 mi of multiple-use horse and hiking trails, 82 mi of motorcycle trails, 202 mi of mountain bike trails, and 129 mi of canoe trails.

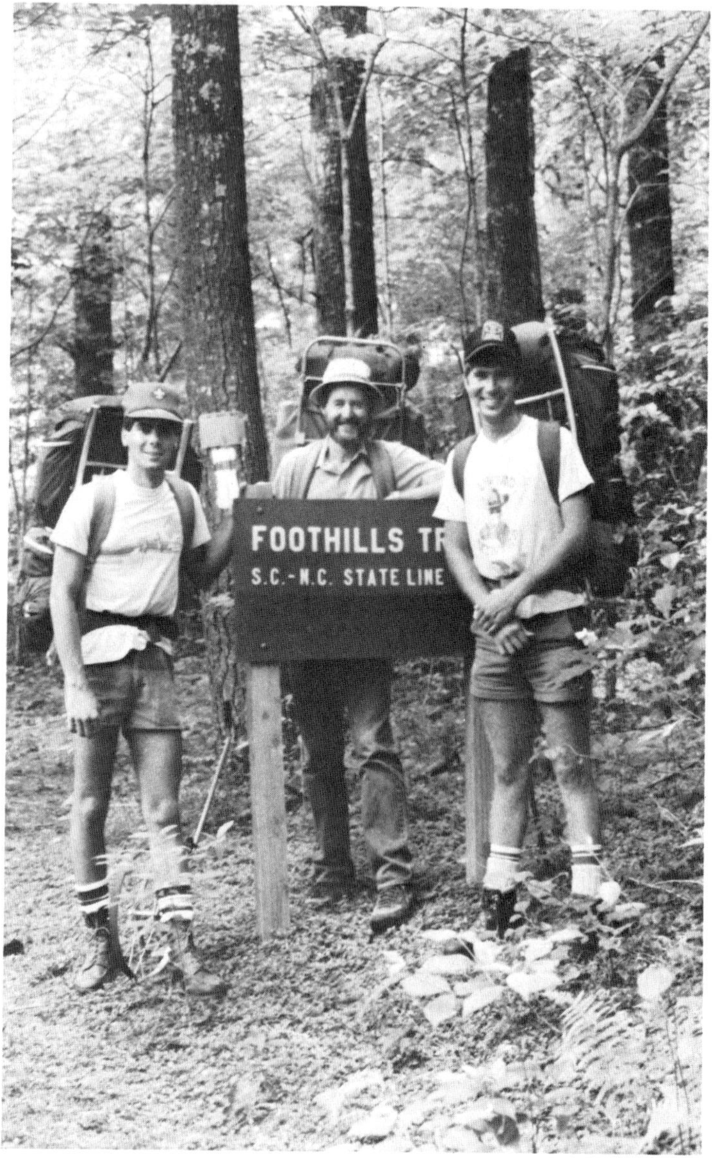
FOOTHILLS TR
S.C.-N.C. STATE LINE

Sumter National Forest

SECTION 1
Andrew Pickens Ranger District
(Oconee County)

The Andrew Pickens Ranger District, "gateway to the mountains," with 78,220 acres, is the only mountainous part of Sumter National Forest. Elevations range from 800 to 3,400 ft. Its W boundary is the Chattooga Wild and Scenic River corridor, the state line with Georgia. At the NW corner of its boundary with North Carolina is the Ellicott Rock Wilderness Area, and NE is scenic, 7,656-acre Lake Jocassee. Federal and private lands are interspersed.

There are 15 dispersed camping sites in the district, four with camping facilities: Burrells Ford on FR 708 near the Chattooga River; Woodall Shoals on FR 757, south of US 76 near Long Creek, with primitive campsites (no water or tables); Cassidy Bridge Hunt Camp on SR 290 (available for group reservations year-round, except during big-game season in the fall); and Cherry Hill on SC 107, with a campground for trailers and tents (but no hook-ups). Most NFS facilities close in November for the winter, but visitors may use the year-round camping facilities, including hook-ups, at Oconee State Park on SC 107. Primitive camping is allowed in the Ellicott Rock Wilderness or Chattooga River corridor anywhere that is more than 0.25 mi from the road and 50 ft from a trail, stream, or river. Other campsites in the general forest area require a permit from the district ranger. Camping is popular in the district because of fishing on the Chattooga River and on 16.7 mi of approach or main trails. The scenic slopes, gorges, and mountaintops are both a mental and physical challenge to hikers.

Picnicking areas are at Burrells Ford on FR 708 near the Chattooga River; Burrells Place on SC 107; Chattooga at the Walhalla Fish Hatchery W of SC 107; Cherry Hill Campground on SC 107; Moody Springs on SC 107 near Cherry Hill; Rose Bud on SC 107;

Sloan Bridge on SC 107; and Yellow Branch on SC 28 near the ranger station. Wildlife in the district is mainly deer, wild turkey, quail, grouse, rabbit, squirrel, raccoon, fox, and beaver. Brown and rainbow trout are N of the SC 28 bridge over the Chattooga River, and redeye bass are more plentiful S of SC 28.

Probably no place in the district is more popular with hikers or river floaters than the Chattooga River. This powerful, wild, blue-green river foaming with white turbulence drops nearly 2,500 ft in less than 50 mi (40 of which are in South Carolina). It was designated a "Wild and Scenic River" by Congress in 1974, and strict regulations protect canoeists, kayakers, and rafters. If you plan a river trip with your hiking trip, know the safety regulations posted on bulletin boards and on the back of permits. You may contact one of the five commercial rafting services licensed by the USFS, listed in the Appendix, or the district ranger office listed at the end of this section.

The district has 13 trails, the shortest a round trip of 0.4 mi from the Chattooga River Information Station to Bull Sluice. The longest is the **Foothills Trail** (25 mi), which stretches from Oconee State Park to the North Carolina state line. Although the trail winds through several other parks that are covered in this book, it is described in this chapter in its entirety. Other district trail descriptions follow. For a small fee you can buy the district trail guide, a folding map with trail directions and forest facilities information.

(An additional trail that equestrians will enjoy is the recently developed, 12.5-mi **Rocky Gap Trail,** which begins in South Carolina and connects with the 15-mi **Willis Knob Trail** in Georgia. The two wind across deeply dissected ridges and descend to ford the Chattooga Wild and Scenic River at Adline Branch, Moss Mill, and Big Island. Because these trails cross a number of secondary roads, trips can be planned for diverse distances. In Georgia camping facilities are at Willis Knob Horse Camp off Gold-mine Road, 11.6 mi E of Clayton on Warwoman Road. Riders in South Carolina may camp at Whetstone Road Base Camp near the

Chattooga River. For access from Walhalla, drive N on SC 28 for 7 mi to Whetstone Road. After the pavement ends it is about 0.6 mi to the camp. Reservations for both camps must be made at least 10 days in advance. In Georgia contact the Tallulah Ranger District Office at (706) 782–3320. For South Carolina see the information below. Both district offices will also provide detailed information on fees, regulations, and primitive campsites, as well as trail use guidelines and trail route maps.)

Information: District Ranger, Andrew Pickens Ranger District, 112 Andrew Pickens Circle, Mountain Rest, SC 29664; (864) 638–9568.

Access: The office is on SC 28, 6 mi NW of Walhalla and 10 mi E of the Chattooga River.

Bartram Trail

Length: 6.9 mi (11 km); **easy;** USGS Maps: Satolah, Tamassee; trailhead: jct of SC 107 and FR 710.

The "unofficial" **Bartram Trail** in South Carolina overlaps the **Chattooga Trail** and the **Foothills Trail,** which are described elsewhere in this chapter. However, William Bartram and his travels are of great significance. Perhaps the following information will stimulate new interest in extending the South Carolina portion of the **Bartram Trail.**

William Bartram (1739–1823) of Philadelphia was the son of John Bartram (1699–1777), the first Native American botanist to receive international recognition for botanical research. William, who often traveled with his father, became renowned as a naturalist and writer, and his *Travels* (1791) greatly influenced English Romanticism. His explorations in the SE states included at least 14 counties in South Carolina; it is known that he traveled through Anderson, Pickens, and Oconee Counties, but his route mainly covered valleys now covered by Hartwell Reservoir and Lake Keowee.

Former district ranger Joseph Wallace told me that the Bartram Trail "officially ends on the Georgia side of the Chattooga River." In the mid-1970s there was talk of extending the trail into the

Sumter National Forest to "an unknown location east of the Oconee State Park." In preparation for that extension, the district used the **Chattooga Trail** and **Foothills Trail** routes from the Chattooga River at SC 28 to SC 107 for 6.9 mi (13 mi if to the Oconee State Park).

"We were never informed of the proposed turning-off point in our district," Wallace said. "We were told that the Department of the Interior was going to study the feasibility of locating the Bartram Trail in this area, but that department never gave us any recommendation."

In September 1975 parties interested in the "Bartram Trail in South Carolina" met in Greenwood and discussed 10 major localities, most of which were along the Savannah River basin and the Lake Keowee area. Their report stated that the trail across Sumter "from Oconee Station to the Georgia line was agreed upon." It was further stated that much of the "desirability" and "feasibility" would be "handled by local garden clubs and historic societies in a county by county study."

At present 75 mi of the **Bartram Trail** are in Georgia, 37.6 mi are on the S border of Thurmond Lake (formerly Clarks Hill Lake), and 37.4 mi run from the Chattooga River through the Chattahoochee National Forest to the North Carolina state line, where more than 70 mi extend through the Nantahala National Forest.

For information about the **Bartram Trail** in North Carolina, read *North Carolina Hiking Trails,* by Allen de Hart (Appalachian Mountain Club Publishers, 5 Joy St., Boston, MA 02108). Also, there are maps and trail descriptions from the North Carolina Bartram Trail Society, P.O. Box 144, Scaly Mountain, NC 28775; (828) 526–4904.

Chattooga Trail (Sumter Section)

Length: 16.7 mi (26.7 km); **moderate;** USGS Maps: Cashiers, Tamassee, Satolah; trailhead: Russell Bridge, SC 28.

The total length of the **Chattooga Trail** is 36.9 mi, 20.2 mi of it in Georgia's Chattahoochee National Forest, and 16.7 mi in

Sumter National Forest (4.3 mi are within the Ellicott Rock Wilderness Area). The Chattahoochee section has termini at the US 76 bridge and the SC 28 bridge. The Sumter section has termini at the SC 28 bridge and other trails in the Nantahala National Forest in North Carolina.

From SC 28 at the parking area E of Russell Bridge, the trail headed upriver. The black-blazed **Chattooga Trail** and yellow-blazed **Bartram Trail** markers led on a gradual slope through white pines. The trail is well designed and graded. At 0.4 mi it crossed a stream and wove in and out of coves. A rocky stream was at 0.7 mi. Wildflowers were prominent. In the spring maidenhair ferns mix with wild geraniums, Indian cucumber root, trillium, and showy orchids. At 0.8 mi and at 1 mi, I crossed streams in coves; at 1.8 mi the trail was on a slope, and I heard the continuous sound of the river.

The trail curved around Reed Mountain and came to an old roadbed at 3 mi. Gradually descending, it approached the riverside and followed the river on the roadbed. At 3.4 mi it crossed Ira Branch, an area good for camping. Yellow root, galax, and pink lady's slippers grew along the trail, and hemlocks, a haven for songbirds, reached silently into the sky. At 4.3 mi I saw a steep slope on the L, where Lick Log Creek fell with a roar into the Chattooga, and another Lick Log waterfall was ahead on the R. At 4.6 mi I reached the **Foothills Trail** jct.

I followed the black-blazed **Chattooga Trail** and the white-blazed **Foothills Trail** over a ridge and down to the Chattooga River again at 6.7 mi. At 9.1 mi was the 40-ft cascading Big Bend Falls. In a picturesque cove at 9.9 mi, the rust-blazed **Big Bend Trail** turned R for 2.7 mi to SC 107. At 12.3 mi was the jct with an 0.2-mi spur trail up to 80-ft King Creek Falls. I reached the Burrells Ford parking area at 12.3 mi.

With some Sierra Club friends I hiked from the parking area on the **Chattooga Trail** to Ellicott Rock. We passed the **Foothills Trail** jct at 12.9 mi and entered the Ellicott Rock Wilderness Area. We curved L at the headwaters of Spoon Auger Falls at 13.3 mi and descended gently to an old roadbed with ferns at 14 mi. (A rust-blazed spur trail here is L to Spoon Auger Falls for 0.3 mi, and it is a total of 0.8 mi out to FR 708 at Burrells Fork Bridge.)

Continuing upriver, we reached a jct with an old wagon road and, at 14.6 mi, we encountered sandy beaches by the river. A log footbridge with a cable crossed East Fork Creek; the **East Fork Trail** jct was at 15 mi. (The **East Fork Trail** gradually ascends for 2.4 mi to the Walhalla National Fish Hatchery and an exit to SC 107. See the section on the **East Fork Trail** later in this chapter.)

From this point we passed through a white pine stand. At 15.5 mi we saw what is claimed to be the state's champion white mountain camellia (*Stewartia ovata*). As two members of our team were bird-watchers, three were fishermen, and another was a wildlife photographer, the Chattooga Trail was providing something of interest for all. At 15.6 mi the trail crossed Bad Creek, hugging the river as it stayed on a generally even contour upriver. At 16.4 mi on the R is the state-champion rosebay rhododendron (*Rhododendron maximum*), more than 2 ft in circumference and 40 ft tall.

At 16.7 mi we reached Ellicott Rock. In 1811, when this was still Cherokee country, Andrew Ellicott surveyed and chiseled a marker NC to designate the tri-state corner of the Carolinas and Georgia. A few feet before reaching Ellicott Rock is the true tri-state intersection: Commissioners Rock, another chiseled marker on a rock that extends into the river. It bears the inscription LAT 35 AD 1813 NC-SC.

Upstream 0.1 mi into North Carolina is a campsite area and a jct L, with the 3.5-mile **Ellicott Rock Trail** that fords the river and ascends to FR 1178 at Ammonds Branch. To the R is the 3.1-mi **Bad Creek Trail,** which ascends to SR 1100, 2.6 mi W of NC 107. On the **Bad Creek Trail,** after 1.2 mi, is the jct R with the 6.4-mi **Fork Mountain Trail,** described later in this chapter. (This trail is also described in Chapter II in *North Carolina Hiking Trails*.)

Cherry Hill Recreation Area

The Cherry Hill Recreation Area includes the Cherry Hill Campground, which has camping sites (but no hook-ups) for RVs and tents, picnic tables and grills, flush toilets, hot showers, drinking water, and sewage disposal. It is an excellent base point for short hikes, and it has a connecting trail to the long **Chattooga Trail.** The campground is usually open from May 1 through October.

Access: On SC 107, 5.8 mi N from Oconee State Park, and 7.5 mi N from the SC 107 jct with SC 28.

Cherry Hill Nature Trail

Length: 0.5 mi round-trip (0.8 km); **easy;** USGS Map: Tamassee; trailhead: Cherry Hill Campground.

We followed the trail signs at the far end of the campground through a thicket of rosebay rhododendron and New York ferns, crossed West Fork Creek on a footbridge, entered a stand of buckberry, and passed under large white pines. We recrossed West Fork Creek at 0.3 mi and returned to the point of origin.

Big Bend Trail

Length: 2.7 mi (4.3 km); **easy;** USGS Map: Tamassee; trailhead: on SC 107 near Cherry Hill jct.

From the jct of SC 107 and Cherry Hill Campground, we went S on SC 107 for a few yards to a rust-blazed trail entrance on the R. The trail descended in a hardwood forest to a crossing of Cane Creek in a forest of rhododendron, hemlock, and oaks at 0.1 mi. Ferns and galax grew along the stream. For the next 0.6 mi, the trail paralleled the S side of Big Bend Road. At 1.2 mi the trail curved around the headwaters of Pig Pen Branch in a mixed forest and ascended to a jct with a spur trail, R, to Big Bend Road at 1.6 mi. From here the trail descended gradually to the E side of a stream with rhododendron and followed the stream to a jct with the **Foothills Trail.** We backtracked, but we could have hiked R on the **Foothills Trail** for 2.5 mi to Burrells Ford parking area for a vehicle shuttle.

Winding Stairs Trail

Length: 3.4 mi (5.4 km); **easy** to **moderate;** USGS Map: Tamassee; trailhead: corner of SC 107 and Cherry Hill Campground entrance.

We followed the rust-colored blaze through buckberry and blueberry in an oak forest. It was fall, and the red oaks were reddish brown, and the white oaks were golden. After crossing a smooth ridge, Taylor Watts, Les Parks, and I descended to a trail jct at 0.2 mi. (The trail to the L goes to the Cherry Hill Campground.) We turned R, following cascading West Fork Creek. Autumn colors were spectacular—ochre, orange, scarlet, and yellow in a generally open hardwood forest. There was a sharp L at 0.9 mi at a jct in the old roadbed. On the L at 1.2 mi was the hypnotic sound of a gentle but high waterfall in a beautiful spot that would be a good campsite. We crossed trickling streams at 1.3 mi and 1.7 mi on a pleasant, wide old roadbed and rushing streams at 2.1 mi and 2.4 mi. At the 2.1-mi stream, many wildflowers bloom in the spring. At 2.4 mi Carolina lily and phlox grow. We heard cascading Comers Creek on the R at 2.8 mi. We surprised a wild hog in a wallow as much as he surprised us. After his fast disappearance we saw evidence of others in the area. Sheets of mica glistened along the old road as we approached an embankment and a stream; at 3 mi we were surrounded by fetterbush, papaw, sweet pepperbush, and ferns. At this point we began to hear West Fork Creek again. We reached FR 710, Tamassee Road, at 3.4 mi. Our shuttle vehicle was there with Kevin Clarey and Dick Hunt. "What's that on your cap?" Kevin asked Taylor. Taylor had two hairy, yellow-and-brown orb-weaving spiders starting a new web on the bill of his cap.

Ellicott Rock Wilderness Area

There are 7,012 acres in the Ellicott Rock Wilderness Area. One section lies in the NW corner of the state, in the Sumter National Forest; another in the NE corner of Georgia, in the Chattahoochee

National Forest; and a third in the Nantahala National Forest, in North Carolina. Falling through this marvelous preserve is the rugged Chattooga Wild and Scenic River. This wilderness area received its name from Andrew Ellicott, a famous land surveyor who completed the boundary between Georgia and North Carolina in 1811. (See **Chattooga Trail** earlier in this chapter). The **Foothills Trail** follows the S edge of the wilderness boundary; the **King Creek Falls Trail, Spoon Auger Trail,** and part of the **Chattooga Trail** are near the Chattooga River. The **East Fork Trail** is completely in the wilderness area, and the **Fork Mountain Trail** is about 80 percent inside the boundary. Although there are no developed campgrounds in the wilderness area, campgrounds and picnic areas are on SC 107, near the E boundary. The Walhalla National Fish Hatchery is also at the boundary. The nearest stores for groceries and gasoline are in Cashiers, North Carolina, 8 mi N on SC 107.

East Fork Trail

Length: 4.8 mi round-trip (7.7 km); **easy;** USGS Map: Tamassee; trailhead: Walhalla National Fish Hatchery parking lot.

From SC 107 (3.4 mi S from the state line), we drove down the Fish Hatchery Road for 1.8 mi to the parking lot. After viewing the fish hatchery, which is open daily from 8:00 A.M. to 4:00 P.M., we saw the state-champion Eastern white pine (*Pinus strobus*) in the picnic area (more than 29 in in circumference and 170 ft tall). Also in the picnic area is the state-champion mountain winterberry (*Ilex montana*), 1 ft in circumference and 28 ft tall. The national-champion sweet pepperbush (*Clethra acuminata*) is also here. It is 11 in around and is also called white alder or cinnamon *Clethra.* Near the fish hatchery is another in the "big tree" league, the Eastern hemlock (*Tsuga canadensis*) with a 12-ft, 10-in circumference and a 141-ft height. And 0.2 mi above the fish hatchery trail is the national co-champ, the beautiful mountain laurel (*Kalmia latifolia*), growing 28 ft tall and 4 ft in circumference.

We began the **East Fork Trail** on the R loop route through a tunnel of rhododendron and under tall hemlocks in the picnic area. We crossed East Fork on a bridge and continued R at a jct of the loop at 0.3 mi. We descended on an old wagon road and crossed a stream cascading from the R, with cement stepping-stones for crossing at 1 mi. Hemlock, maple, oak, and hickory were prominent at 1.3 mi and rhododendron at 1.6 mi. The jct with the **Chattooga Trail** by the Chattooga River was in a stand of white pines at 2.4 mi. To the L it is 2.7 mi to Burrells Ford parking area, and to the R it is 1.7 mi to Ellicott Rock.

(Backtrack, make a loop downriver, or use a shuttle for connecting trails upriver. If downriver, go 1.2 mi to jct with the **Foothills Trail** on L, and go 3.2 mi to Fish Hatchery Road. There, turn L and hike down the Fish Hatchery Road for 1.7 mi for a total of 9.4 mi. If upriver, follow the **Chattooga Trail** for 1.7 mi to Ellicott Rock jct at the state line. Here you have a choice of taking the 3.5-mi **Ellicott Rock Trail** out to Nantahala National Forest road 441F and 1178 to SR 1100 and SC 107 for the shuttle, or from Ellicott Rock taking E route on **Bad Creek Trail** for 3.1 mi to SR 1100 and SC 107 for shuttle. For another potential loop, see **Fork Mountain Trail** below.)

Fork Mountain Trail

Length: 6.4 mi (10.2 km); **easy** to **moderate;** USGS Map: Cashiers; trailhead: Sloan Bridge Picnic Area parking lot on SC 107.

This is a well-graded trail that weaves in and out of more than 20 coves. Robert Ballance and I began at the picnic parking area and hiked N 0.1 mi on SC 107 to cross the East Fork of the Chattooga River bridge, then turned L into the forest at a trail sign. We followed a rust blaze upstream of the Slatten Branch in an outstanding virgin grove of rhododendron and laurel and crossed the branch at 0.7 mi.

After entering an open hardwood forest, we crossed a ridge at 1.2 mi. At 2.5 mi we crossed Indian Camp Branch and beyond entered a grove of large hemlocks before passing through a fern glen. We entered an arbor of laurel at 2.8 mi. Crossing a ridge at 3.4 mi, we noticed large yellow poplar and hemlock (near the N.C./S.C. state line) en route to the dual forks of Bad Creek at 5 mi and 5.2 mi. Wildflowers, such as pink lady's slippers, grow along the trail.

At 6.4 mi we made a jct with the **Bad Creek Trail.** (A loop can be made here by descending on the **Bad Creek Trail** L, steeply, for 1.2 mi to the **Chattooga Trail** at the Chattooga River. The **Chattooga Trail** jct with the **Foothills Trail** is 3.8 mi downstream.)

King Creek Falls Trail

Length: 1.2 mi round trip, combined (1.9 km); **easy;** USGS Map: Tamassee; trailhead: Burrells Ford parking area.

From SC 107 and FR 708, start your hike at the trailhead in Burrells Ford parking area. We followed the Chattooga River Trail S for 0.4 mi to the jct with this trail. Here we turned L on the rust-blazed trail for 0.2 mi to see the 80-ft King Creek Falls. The area has large hemlocks and white pines as well as dense rhododendrons. Backtrack.

Spoon Auger Trail

Length: 1.2 mi round-trip (1.9 km); **easy;** USGS Map: Tamassee; trailhead: Burrells Ford bridge.

From SC 107 jct with FR 708, Burrells Ford Road, take FR 708 for 2.7 mi to the parking area on L. To approach this 0.1-mi trail, walk down FR 708 for 0.3 mi to trail entrance on R. Follow the rust blaze to signs explaining the Ellicott Rock Wilderness Area, cross Spoon Auger Creek, and turn R at 0.2 mi for an 0.1-mi section of switchbacks to the scenic falls. There are massive hemlocks in the gorge. Backtrack.

(A loop can be made by continuing upriver, where there is evidence of beavers, to the jct with the **Chattooga Trail** at 0.6 mi. Turn R and follow the **Chattooga Trail** back to the parking area after a 2.5-mi round trip. Outstanding views of large hemlock and white pine are on this route.)

Other Pickens District Trails

Bull Sluice Trail

Length: 0.4 mi round-trip (0.6 km); **easy;** USGS Map: Rainy Mtn; trailhead: Chattooga River Information Station.

The trail begins at the parking area on the E side of the US 76 Chattooga River bridge. The shortest trail in the district, this 0.2-mi walk to Bull Sluice is also the trail from which you can see the best white-water action. At the information station are large interpretive displays about the river and the general area, regulations, and other information. Follow the signs on a paved area through a forest of white pine, black gum, hemlock, and by a bank of galax to the outcroppings at Bull Sluice. The rapids are rated Class 5.

Tamassee Knob Trail

Length: 4.2 mi round-trip (6.7 km); **easy;** USGS Map: Walhalla; trailhead: Oconee State Park.

From the FOOTHILLS TRAIL sign in Oconee State Park (see Oconee State Park in Chapter III), we followed the trail for 0.4 mi to a jct. The **Foothills Trail** forked L with white blazes, and the **Tamassee Knob Trail** forked R with rust blazes. Fall colors were excellent in a mature hardwood forest on this well-maintained trail. At 0.7 mi we entered an old wagon road into the Andrew Pickens Ranger District of the Sumter National Forest. Mountain laurel and rhododendron were prominent among locust and oak at 1.2 mi. At 1.3 mi we crossed a ridge to the SE side, where huge dogwood and redbud grew. In the springtime wildflowers are prevalent on the slopes. Some of the Solomon's seal were bending over with bright red berries and golden leaves. We began a climb at 1.7 mi, reached a crest for a view of Tamassee Creek Valley, and at a large rock saw a sign painted on an oak, END, at 2.1 mi.

Yellow Branch Nature Trail

Length: 0.5 mi (0.8 km); **easy;** USGS Map: Whetstone; trailhead: SC 107 entrance.

Yellow Branch Picnic Area off SC 28, 0.3 mi SE of the Andrew Pickens Ranger District hq, or 6 mi NW of Walhalla. Near the picnic-area entrance, we followed the trail sign and descended through a large hardwood forest with mountain laurel and rhododendron understory. We crossed a stream at 0.3 mi and passed beds of galax and trailing arbutus by a cascading stream. Ascending, we passed large hemlocks and loblolly pines. On reaching the paved road, we turned R to the point of origin.

Foothills Trail

Length: 85.2 mi (136.3 km); **easy** to **strenuous;** USGS Maps: Tamassee, Satolah, Cashiers, Reid, Eastatoe, Table Rock, Cleveland, Standingstone Mountain; W trailhead: Oconee State Park; E trailhead: Table Rock State Park, or former Jones Gap State Park.

The **Foothills Trail** is interstate (South Carolina and North Carolina); it is intercounty (Oconee, Pickens, and Greenville in South Carolina and Jackson and Transylvania in North Carolina); it is intrastate park (Oconee, Table Rock, and former Caesars Head and Jones Gap State Parks in Mountain Bridge State Natural Area); it was designed and constructed in South Carolina from private sources (Duke Power Company); it is the first trail about which an entire guidebook has been written (by the Foothills Trail Conference); it is the most spectacular in variety of topography, flora and fauna, water sources, and natural beauty (Chattooga River, Upper Whitewater Falls, Lake Jocassee, Toxaway River, Laurel Fork, Sassafras Mountain, Drawbar Cliffs, Raven Cliff Falls, and Middle Saluda River Gorge); and it is the most potentially adaptable for inclusion in a network of other mountain trails (in the Mountain Bridge State Natural Area, Horsepasture River Gorge, Eastatoe Creek Gorge, and the Pisgah and Nantahala National Forests).

The idea for an upstate mountain trail developed in the 1960s. Discussions between the NFS, the Sierra Club, PRT, Clemson University Recreation and Parks Administration Department, and Duke Power Company led to planning and eventual construction. When Duke Power Company decided to build a trail of more than 40 mi to satisfy its recreation plan ("Exhibit R") in fulfillment of the government requirements for the Bad Creek pumped-storage project, funds, dreams, and hard work came together to create a scenic ribbon through the former Cherokee Nation lands (which the Cherokee called "The Blue Hills of God"). The trail passes through rugged back country and offers sufficient hiking space to once and for all silence the allegation that "South Carolina doesn't have any trails."

Although "it is entirely Duke's responsibility to maintain" the trail section it built, either "by itself or through cooperation with the Foothills Trail Conference or others," volunteer help is encouraged, according to Charles Borawa, supervisor of Duke's Project Recreation. "We are working with the Foothills Trail Conference to assign groups to maintain segments of the trail."

For additional information, order the *Guide to the Foothills Trail,* published by the Foothills Trail Conference, Inc., P.O. Box 3041, Greenville, SC 29602; (864) 467–9537; or contact Charles Borawa, Senior Lake Management Representative, Duke Power Company, P.O. Box 1006, Charlotte, NC 28201–1016; (800) 443–5193, option #5, or (828) 382–1567. (Because I had hiked the entire trail before the guide was published, the directions and descriptions that follow were created without its materials, maps, or manuscripts for guidance. It is coincidental that the conference describes the trail from the former Caesars Head and Table Rock State Parks to Oconee State Park, while I describe it from the opposite direction and find them equally exciting. The Duke Power Company map is color-coded to show which sections of the trail are in Sumter National Forest, company property, and the state parks.

From Oconee State Park to SC 107 (6.1 mi)
From Oconee State Park Campground, my Chattooga River whitewater friends took Lee Little and me on the cottage road to the FOOTHILLS TRAIL sign. At 0.4 mi we faced a jct R with the rust-blazed Tamassee Trail. We turned L and followed the white-blazed FOOTHILLS TRAIL sign through a mature forest, intercepting a few ravines with wildflowers and galax on a well-designed approach to

the boundary of the Andrew Pickens Ranger District of the Thomas Sumter National Forest at 1.2 mi. We soon entered an open area with hardwood saplings, red cedar, birdfoot violets, and huckleberry patches. (A sign here read BARTRAM TRAIL, but that trail's E terminus remains in the planning stage.) Reentering the main forest, we skirted the E side of Long Mountain (2,080 ft), gradually ascending and curving around the ravines. At 2 mi a trail signpost pointed to Oconee State Park, Long Mountain Lookout Tower, the **Foothills Trail,** and **Bartram Trail.** We took the spur of 0.1 mi to the firetower. We could see the mountains in Georgia and North Carolina as the early sun cast shadows over the Chattooga gorge. It was a May sky as blue as October, calling to mind Byron's description—"deeply blue, as someone somewhere sings about the sky."

Continuing ahead, we crossed an old road bed at 2.2 mi, then a small bridge over a stream where galax spotted the banks. Ahead was a timbered area with scrub pine. Reforestation had begun, but 0.2 mi of sunny open space is a haven for huckleberry, loosestrife, and bristly locust. At 2.8 mi we entered a tall pine forest and descended into a rosebay rhododendron thicket near a stream on the L. Beyond this was our surprise of the morning. Thousands of trillium covered the hillsides, many forming a display with fern crozier, fresh and wet green.

We crossed two small streams among white pines and mature hardwood, fetterbush, running cedar, and pink lady slippers (*Cypripedium acaule*) at 3.5 mi, then veered L on a gentle ascent beside cascading Tamassee Creek at 3.7 mi. After leaving the low areas we ascended gradually. For the next 1 mi we saw evidence of the 1973 tornado and the April 7, 1978, Jumping Branch fire, which roared across SC 107, and destroyed more than 2,800 acres of the forest. In the open spots left by the fire grew gardens of bristly locust, thick patches of bracken, and scattered crested dwarf iris. A good view of Long Mountain firetower was at 4.2 mi. At 4.7 mi we reached SC 107, where a member of Lee's rafting team picked him up, and I hiked alone to Burrells Ford Campground.

Continuing E of the highway, I passed a tributary of Tamassee

Creek on the incline to Dodge Mountain (2,380 ft). Skirting the E slope, I had excellent views at 5.6 mi. Flame azaleas were scattered in a mixed forest. At Tamassee Road, FR 710, was the first yellow blaze for the **Bartram Trail.** (See Chapter 1, Section 1.) I turned L on the graveled road and at 6.1 mi reached SC 107. (To the L on SC 107, it is 3.6 mi to the entrance of Oconee State Park.)

From SC 107 to Burrells Ford (10.4 mi)

The trail continued across SC 107, entered a mature forest, and gradually descended. A cascading stream was on the L; buckberry was abundant, with rosebay rhododendron in spots. The trail entered a stand of large white pine and at 7.5 mi crossed a cul-de-sac of a fire road. Again it entered a stand of white pine where the duff was thick and soft. Log footbridges crossed Lick Log Creek banks and Pig Pen Creek; the remnants of a primitive cabin were on the L. At 8.4 mi I reached a jct with the **Chattooga Trail.** (From here on the L it is 4.5 mi to SC 28, though the sign has 3.7 mi. To the R it is 8.1 mi to Burrells Ford Road.)

I turned R and, shouldering my backpack, ascended to a ridge crest at 9 mi. Soon I turned L on an old wagon road and descended, but I turned R from the road after 0.2 mi. I could hear the distant roar of the Chattooga River. Towering above were magnificent oaks, maple, and white pine, with buckberry and galax covering the earth. Scattered sourwood sought what sunlight it could find, like Kahlil Gibran's "slender reed and oak tree, side by side striving upward." At 10.5 mi I was on the E bank of the Chattooga, refreshed by its mist. Soon the trail was on a flat terrain providing excellent camping spots near the river. I went out on a spur trail to photograph the river. Upstream was a fishing party who invited me to share their noonday meal, prepared over an open fire. "We would have fish if we had caught enough," said Ricky Baumgarner. Out on a broad shaft of granite was Will John Rogers, catching small- to medium-size rainbow trout. "I don't know how he is so lucky," Terry Simmons said. "It's his first time up here fishing . . . look at that smile on his face." They were all from the Walhalla

Merchants Softball Team—Will John, Ricky, Ricky Pate, John Thompson, Robert Cowan, Tim Gillespie, Jess Neville, and Terry, the coach and manager. "It's peaceful here, only natural sounds," Terry said.

Continuing ahead, the trail ascended from and descended to the river occasionally on the sandbars or rocky, sometimes slippery, borders. Rivulets trickled down from the slopes and switchbacks cut through the *maximum* and *minus* pink rhododendron. The trail curved around Round Top Mountain to 12.9 mi, where Big Bend Falls thundered over a 40-ft cascade before dropping in a 12-ft powerful hydraulic. The trail is about 100 vertical ft above the falls. Rocks and roots are usually slippery here.

At 13.7 mi is a jct with the rust-blazed **Big Bend Trail.** (From here on this trail it is 2.7 mi to Cherry Hill Campground; **Big Bend Trail** also connects with Big Bend Road, FR 709, from SC 107.) A footbridge crossed a stream with a flume on the L. After 0.2 mi I reached the river and hiked 175 ft on the river rocks. Yellow root, crested dwarf iris, and fetterbush grew near some excellent spots for a campsite. An exceptionally fine view was at 14.4 mi, with waterfalls, sandbars, and huge rock formations. From here I ascended on switchbacks; some parts of the trail were steep and narrow—steep enough to prevent a motorcyclist, who had damaged the trail here, from going farther. I ascended on an old wagon road at 15.3 mi and, 0.3 mi farther, reached a jct veering R off the old road. (Straight ahead is Burrells Ford Campground.) At 16.1 mi I crossed a creosote and rail bridge over cascading King Creek. (On the R is a rust-blazed trail for 0.2 mi to the 80-ft King Creek Falls. To the L is the old wagon road to Burrells Ford walk-in campground.) The **Chattooga Trail** and the **Foothills Trail** go straight ahead after a turn from the wagon road, R. I ascended on a gradual incline to the Burrells Ford parking area at 16.5 mi.

From Burrells Ford to Walhalla Fish Hatchery Road (3.8 mi)

On the second day I was joined by my white-water–river companions, Steve Harris, Steve Cosby, Robert Kistler, and Eric Tang. We were to hike the **Foothills Trail** to Sloan Bridge and shuttle back to complete the **Chattooga Trail** to Ellicott Rock and return on the East Fork Trail to the Walhalla National Fish Hatchery. This way we retained our campsite at Burrells Ford Campground for the second night.

From the parking area at Burrells Ford, we crossed the graveled FR 708, ascended to a stand of exceptionally tall hemlocks, and crossed a creek with cascades at 16.8 mi. We crossed a rocky area in a dense section of rhododendron at 16.9 mi and reached the fork of the two trails at 17.1 mi. (The Chattooga forked L, 3.8 mi to Ellicott Rock.) We forked R on the **Foothills Trail** and ascended gradually on a wide ridge through mountain laurel. Undulating, we curved SE and NW on slopes to switchbacks at 19 mi. Ascending in tall hardwoods, we saw flame azaleas rising from the understory like large orange forest lanterns. At 19.3 mi we reached the ridge crest of Medlin Mountain along the boundary of the Ellicott Rock Wilderness area and began to descend gradually on the slope at 19.7 mi. At 20.3 mi we reached the parking area at the Walhalla Fish Hatchery Road.

From Walhalla Fish Hatchery Road to Sloan Bridge, SC 107 (3.3 mi)

Across the road, the trail entered a hardwood forest, ascending through rosebay rhododendron. At 20.9 mi we crossed a stream, the first of more than a dozen in the next 3 mi, and noticed disturbed earth, probably from an old homestead. At 21.5 mi we crossed a large rocky area with moss and lichens before reaching a small cascade on the R at 21.9 mi. Switchbacks in rhododendron and mountain-laurel thickets, then a stand of hemlocks, were followed by a power line at 22.8 mi. At 22.9 mi the trail went around a huge rock, where we were sprinkled with spray from a waterfall. At 23.1 mi on the L was the East Fork of the Chattooga River, which we followed to Sloan Bridge Picnic Area and the jct with the **Fork Mountain Trail,** L, at 23.6 mi. (A shuttle took us back to Burrells Ford to complete the Chattooga Trail. See **Chattooga**

Trail, East Fork Trail, and **Fork Mountain Trail** elsewhere in this chapter.)

From Sloan Bridge, SC 107, to Whitewater River Bridge, NC 281 (3.9 mi)

The next day our white-water team had to return home, and replacing them were Ray Matthews and Sammy Gooding. We continued on the Foothills Trail from the Sloan Bridge Picnic Area on SC 107 (0.5 mi N on SC 107 is the state line, and 8 mi farther is Cashiers, North Carolina), gently ascending the slope of Chattooga Ridge to 25 mi at the state line. Here we left Sumter National Forest and entered the Nantahala National Forest.

At 25.3 mi we began a switchback, reached a ridge crest for partial views of Lake Jocassee, and started a decline into coves on the E slope. At 25.7 mi the trail descended steeply, then ascended near large rocks on the L. The gap between Grassy Knob and Round Mountain was at 26.1 mi, with banks of ferns, rhododendron, buckberry, fly poison, and trillium. At 26.3 mi we entered an old roadbed, turned R, and crossed a small stream. On the R in a dense area of evergreens was a tributary of Whitewater River. At 27.3 mi the trail turned sharply R (ahead on the old road it is 100 yd to a campsite) and ascended to NC 281 (SC 130 in South Carolina) at 27.5 mi. (About 1 mi S on NC 281 and over the South Carolina border is the entrance to Bad Creek Visitor's Center, where **Coon Branch Spur Trail** offers scenic views of Whitewater River Gorge.)

From NC 281 to Horsepasture River (12.7 mi)

We crossed the paved road, climbed over the guard rail, and descended on a N slope by Whitewater River. The trail passed the "Big Tongue," a rock formation on the R in a road bordered with fragrant rhododendron and wild hydrangea. At 28 mi was the overlook for the Upper Falls of Whitewater River, which cascades more than 400 ft (some descriptions have from 400 to 600 ft) into the gorge. (To the R is an 0.2-mi paved trail to a paved parking area and excellent views of Lake Jocassee.)

After the first 100 steps (in a series of 400) down into the gorge, there was another superb view of the falls. A series of steps and steep treadway led to the river with huge boulders at 28.5 mi. We crossed the rapids by rock hopping and wading. (Now there is a footbridge.)

Safely across the river, we crossed Corbin Creek on a hemlock footbridge. Extremely tall hemlocks stood in this area; yellow root and fetterbush grew in clusters on the forest floor. It was "shady depths," like those described by John Muir, "where subdued light makes a perpetual morning." We joined an old wagon road and left it at 28.9 mi. We reentered South Carolina at 29 mi, leaving the Nantahala National Forest. A series of wooden steps, the first of thousands installed by Duke Power Company on the trail, began 0.2 mi after the state line. (Each step is 4 in x 6 in x 18 in, with a 24-in rebar.) After the steps and stairs, we came to a generally level area. At 30.1 mi we reached a trail jct R to the **Lower Whitewater Falls Overlook Spur Trail,** by the Whitewater River. Here we met Carolyn and Jesse Hartley and their three children, Pam, Andrea, and Tiffany, from Greenville.

(Ray and Sammy had explored the cable bridges at the river, and I joined them on the blue-blazed trail on the W side of the river for a round trip of 2.3 mi. We followed a spur trail downstream to a graveled road at 0.1 mi and then 0.4 mi farther to view the Lower Falls of the Whitewater River. This area can be extremely slippery and dangerous when wet.)

Back on the main trail and heading E, we entered a mature hardwood forest with scattered pines. At 30.3 mi we reached a ridge crest and ascended gradually, crossing a dirt road at a R angle at 30.5 mi.

A series of footbridges over ravines followed in an open oak and hickory forest; red clay showed in a sparse understory. At 31 mi we reached a gap, crossed over, and descended through a fern patch to an old wagon road, steep in parts. The trail followed an old roadbed on the S slope of the mountain. We left the road at 31.4 mi and began a steep ascent to the North Carolina state line.

A ridge crest, rhododendron thicket, two streams, and timbered area followed, but we reentered the forest after a few yards. At 31.8 mi we turned R at a locked gate, crossed a small stream, and followed a road R, into the forest, crossing a ridge and a small stream. An old road took us through mixed forest into the Thompson River gorge. At 32.8 mi we reached the exceptionally scenic Thompson River and crossed on a well-designed footbridge. (Rocky sections here on the trail require caution in wet or icy weather.)

From here we ascended through rhododendron, holly, and oaks to a ridge, reached a jeep road, turned R and continued to ascend. At 33.4 mi we reached another ridge, turned on the crest, and followed a slope.

After crossing a rivulet and passing a rocky face on the L, we changed to the L side of the ridge and reached a timber road gate of the Crescent Land and Timber Corporation at 34.3 mi. After another gated road at 35 mi came a hardwood forest with an understory of mountain laurel, small hemlocks, locust, and dogwood. Cascades were audible on the R.

A footbridge crossed over a ravine, followed by two log bridges and an ascent to a ridge at 36.1 mi. From here we followed an old wagon road, but we left it to descend on a section of 100 steps. At 36.4 mi we reached Bearcamp Creek. After crossing the creek **Hilliard Falls Spur Trail,** a 0.7-mi spur route, is L to the waterfalls and pool. Farther on we crossed the creek again to a primitive campsite.

Back on the trail, for the next 0.7 mi we could hear Bearcamp Creek on the R, but we turned sharply and ascended to cross a ridge. An old roadbed took us along an S slope. We climbed steep steps (unnecessary had the trail been graded) and descended on more steps. At 39 mi large boulders were on the R. At an old road jct on a ridge, we turned L, reached another old road jct, and turned R to continue the descent.

At 39.5 mi we turned off the road on a steep climb L, crossing two footbridges over ravines. We crossed a ridge and followed an S slope. (At 39.9 mi is another example of unnecessary steps, where a graded trail would have been better for backpackers.) At 40.2 mi we crossed a 50-ft suspension bridge over the scenic Horsepasture River Gorge. The edge of Lake Jocassee was on the R. The beautiful view was made possible by Duke Power Company engineering skill. (For boat shuttle to this and other points mentioned for Lake Jocassee accesses, contact Hoyett's Tackle Store in Salem, SC 29676; 864–944–9016.)

From Horsepasture River to Toxaway River (6.7 mi)

We crossed a small stream heavily shaded by rhododendron and bordered with fetterbush, turned R on an old road, descended, then ascended to a ridge. More horse tracks. "They must bring in these horses with helicopters," we speculated. At 41.1 mi we turned R on a ridge road, then turned L from the road, crossed an old road, and reached a much-used dirt road at 41.5 mi. Here was a fork road jct; the trail followed the second gated road on the L. We crossed Bear Creek on an excellent steel-bolted, 30-ft bridge at 41.6 mi, reaching a hemlock forest, a good place to camp. After ascending to a plateau, we met two backpackers, Mark Looper and Chuck Posey, from Easley. "We are going as far as our food lasts," Mark told us.

By now the sun had burned off the heavy fog and was shining against a bank, a good place to dry out our tent from the previous night's rain. After drying out we were on a ridge when we met two more backpackers—Tommy and Debbie Byers from Clover.

At 43.6 mi we crossed Cobb Creek in a rhododendron thicket near beds of Oconee bells (*Shortia galacifolia*), an evergreen with small white flowers. It grows only in a few mountain counties. We passed a landslide at 43.7 mi in a forest of pine and mountain laurel. From here we ascended on a ridge and for the next 2.5 mi undulated, following and crisscrossing old logging roads and crossing small streams SE of Grindstone Mountain. One stream was at 45.2 mi, where rhododendron, galax, and Oconee bells were abundant. Continuing the descent, at some points steep, we turned R at 46.4 mi, crossed another small stream, and reached the edge of beauti-

ful Lake Jocassee at 46.9 mi. This is Cane Break, a boat access to the trail and a campsite.

From Cane Break, Toxaway River, to Laurel Fork Creek (5.8 mi)

Thunder shook the mountains, and dark angry clouds moved in swiftly from the NW. Rain poured on us as we made a steep climb in the final approach to the spectacular view at the bridge. The rain made the rhododendron and Oconee bells shine as if they had been waxed. As sheets of rain fell, we crossed the extraordinary 200-ft suspension footbridge, which some say is the longest bridge of its type in the East. The bridge was designed and built by Duke Power Company. Across the bridge the rain suddenly stopped, the storm passed, and the sun came out. A campsite near the lake is allowed by the Crescent Land and Timber Corporation if you stay at least 1,000 ft from the shore.

We entered a hemlock stand with good views of the lake on the R. At 48 mi the trail went straight up the mountainside on more than 250 wooden steps. Some of these steps are too high for an ordinary hiker with a full backpack, and climbing them requires the exertion and patience of a Sisyphus. Almost at the top was a welcome "resting bench." At 48.1 mi we reached the ridge, followed it to a sharp turn L on a switchback, and descended to Rock Creek at 48.7 mi. We found a campsite under the hemlocks, sweetgum, and white pines, by a cascade. We walked downstream and took a swim in the lake.

The next day we followed the trail for 0.1 mi along the lakeside. Near the return to the South Carolina state line, we began ascending on switchbacks at 49.1 mi. Rhododendron, beech, and hemlock were the major foliage on the mountainside. Galax was profuse. On an eroded red-clay road, the trail was steep. After a short plateau the trail ascended again, finally reaching a ridge crest at 49.6 mi. It took erratic turns, and the blazes were easy to miss. We hiked through patches of bristly locust, gold star, trailing arbutus, wild hydrangea, and calicroot (*Aletris farinosa*). At 50.7 mi we exited from a gated road, turned R, followed a more recently used road to another gated road, and turned L at 51.6 mi. The roadside had large banks of blooming blackberry bushes, a feast for summer hikers. We changed roads, R, at 52.2 mi. A cascading stream was audible on the L. At 52.7 mi a spur trail came in from the R; it led to a Lake Jocassee access.

From Laurel Fork Creek to US 178 (8.4 mi)
The trail follows an old road, wide enough in its construction to have once been a public road. (A spur trail up a hill at 53 mi leads to an excellent view of Lake Jocassee.) The sound and views of Laurel Fork Creek Falls were impressive at 53.1 mi. At 53.2 mi a suspension bridge across Laurel Fork Creek led to an ideal campsite, with evidence of former buildings in the area.

After leaving Laurel Fork Creek, the trail ambled from one side of the road and the stream to the other for 3 mi. Logging had altered the natural beauty in the area. Permanent bridges make it unnecessary to rock-hop. Forests of hemlock, white pine, oaks, and poplar included some virgin stands of hemlock. In addition to acres of rhododendron, there were borders of spice bush, witch hazel, and wild hydrangea, and beds of partridge berry, maiden hair and Christmas ferns, Oconee bells, and Indian pipe (*Monotropa uniflora*), a herbaceous perennial without chlorophyll. On one of the logging roads, we met lumbermen hauling out large hemlocks. At 56 mi we sat on a bench to observe a 60-ft cascade.

At 57 mi the trail crossed the last bridge before ascending S on a slope from Laurel Fork. Here we saw a copperhead, the first poisonous snake spotted on the trip. We climbed through dense rhododendron to a hilltop at 57.5 mi and descended in a deciduous forest to a small stream, where, at 58 mi, there is a designated campsite area W of an old road. Boulders dominated the landscape at 59.2 mi. At 60.2 mi the trail made a horseshoe curve near a used graveled road and reached a parking area at 60.8 mi.

(At the parking lot is the yellow-blazed **Eastatoe Gorge Trail** [5-mi round trip], a spur that descends 2.5 mi to Eastatoe Creek in the Eastatoe Gorge Natural Area. From the parking lot walk up the road 0.2 mi and turn L on an old gated logging road. Follow it through a cut in a low ridge, turn L at a fork, and ascend through an area of grass, locust, and blackberry. At 0.7 mi cross Narrow Ridge, an area that has been clear-cut; follow signs and blazes to avoid side-logging skid roads. Here is a view of Roundtop Mountain to the E. Descend gradually on old roads through a scenic forest of large poplar, hemlock, beech, birch, and oak. Fetterbush, rhododendron, ferns, and wildflowers are prominent. The area has a number of rare ferns, one of which is the Tunbridge fern, *Hymenophyllum tunbridgense,* which, according to botanist Richie Bell, is not found elsewhere in North America. At 1.5 mi, L at a bench, leave the road and descend on a foot trail. There is a campsite at Eastatoe Creek. Backtrack.)

We followed the graveled road to US 178, near the community of Rocky Bottom, at 61.1 mi. Laurel Valley Lodge was on the R, and as we filled our canteens, the smell of home-cooked food tempted us to stay for dinner. We compromised and purchased tomatoes and cucumbers to freshen up our freeze-dried food menu. The motel is open all year, but in the winter the restaurant is usually open only Thursdays through Sundays (864–878–4615). We returned to US 178. (For groceries and gasoline turn R on US 178 and proceed down the mountain 7 mi to the jct with SC 11, or turn L and go 8 mi up the mountain to Rosman.)

From US 178 to SR 199, Chimneytop Gap (2.0 mi)

At US 178 the trail crossed a bridge over Eastatoe Creek and ascended to Chimneytop Mountain. A massive rock formation and an excellent S view were at 61.8 mi. The trail skirted SW of the peak.

From SR 199, Chimneytop Gap, to Sassafras Mountain (2.5 mi)

From Chimneytop Gap, at 63.1 mi, the trail crossed the paved SR 199, ascended steeply to an old road, and turned toward the N side of the slope. After a return to the ridge, we climbed steeply, passing large rocks, good views, and pink lady's slippers and twisted stalk blooming in a hardwood forest. Leaving the old roadbed at 63.9 mi, the trail entered an open forest with a profusion of New York ferns. We met Myron Aycock and Joel Dowis from Anderson on our climb.

We returned to the ridge at 64.2 mi and turned L on an old open grassy road. White pines bordered the trail, and a plump copperhead was enjoying the morning sun. The measuring wheel, "Clicker," nudged him out of the way. At 64.8 mi the trail led to a jct; we angled R and up. Three deer bolted down the old road to our L. Wild quinine (*Parthenium integrifolium*) grew on the banks of a paved road at 65.2 mi. After crossing it and climbing steeply, we saw locust, black birch, sassafras, witch hazel, and chestnut oak in a rocky area. Steps led to the top of Sassafras Mountain (3,554 ft), the state's highest peak, and a sheltered sign provided information on the trail routes. (The firetower has been dismantled and removed.) A paved road descended to the parking area at 65.6 mi. At the parking lot is an option to take the original **Foothills Trail** for 9.2 mi to Table Rock State Park, or to take the blue-blazed **Foothills Trail** spur for 14.2 mi to US 276 in former Caesars Head State Park and another 5.4 mi to former Jones Gap State Park. The original **Foothills Trail** is described first.

(If planning a vehicle shuttle from here to Caesars Head, there are two routes. The longer one, all on paved roads, 29.7 mi, is down from Sassafras Mountain 4.2 mi to Rocky Bottom and the jct with US 178. A turn L on SC 11 from US 178 and another turn L on US 276 from SC 11 will take you to the trail jct at Caesars Head. The other route is approximately 20 mi, depending on which county road you take, and it is mainly in Transylvania County, North Carolina. One advantage of this route is the avoidance of the repetition of mountain ascents from SC 11. To follow it, descend from Sassafras Mountain but leave the paved road after 1.5 mi, R, at the first road, Glady Fork Road, SR 1105, a gravel road that runs 4.2 mi to East Fork Road, SR 1107. Here you may go R or L on SR 1107 to reach US 276, but the road conditions are usually better to the L, where it takes you through Connestee to US 276.

Either way, when you reach US 276, turn R. After you reach the South Carolina line, S of Cedar Mountain community, it is 1.6 mi to the **Raven Cliff Falls Trail [Foothills Trail]** parking area.)

From Sassafras Mountain to Table Rock State Park (9.2 mi)
A few yards down the paved road, the trail turned L on a slope, where some remarkably large pink lady's slippers grew. Following an old roadbed among stands of mountain laurel and scattered holly, sourwood, and Virginia pine, the trail crossed a ridge at 66.6 mi. Here were large patches of trailing arbutus. At 66.8 mi there was an old homesite and what appeared to be an old mining area. Rhododendron thickets and large beds of galax grew nearby. We reached Hickorynut Mountain Gap at 67.3 mi where we saw cancer root (*Conopholis americana*), a yellow-brown parasite, at the base of oaks, and outstanding examples of downed American chestnut logs. At 68.5 mi a short section of the old Emory Gap toll road began, passing through a beautiful forest of both deciduous and evergreen trees. A footbridge crossed a small stream at 69 mi, where rhododendron and hemlock provided a heavy shade. The trail entered another open hardwoods forest with chestnut logs at 69.2 mi. Turning L on a ridge near boulders, it descended to a small bridge and a trickling stream. Legend has it that Marion Castles had a rock house there to hide from service in the Civil War; now there are campsites. A large rocky cliff is on the L at 69.4 mi. Rocks, streams, and picturesque topography make this area at 70.1 mi unusually attractive. On the L at 70.2 mi can be seen the "Lighthouse" on the lower area of the Drawbar Cliffs.

From here we followed an old roadbed among young poplars and through an open grassy area, turned L on another old road, and ascended to an exceptional view from Drawbar Cliffs at 71 mi. We could see Lake Keowee and the foothills beyond. We stayed an hour, observing the magnificent scenery and the plants on the outcrops.

Still ascending, the trail turned L on a ridge and took an S slope off the ridge at 71.1 mi. Mandrakes, cohosh, and Canada violets

(*Viola canadensis*) grew in an open forest of large oaks.

At 71.4 mi we reached a jct with the yellow-blazed **Pinnacle Mountain Trail** and the boundary of Table Rock State Park. (To the L, the **Pinnacle Mountain Trail** extends for 0.2 mi to the summit of the peak, where, except in the winter, there are no views. See Table Rock State Park.) The **Foothills Trail** and the **Pinnacle Mountain Trail** joined, turned R, and descended to a magnificent view from a granite cliff at 72 mi. The descent from here was steep, narrow, and in some places eroded. At 72.7 mi were flumes and rhododendron; the trail descended on a precipitous area among rhododendron roots at 73.2 mi. At 74.1 mi are more flumes, cascades, falls, slides, and pools along Carrick Creek. At 74.7 mi the trail crossed a bridge at a waterfall and became paved before it reached the Nature Center at 74.8 mi. Across the road is a parking area. (Remember that camping is allowed in Table Rock State Park only at the designated campgrounds, and the park superintendent must be informed if you plan to leave your vehicle overnight in the parking area. See Table Rock State Park in Chapter III, Section 1, for support facilities.)

From Sassafras Mountain to Caesars Head, US 276 at Raven Cliff Falls Trail Parking Area (14.2 mi)

This section of the trail is rugged, remote, and strenuous. It is partially footpaths and partially timber-industry and settlers' roads. Deer, turkey, fox, raccoon, hawks, and songbirds frequent the route; wildflowers are prominent, including trailing arbutus, galax, orchids, Indian pipe, asters, and azaleas. Dense beds of wild berries and ferns are common, and the varied hardwoods make an unforgettable display of color in October. Blazes and markers are blue for the **Foothills Trail,** red for the Greenville Lake watershed boundary, and white for survey markers or private-property boundaries. Also, from here to Gum Gap, where the trail leaves the state boundary, there are metal stakes that identify the state line—North Carolina (N) and South Carolina (S). Sometimes markers are on the stakes.

Hiking this section with me were John Matthews, Mark and Kevin Zoltek, Nile Spiegel, Tate Hayman, and Greg Hippert. (Although this hike took place later in the season, it was our bad luck for it to rain all day, with a strong SW wind howling across the ridgeline.) We crossed the road from the Sassafras Mountain parking lot to a narrow dirt road that serves two radio towers. After passing L of the towers, we descended through a dense forest of oak, rhododendron, and hemlock to Sassafras Gap at 66.4 mi. (Here is evidence of the old Emory Gap toll road that ascends from Pickens County, South Carolina, to Transylvania County, North Carolina. There is a water source 0.3 mi N on the old road.) From here we ascended to skirt the N side of White Oak Mountain (3,297 ft) at 66.7 mi to find views of Glady Valley and the Blue Ridge Mountains beyond. After returning to the ridge crest, at 67 mi, we followed, crossed, or paralleled a variety of old roads for 6 mi to Slicking Gap.

Along the way, at 67.9 mi, we passed through a former clearcut where white pines were abundant, and at 68.5 mi we reached the top of Bigspring Mountain. After a gap and knoll, we descended steeply to a briar patch and wet area at 69.7 mi. Jane Cantrell Creek is L, and the N end of Little Table Rock Mountain is ahead. At 69.9 mi is a good campsite at an old logging road. To the L (N) at 71 mi, on Dolves Mountain, is an excellent view of the East Fork of the French Broad River valley. We reached Slicking Gap at 72.8 mi and began the climb on a timber road to the top of Slicking Mountain. At 73 mi there is a blue arrow painted on a flat rock to remind us that the trail follows R at the fork. At 73.6 mi are overlooks. Descending on switchbacks from Slicking Mountain, we reached Gum Gap at 74.9 mi. (Here we left N.C. and entered the preserved area of the S.C. Wildlife and Marine Resources Department. Camping is not allowed on this or other properties for the remainder of this trail segment.)

We climbed over the earthen barrier, R, and descended on a rocky (and closed-to-vehicles) road. Soon the trail paralleled Julian Creek until near its mouth, at 76.2 mi, where we rock-hopped

Matthews Creek. After passing a gate we came to a curve in the road, L, at 76.9 mi. (This connects with 9.6-mi. **Naturaland Trust Trail,** R, and 3.3-mi **Gum Gap Trail,** L. [See Mountain Bridge State Natural Area in Chapter III.] At 0.3 mi on the **Naturaland Trust Trail** are spectacular views of Upper Raven Cliff Falls.)

We continued on the road, **(Gum Gap Trail)** and at 78.1 mi we turned off, R, at a trail sign in former Caesars Head State Park. We ascended gradually to a jct with the **Raven Cliff Falls Trail** at 78.4 mi. (To the R it is 0.8 mi to the observation deck for viewing the 420-ft Lower Raven Cliff Falls, a popular area for day hikers.) A turn L takes you 1.4 mi to the parking area at US 276, 1.1 mi N of Caesars Head . (For more information see Caesars Head in Chapter III.) For food, supplies, and services, it is 14 mi N on US 276 to Brevard; on US 276 S, it is 14 mi to Cleveland.

From Caesars Head, US 276, to Jones Gap at River Falls Road (5.4 mi)

From the parking area on US 276, Nile Spiegel, Kevin Zoltek, and I continued on to complete the **Foothills Trail** (which follows the **Tom Miller Trail** to the **Jones Gap Trail**) at its E terminus in the former Jones Gap State Park. We descended to the Middle Saluda River at 80.5 mi, crossed a log bridge at 80.8 mi, and followed the old toll road, engineered and built by Solomon Jones in the mid-nineteenth century. Champion trees, ferns, and wildflowers garnish the trail. The river and its tributaries cascade over huge boulders and splash into numerous pools for nearly 4 mi in a drop of nearly 1,700 ft. At 83.1 mi the trail made a jct, R, with the **Coldspring Branch Trail,** and at 84.2 mi we crossed another log bridge over the river. Passing a number of designated campsites, we reached the former Jones Gap State Park parking lot at 85.2 mi. (For detailed information on this section of the **Foothills Trail,** adjoining trails, and access descriptions, see the Caesars Head and Jones Gap sections of the Mountain Bridge State Natural Area in Chapter III.) Access to the E terminus is on the River Falls Road, 5.8 mi in from US 276/SC 11, 1 mi W of Cleveland.

**Foothills Trail
Map 1**

Foothills Trail
Map 2

N

Mill
Mtn

BM
259

Big Bend
Falls

Round
Top

Rand Mtn

alt Trough
ap

CHATTOOGA

GA
EABON CO

BIG

BEND

RIDGE

Crane
Mtn

CHATTAHOOCHEE

NATIONAL FOREST

Ford

GEORGIA
SOUTH CAROLINA

FOREST
BOUNDARY

Rock Gorge

Branch

Pigpen

Morton
Mtn

BM
2213

Big Stakey Mtn

NICHOLSON

CHATTOOGA

TAMASSEE

Dodge
Mtn

UMTF

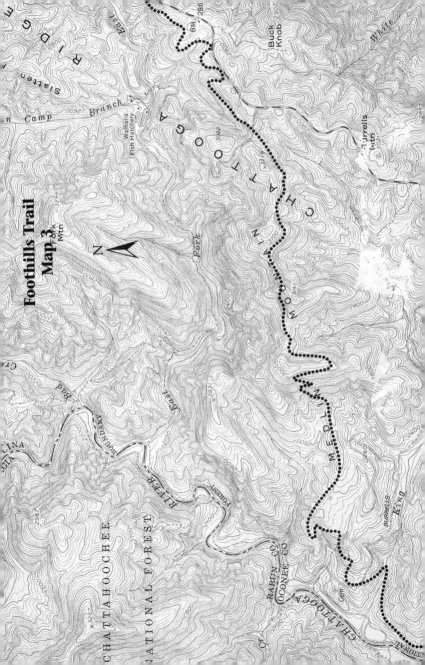

**Foothills Trail
Map 4**

JACKSON CO
OCONEE CO

Indian Camp Br

Walhalla
Fish Hatchery

Indian Camp
Branch

Slatten Ridge

East Fork

Bee

PERSIMMON

SUMTER

CHA

NATIONAL

Slatten Br

Branch

River

N

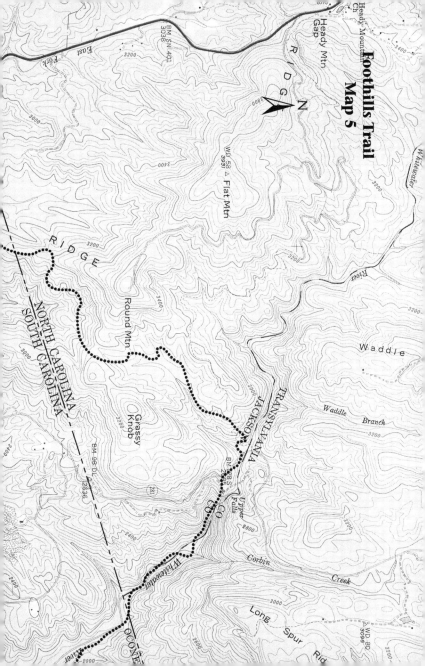

**Foothills Trail
Map 5**

N

Heady Mountain
Ch

Heady Mtn
Gap

BM SN 401
3038

East Fork

R I D G E

3200

3200

Whitewater

3000

3400

WD 52
3391 △ Flat Mtn

3200

3000

Ritter

R I D G E

3200

Round Mtn

3400

W a d d l e

NORTH CAROLINA
SOUTH CAROLINA

JACKSON CO

TRANSYLVANIA CO

3000

Waddle
Branch

3200

Grassy
Knob

3200

BM 98 DL
2636

281

BM 285

3000

3200

Upper
Falls
2800

Whitewater

2400

Corbin

Creek

2600

Long Spur Rid

WD 80
3096

OCONEE

River

2000

2600

3000

3200

**Foothills Trail
Map 7**

N

Turkeypen
Gap

WD 70
2130

2400

2000

1800

Bear

Horsepasture

Bear
Gap

R i d g e

1600

1200

1200

1600

1600

FO

NATIONAL

1400

1400

Crossroads Mtn

NORTH CAROLINA

SOUTH CAROLINA

1400

1200

1200

1200

1200

Reedy

NATION

PICKEN

OCONEE

Mill

Creek

1800

1800

1600

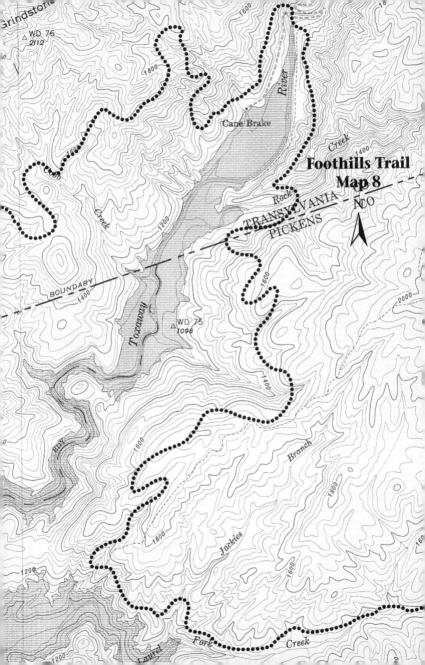

**Foothills Trail
Map 8**

Cane Brake

TRANSYLVANIA
PICKENS

BOUNDARY

WD 76
2112

WD 75
1098

Foothills Trail
Map 9

TRANSYLVANIA CO
PICKENS

N

Chestnut

Ridge

Hog.

Creek

Eastatoe

Flatrock
Mtn

BM

Creek

Fork

Laurel Fork
Gap

Side-of-Mountain Creek

Narrow Ridge

Cane Mtn

Long Branch

Laurel

Branch

Diana Mtn

Eastatoe

Twisting

Pine Mtn

Reedy

Cane

Creek

**Foothills Trail
Map 10**

N

Rock

Bigspring

Creek

Creek

Sunfish Mountai

Sunfish

Saluda

South

2400

USGS 2785
2774

Sassafras
Gap

Whiteoak Mtn
Lake Toxaway 11   3297

GREENVILLE CO

PICKENS CO

Sassafras Mtn

3000

South

Saluda

River

3200

VD 52
3483 △ Hickorynut
Mtn

Emory
Gap

Rock Mtn

2800

2800

2400

2600

(APPROXIMATE STATE

Pinnacle Mtn
△ 3425   2800

2600

Mountain Creek

2400

Ern

N

WD 53A Table Rock

PICKENS

2000

2400

2200

BOUNDARY

Panther
Gap

T A B L E   R O C

2600

Green

S T A T E   P A R

1400

Creek

1800

Carrick   Creek

Falls

2200

1400

1400

STATE

Mill

1200

TANK

PARK

BOUNDARY

PARKWAY

SCENIC

Cr

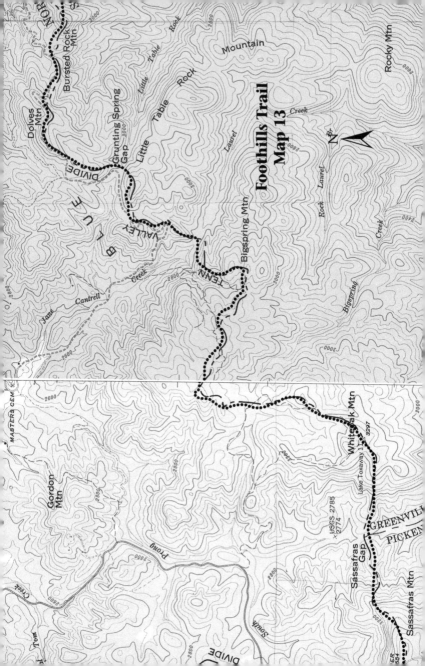

**Foothills Trail
Map 13**

N^{Br}

**Foothills Trail
Map 14**

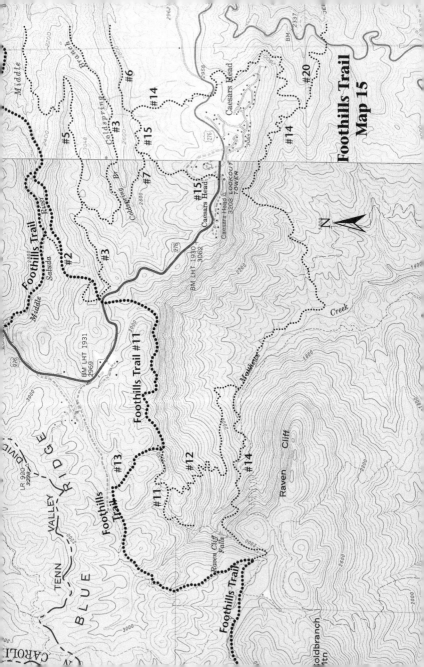

Foothills Trail Map 15

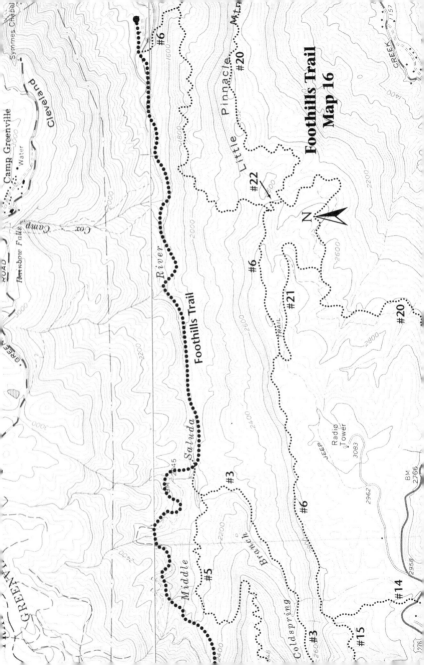

**Foothills Trail
Map 16**

SECTION 2
Long Cane Ranger District

(Edgefield, McCormick, Saluda, Abbeville, and Greenwood Counties)

The Long Cane and Edgefield Ranger Districts have administratively and geographically been combined as the Long Cane Ranger District, with 119,658 acres. The former Edgefield adjoined Long Cane on the W boundary, generally along Stevens Creek, and on the S it bordered Georgia and the U.S. Army Corps of Engineers property border at the Thurmond Reservoir. The N boundary extended to US 178 near Kirksey, and the E side was W of Edgefield. Long Cane originally bordered the South Carolina/Georgia state line at Thurmond Lake in McCormick County, covered the crescent in Abbeville County SE of Abbeville, and included a SE corner of Greenwood County.

The district has the Long Cane Scenic Area, with some of the state's champion hardwoods. There are riverside scenery and hilly topography, with sections of quartz and Carolina slate. Hunting and fishing are allowed. The hunting season is usually from October 1 through December. Wildlife includes deer, turkey, bobcat, raccoon, squirrel, quail, and dove. There are two major recreation areas and two long trails: **Turkey Creek Trail** and **Long Cane Trail.**

Information: District Ranger, Long Cane Ranger District, 810 Buncombe St., Edgefield, SC 29824; (803) 637–5396.

Access: The office is in Edgefield on US 25N.

Lick Fork Lake Recreation Area

The Lick Fork Lake Recreation Area has facilities for camping, swimming, picnicking, boating, and hiking. A new bathhouse with hot showers was constructed in 1992. There is a parking fee for day use of facilities.

Access: From the ranger station take SC 23 W for 8.5 mi to jct with SC 230, Westside Volunteer Fire Department. Turn L on SC 230 and proceed 0.4 mi, then turn L again on SR 263. After 2 mi turn R on SR 392.

Lick Fork Lake Trail

Length: 1.7 mi (2.7 km); **easy;** USGS Map: Colliers; trailhead: Lick Fork Lake parking area.

From the parking area I followed the trail sign on the well-maintained footpath through a young mixed forest. Wildflowers, including pink spiderwort, were prominent. I crossed a stream at 0.4 mi and Lick Fork at 0.5 mi. The fiddleheads of the Christmas ferns had recently uncurled on a moist bank, and on a slope I saw beech, oak, sourwood, pine, and hickory trees. At 1 mi I descended to a dam on the L through a dense cove with copious Virginia creeper and honeysuckle. I rock-hopped the stream at 1.1 mi to the jct with the **Horn Creek Trail** on the R. Turning L to complete the loop, I crossed a footbridge, reached a picnic area, crossed another footbridge, and returned to the parking area at 1.7 mi.

Horn Creek Trail

Length: 5.4 mi (8.6 km); **moderate;** USGS Map: Colliers; trailhead: Lick Fork Lake parking area.

From the parking area I took the **Lick Fork Lake Trail** S for 0.6 mi to the jct with **Horn Creek Trail.** I followed the white-blazed trail downstream in a mixed forest to the graveled FR 640 crossing and alternate parking area at 0.4 mi. I passed a spring and crossed a footbridge at 0.9 mi, then turned L away from Lick Fork Creek. Where parts of the forest have been timbered, penstemon grew and jessamine was spreading. At 1.2 mi the trail ascended to a ridge top in a pine stand and crossed a graveled road, SR 263, at 1.6 mi. Here were blackberry patches and fire anthills.

I followed the trail through a young pine stand, parallel to FR 634, and reached Horn Creek at 2.2 mi. At 2.5 mi the trail crossed two footbridges. The forest was mature, tributary crossings were frequent, and the trail was wide. At 3 mi the forest floor changed. Dozers with KG blades had left their marks, and for 1.5 mi I had to crawl over or through brush left by the stingers. The selective cutting, however, provided some shade and trail-corridor direction.

I had circled the timber harvesters to recross SR 263 at 4.8 mi. Here I disturbed a box turtle eating a mushroom for lunch on a seeded roadbed. There is an inactive colony site of red-cockaded woodpeckers on SR 263. Slightly descending, I reached the picnic area at 5.2 mi, turned R, and completed the loop at 5.4 mi (5.8 mi counting the distance on the **Lick Fork Lake Trail**).

Turkey Creek Trail

The two sections of the **Turkey Creek Trail** are excellent places to see flora and fauna any season of the year. Large stands of climax forest are in this area. Considerable design, planning, and work have gone into its construction. Unfortunately, the trail is segmented by the lack of a bridge at Stevens Creek and an upstream dead-end on the S section (satisfactory arrangements have not been completed with the owners of the property through which the trail must pass). Because the creek rises more than 15 ft during flood stage, a bridge over Stevens Creek would have to be more than 200 ft long, a costly undertaking. (Perhaps an alternative would be to attach two strong guy-wires to sturdy trees for a foot support and hand guidance. Cuts in the NFS budget have greatly limited trail maintenance and reduced construction.)

North Section
Length: 11.9 mi (19 km); **moderate;** USGS Maps: Parksville, Clarks Hill; trailhead: parking area on SC 283.

To avoid backtracking I arranged a vehicle shuttle. I began at the N terminus on SC 283 between the Wine Creek and Turkey Creek bridges at a small parking area, following the white blazes through an open pine forest. Quartz and wildflowers were mixed with the honeysuckle ground cover. At 0.4 mi I heard the rocky Wine Creek on the R. Crows were noisy on the L, in contrast to the towhees overhead. Brilliant pinkroot were at their peak along the creek bank; heartleaf, arbutus, and wood betony had already bloomed. A box turtle was breakfasting on a snail. Across Wine Creek there were wild azaleas and squirrel cups.

I crossed Mack Branch at 1.3 mi, with large beds of wood betony, more like those found in the mountains. The bottomland hardwood forest became more open, with only a scattered understory. At 1.8 mi there was a good campsite near a huge beechnut tree. High water had moved the footbridges at three ravines. At 2.3 mi I crossed a mudsoaked footbridge, evidence that the creek had risen surprisingly high. The trail continued on a slope, then descended to a floodplain. Cypress, papaw, hackberry, large grapevines, ironwood, and oaks grew along the river bank. One grapevine with a 25-in circumference must be a champion.

The trail crossed a pipeline route and passed a stand of enormous cypress at 3.2 mi. At 3.7 mi switchcane, blackberry, and briars encroached on the trail. Hardwoods gave way to pine forest at 4.2 mi, where coreopsis and rattlebox had survived an earlier controlled fire burn. (The poisonous rattlebox, *Sesbania drummondii*, is the subject of experiments by the U.S. Department of Agriculture; the seeds may be an anticancer agent.) The trail reached SR 227 at the Key Bridge at 4.5 mi. It crossed the road, followed an old roadbed briefly, then followed a high bluff by the river. At 5.3 mi the trail passed dead-end FR 618 on the R. I heard wild turkey calling ahead. A good campsite was near a cement spring on the L at 5.7 mi. At 6.2 mi the trail crossed Coon Creek and for nearly a mile swung from cove to bluff. Turkey Creek tumbled over a row of river water bars. At 7 mi the air was cinnamon-sweet with what local folk call wild mint, or mountain mint (although its fragrance was more like holy basil). Among buckeye and papaw and basswood, in one continuous path of beauty, the trail undulated. The river was dark and slow, brushing slightly against cypress knees. I crossed other tributaries at 8.6 mi and 9.1 mi, then abruptly the trail turned R. It had to: Ahead was the confluence of Turkey and Stevens Creeks. Their silted silence concealed their power to make massive oak and cypress sink their roots deeper.

Eric Tang hiked in from the Stevens Creek trailhead to meet me. At 9.6 mi was a trail jct and sign. To the R was a spur of 0.2 mi to the end of FR 617. We continued ahead to another jct at 9.8 mi, where the trail forked. An alternate route turned L down the bank to Stevens Creek; the blaze was there, but the murky water was too deep to cross. The main trail continued ahead through thick grasses in bottomlands. We saw deer and wild turkey. At 11.5 mi we turned R and began an ascent to a more xeric area, to end at 11.9 mi.

From the trail's end at FR 617-A, we drove to SR 138, turned L, and went 1.3 mi to J. M. Price's water-ground, sifted, white, self-rising cornmeal gristmill at the Stevens Creek bridge and dam. John Henry Tolbert, who for more than 25 years has been the mill's operator, told us how "all that water comes down from Hard Labor Creek; in years back, can't say when, it washed away the mill . . . a cotton gin used to be here . . . I've seen the water up to the porch." From across the bridge on SR 138, it is 1.4 mi to US 221–SC 28.

South Section

Length: 11 mi round-trip (17.6 km); **moderate;** USGS Maps: Parksville, Clarks Hill; trailhead: Modoc Bridge parking area.

(The center of this trail can be reached from US 221-SC 28 by taking SR 93 [E of Hamilton Branch State Park entrance] for 0.5 mi to FR 632, then R for 2.1 mi to a cul-de-sac. FR 632-A is another route to within 0.2 mi of the trail's N dead-end.)

From the Modoc Bridge parking area at SR 23, 1.4 mi E of US 221–SC 28 in Modoc, Eric Tang and I followed the trail blaze upstream, crossing a footbridge, through a timbered area to a good campsite at 0.3 mi. At 0.4 mi we crossed a rocky area over Key Branch, followed by a stand of dwarf palmettos. Fire and timber harvesting had opened an area for the next 0.2 mi. We turned away from the river at 0.6 mi to avoid a floodplain and wet bottomland to curve back at 1.3 mi. Timbering on the L had increased the trail vegetation. After a slight ascent we reached a jct with a spur trail to the L for connecting FR 632 at 2.1 mi. We were on a

Turkey Creek Trail
Map 1

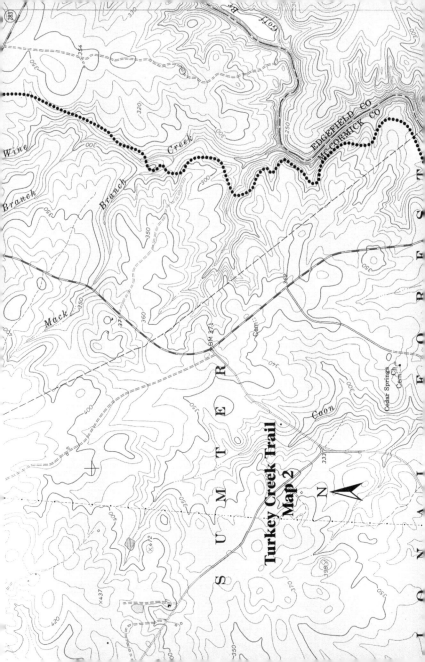

Turkey Creek Trail Map 2

**Turkey Creek Trail
Map 3**

bluff that became higher at 2.2 mi. It was refreshing to hear Turkey Creek splashing over rapids after 2 mi of hardly knowing it was there. Trees were tall upland hardwoods. We soon left the river and wound around another tributary from a ridge. At 2.6 mi and 3 mi, we could see the river after traversing a cove and ravine to follow a slope.

The best view of the river came at 3.2 mi. Here we could see the rapids through an open forest. At 4 mi we crossed a ravine, where buckeye, papaw, and meadow rue grew. From here the trail twisted N, then W, then S, then W away from the river to cross a small stream. While we were looking at a garden of wildflowers, a buck came down the trail but bolted when I moved for my camera. In a clearing at 4.6 mi, sundrops, phlox, and wild mint gave color and fragrance. From here to the end of the forest boundary, we saw the river intermittently, probably best at 5.3 mi, where a large patch of black cohosh grew. The trail dead-ended at 5.5 mi, at private property. Dead-ends are frustrating, but we knew that if we got through the briars and thistles, there would be another dead-end at Stevens Creek. Looking on the bright side, Eric said, "I like to backtrack; we'll see what we missed."

Parsons Mountain Lake Recreation Area

There is a paved road through the campground, lake-swimming facilities, picnic areas, a boat launch, sanitary facilities, hot showers, and a sewage-disposal station. Visitors can hike to the firetower on Parsons Mountain or go backpacking (or horseback riding) on the 22.2-mi-long **Long Cane Trail.** There are also two motorcycle trails: **Parsons Mountain Cycle Trail** (11.2 mi) and **Cedar Spring Cycle Trail** (10.9 mi). (Maps are available from the ranger's office.)

Access: From Abbeville take SC 28 S to Rock Buffalo Church at SR 251. Turn L on SR 251 and continue 1.5 mi to the park entrance on the R.

Parsons Mountain Trails

Length: 2.9 mi round-trip (4.6 km); **moderate;** USGS Map: Verdery; trailheads: parking area across the dam, or the picnic area.

Access to Parsons Mountain is from the **Living on the Land Trail** or from the campground area. The following description is from the campground area, near the boat ramp at the lake. At the trail sign we entered a forest of large hardwoods with an open understory. After 0.4 mi we passed a small pond and descended to a small stream with a natural spring. We turned R through an area of large poplar, red and white oaks, hickory, and beech at 0.6 mi. Wildflowers are usually blooming in this area—fly poison, phlox, pinkroot, green-and-gold, black-eyed Susan, asters, indigo, and goat's rue. Among the flowering shrubs are papaw, dogwood, wild azaleas, redbud, and New Jersey tea. To the R is a jct with the **Audubon Trail,** a 1.1-mile route to the **Living on the Land Trail** (described below). At 1.1 mi we crossed a gravel FR road and ascended steeply to the Civil War gold-mine shafts. From here we ascended to a ridge crest toward the top of Parsons Mountain (832 ft) and the 80-ft firetower at 1.4 mi. The mountain is named in honor of James Parson, a pioneer of the piedmont, who was granted the land from King George III in 1772. We backtracked to the parking area.

Living on the Land Trail

Length: 0.5 mi (0.8 km); **easy;** USGS Map: Verdery; trailhead: parking at swimming area.

From the parking area near the bathhouse, we entered the trail by a large trail sign. Twelve interpretive stations described the trees and animals and told how the pioneers lived off the land. We turned R on a gradual incline to a jct with the **Audubon Trail,** or a loop back to the parking area.

Long Cane Horse and Hiking Trail

Length: 22.2 mi (35.5 km); **moderate to strenuous;** USGS Maps: Verdery, Abbeville E; trailheads: recreation area campground and Fell Hunt Camp.

This is a hiking and horse loop trail that twice crosses scenic Long Cane Creek and a number of its tributaries. About halfway in the loop is a 2.6-mi connector trail that can shorten the distance to 14.8 mi.

Dick Hunt, Bob Brueckner, and I took the Long Cane loop clockwise. We followed an old roadbed for 0.5 mi and crossed paved SR 251. We entered a young forest mixed with spots of pine barrens and gradually descended to SR 33 at 1.2 mi. After crossing the road we continued a slight descent to a sticky mud trail at floodplain level. At 2.3 mi we reached a jct (to the R it is 125 yd to the cul-de-sac of FR 530). To the L was the Long Cane Scenic Area boundary, which many had hoped would be designated a wilderness area under the RARE II program. Within a few yards flowed the silent silted Long Cane Creek on its way to the Savannah River, and a steel bridge for hikers stood slightly upstream from the horse crossing. River birch, sycamore, ironwood, and elm hugged the stream banks. When we crossed the bridge, our noise sent two wild turkeys flying from the floodplain. We ascended to a ridge and then descended at 2.7 mi to a cove. The terrain and the hardwood forest were becoming more like the mountains than the piedmont. At 3.3 mi a sign indicated that the hardwoods in the cove were a holdover from the time when the Appalachian Mountains reached this far east; though the mountains wore down, this type of cove trees continued to grow. Sunlight was at a premium in this beautiful forest of tall poplar, oaks, elm, beech, maple, and hickory. Healthy patches of jack-in-the-pulpit and wood betony were between us and the floodplain. False downy foxglove bloomed on the drier slopes.

At 3.4 mi we saw the state's largest shagbark hickory (nearly 11 ft in circumference and 135 ft tall). Other large shagbarks were on the slope. The next mile was on the floodplain, some of which was swampy. As we rounded a curve in the trail, a raccoon, ignoring his nocturnal nature, ran up a tree when he saw us. Dark clouds caused the forest to darken. Dick said that when he was a little kid he "thought all forests had scary walking trees with huge arms . . .

ready to grab me, just like in the *Wizard of Oz*."

At 4.5 mi we left the Long Cane Scenic Area at FR 505. (After crossing the road, there is a jct, R, with the 2.6-mi connector that joins the main trail at the S side of Little Muckaway Creek. This connection shortens the distance from 22.2 mi to 14.5 mi. The trail descends to follow a natural-gas pipeline and cross Curltail Creek in a flat area at 1.3 mi. It leaves the pipeline to cross Little Muckaway Creek before turning E.)

Continuing ahead on the main trail, we entered a small grazing field, then a pine forest that merged into a stand of hardwoods. There were more pines before we crossed FR 505 again at 5.2 mi. Cicadas were becoming louder and more singsong as the heat of the day increased. Patches of rose pink grew where we crossed a natural-gas pipeline at 5.4 mi. At 5.5 mi we reached FR 505 again and turned L on the road to cross the Seaboard Coastline train tracks. We continued on the road, originally the Old Charleston Road, for half a mile and entered a young pine forest on the R.

At 6.6 mi a number of white oaks had been splintered by lightning. After passing extremely large loblollies, we continued to descend through a mixed forest. Honey locusts and beauty bushes were near the trail, then a mixed forest at 8.4 mi and finally a stand of immense hardwoods similar to those in the Long Cane Scenic Area. Christmas ferns and rattlesnake orchids grew in a floor of honeysuckle. At 8.9 mi we crossed a small tributary to Big Curltail Creek and entered a clear-cut, where trumpet vines and woodland sunflowers grew. We crossed FR 505 again at 9.2 mi and took what was apparently an older trail. In open forest in places, the trail was of excellent design and quality. Rocks, streams, slopes, small cascades, wildflowers, and even a cement bridge made this an ideal campsite.

We reached a jct of FR 505 and FR 506 at 10 mi. (To the L it is 1 mi to the Midway Hunt Camp, where there is public drinking water.) We crossed the jct into a pine forest where the flash of a dove covey startled us. Prior timber harvesting had opened new grazing fields here for wildlife; as a result, the trail had been relocated. We turned L on FR 506 and followed the road over two bridges of the Big Curltail Creek and swamp to a red-clay unnumbered FR at 11.7 mi. At 12.4 mi a huge white oak was on the R, and at 12.5 mi the Little Adams Cemetery was on the L. We counted some 20 gravesites, many those of children.

At 12.8 mi the old road ended, and we walked under the Seaboard Coastline railroad to cross Gray's Creek. Emerging from the forest at 13 mi to a cul-de-sac of FR 509-C, we hiked it for 0.9 mi to the jct with FR 509.

From here we ascended through a pine forest on a gentle old jeep road and then gradually descended to Little Muckaway Creek at 15.2 mi. A good campsite, the stream was clear and rocky with sandbars, and papaw and wood betony grew on the banks. (After crossing the creek, there was a jct, R, with the 2.6-mi connector trail that joined the main trail near the edge of the Long Cane Scenic Area.) We passed a grazing field on the R and later entered a stand of cedar. At 15.7 mi we crossed FR 505, Curltail Road. George Devlin Branch was at 16.3 mi, then a large grazing field, and we reached a fork at 16.7. (To the R is an old trail route, closed because of wet bottomlands.) We veered L on a forest road for 0.7 mi to Fell Hunt Camp at SR 47, where public drinking water and a trailhead parking area are located. (Fell Hunt Camp is 1.6 mi S of the SC 10–SR 47 jct, which is 7.7 mi S of Greenwood and 1 mi N of the SR 47–SR 33 jct at Cedar Spring Church.) At 17.7 mi we reached a parking area and cul-de-sac of FR 537, Rogers Road. From here we hiked the graveled road to have a bridge crossing of Stillhouse Branch. After the bridge we turned R and came out to SR 33 near the Long Cane Creek bridge at 19.4 mi.

The trail turned R across the bridge and followed the paved road for 0.7 mi before turning L on FR 518, Candy Branch Road. We passed a grazing field, turned R on a woods road, and crossed a ravine in a hardwood area at 20.8 mi. After ascending and descending through the hardwoods, we reached FR 515 at 21.8 mi, where we saw the state-champion white oak (23-ft circumference). From here we followed the trail to the Parsons Mountain Lake Recreation Area campground.

Long Cane Trail
Map 2

Long Cane Trail
Map 3

N

SECTION 3
Enoree Ranger District

(Laurens, Newberry, Fairfield, Chester, and Union Counties)

The Enoree and Tyger Ranger Districts have merged for a total of 158,350 acres to become the Enoree Ranger District. There are three loop trails, the longest of which is the **Buncombe Trail,** with an equestrian emphasis. Hunting is allowed according to state and federal regulations for turkey, quail, dove, deer, raccoon, red and gray fox, rabbit, and fox squirrel. In the former Tyger Ranger District is Broad River Recreation Area, used mainly as a boat launch for fishing. There are restrooms and a picnic area. Access is 9 mi E of Union on SR 389 to jct with SR 86, then 1.4 mi to a parking area on SR 389.

Information: District Ranger, Enoree Ranger District, 20 Work Center Rd., Whitmire, SC 29178; (803) 276–4810.

Access: The ranger's office is on US 176–SC 121, 6.3 mi S of Whitmire and 10 mi N of SC 121 from Newberry.

Brickhouse Campground Area

Buncombe Trail
Length: 27.8 mi (44.5 km); **moderate;** USGS Map: Newberry NW; trailhead: Brickhouse Campground.

Access: The campground is 7.4 mi SW on SC 66 from jct with US 176 in Whitmire, or 3.6 mi NE on SC 66 from I-26 (exit 60) to Brickhouse Crossroads.

The **Buncombe Trail** was named for the Buncombe Road, an early road between Columbia and Buncombe (Asheville), North Carolina. At the historic Brickhouse Inn, it crossed another important early road, the Chester Road, which was the main route from Washington, D.C., to New Orleans. At the formerly busy intersection, the Brickhouse was built in 1832 as a way station. The private home was constructed from local handmade brick.

This trail has more equestrian use than hiker use, but its design and maintenance enable it to easily accommodate both. Trailheads could be established at a number of road crossings; but to describe the trail, I have chosen the main trailhead at the Brickhouse Campground. That is the site of the only source of drinking water approved by the National Forest Service, and there are picnic tables, restrooms, and horse corrals. The trail has good campsites; a written permit is required from the district ranger to use them. I recommend securing a permit and camping out in the general forest at least one night.

When Jeff Fleming, Bob Brueckner, and I arrived at the Brickhouse Campground, it was a scorching 100°F mid-July weekend. From the Brickhouse Campground near the water pump, we began a SW curve of the camp area. Some campers saw us through the woods. Hearing the clickety-click of the measuring wheel, one camper hollered, "Is everything measuring up?" On many other hikes I have thought about his question. The word *everything* means whatever exists; it sounds so philosophic, so permanent. But the question is a good one for the forest service and for forest users.

Through tall loblolly pines and an understory of maple, dogwood, redbud, and sweet gum, the trail passed a 1976 YCC granite logo, crossed a wooden bridge, and ascended slightly in a stand of hardwood at 0.5 mi.

The trail crossed a tributary of Headley's Creek and ascended on an eroded section to more level ground at 2 mi. Spots of wildflowers such as ironweed (*Veronia acaulis*), alumroot, butterfly pea, woodland sunflower, self heal, wild indigo, leopard's bane, and wild bean gave some color to the trail-border foliage.

At 2.5 mi, at a jct with a motorcycle trail, the trail turned a sharp L and descended to cross Drysachs Branch at 3.8 mi. An open skid road went through a clear-cut section and a young stand of pines for nearly half a mile. Midway through it was being at-

tacked by kudzu, a fast-growing villous vine that thrives in heat and even the poorest soil.

Near the edge of the field, I saw two bluebirds. This beautiful songbird "carries the sky on his back," Thoreau wrote. How appropriate that the trail was lined with beautyberry shrubs as we reentered the woods.

At 4.5 mi we began to hear I-26 traffic. At 5.9 mi we took a sharp L on an old logging road, crossed FR 359, and went L again. After crossing a small stream at 6.2 mi, the trail undulated until leveling off at 7.5 mi, where it crossed FR 359 again. We approached a damp area at 8 mi as we returned to FR 359 to cross Peges Creek. For 0.6 mi we hiked on FR 359 to the jct of FR 361, Bonds Road, at 8.7 mi.

For 2 mi the trail zigzags in a young pine forest. At 10 mi the trail came within 50 yards of Indian Creek, and at 10.9 mi it paralleled Headley's Creek.

After crossing Headley's Creek on FR 361 bridges, we reentered the forest at 11.2 mi. Again the trail wove in and out of a timber harvest area, where quartz shone bright in the sun and the hillsides simmered in summer heat. Occasionally the trail arced toward FR 361, but at 12.7 mi it headed NE in a pine forest. A small stream over rocks, large shade trees, and wildflowers made a spot at 13.7 mi an inviting campsite. After nearly 0.2 mi farther, we entered an open field, exceptionally thick with blackberry and lespedeza, with featherlike leaves taller than our waists.

At Patterson's Creek we hoped we could find a rocky or sandy area other than the usual mud in which to take a bath, but we saw only mud. We crossed the wooden bridge, passed through a stand of extra-large poplar trees, and ascended through a young forest of pine, oak, wild plum, and sumac for half a mile. Poison ivy and honeysuckle hugged the trail. At 15 mi we crossed FR 360. At 15.9 mi we reached a clear tributary of Patterson's Creek, with low cascades over mossy rocks and pools the size of a Roman bath—a fine campsite. Black cohosh, ferns, and climbing hydrangea were on the stream banks, and enormous loblolly and poplar helped shade the area. The trees appeared to be the oldest we had seen on the trail. I longed to place a placard on the trail with poet George Morris's words: "Woodman, spare that tree! Touch not a single bough!"

The next day we crossed a stream on a large flat rock at 16.4 mi and came within sight of FR 420. Another good campsite was at 16.7 mi. We ascended through a pine forest to reach SC 66 at 17.9 mi, crossed the paved road, and took the L fork at 18.7 mi and again at 18.8 mi. At 19.5 mi the trail turned sharply R and descended toward Sandy Branch. Two deer ran ahead of us in patches of black-eyed Susan, ferns, wild ginger, and wild orchids. At the branch was a flat dry area near the bridge, another good campsite. After crossing the wooden bridge, we ascended to FR 363 at 20.1 mi.

Across FR 363, we noticed that trees with blazes were being cut down by a timber contractor. Near Mulberry Branch we saw deer and wild turkey at 21.5 mi. This branch also could be a campsite. From here the trail led up a gradual incline to FR 364, Duncan Road, at 22 mi. After we crossed FR 364 and entered the woods, we saw a timber cut. But in the middle of this, a lone rose pink (*Sabatia angularis*) near a tender pine offered an example of forest regeneration and succession. Within three years the area would be thick with new pines.

We crossed a wooden bridge at 22.4 mi and began a 2.5-mile winding path along the W side of Flannigan Branch. We saw and heard more wildlife in this area than anywhere else on the trail. Spicebush swallowtail and metal mark butterflies were prominent, and sumac, beautyberry, phlox, horsemint, ironweed, button bush, and creeping bush clover flowered. In a quick turn around a corner of the trail, the thorns of a hawthorn spiked my hand just as a covey of quail flew up in my face. I thought I had been shot.

At 24 mi we passed an appealing area where the creek flows over smooth rock slabs. Soon we turned W, gradually ascending, and at 25.2 mi crossed FR 365, Fendley Road. For the next 0.6 mi in a pine forest, we paralleled the gravel road; then we crossed SC 66. The understory was sourwood, holly, cedar, and small oaks on the

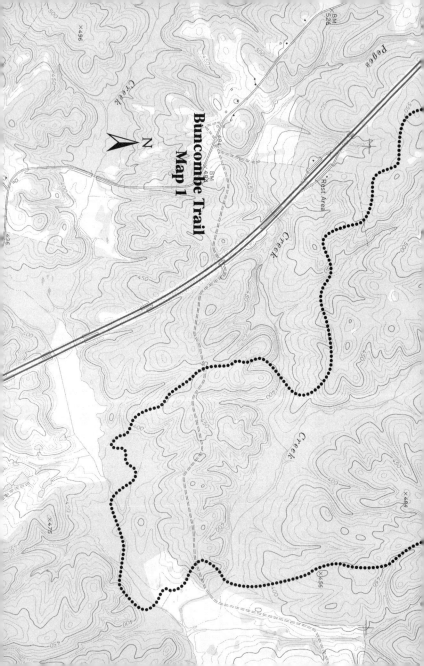

Buncombe Trail
Map 1

N

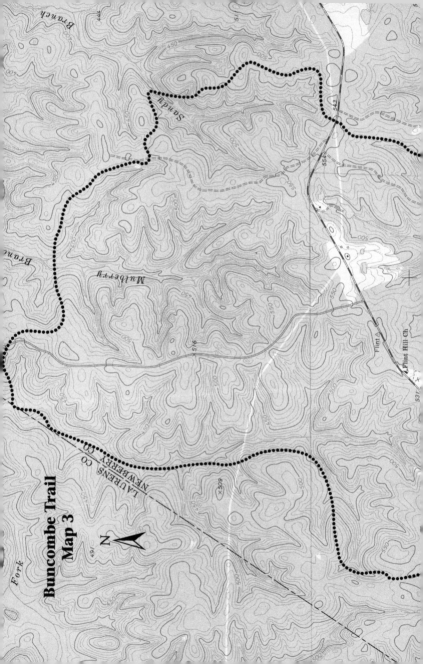

Buncombe Trail
Map 3

way to FR 356 at 26.6 mi. We turned R and followed the blaze up the gravel road for 0.3 mi, turned L on FR 356-F, and reentered the woods on the R. A small cirque was on the L in a hardwood forest at 27 mi. We began to hear sounds from the Brickhouse Campground as we approached FR 358, crossing to the campground area and point of origin at 27.8 mi. Hot and dusty, the first thing we did was put our heads under the campground hand water pump.

Molly's Rock Picnic Area

Molly's Rock Trail
Length: 0.7 mi (1.1 km); **easy;** USGS Map: Newberry E; trailhead: parking area.

Access: From US 176 (11 mi NE of Newberry and 3.5 mi N of SC 34) and FR 367. Turn onto FR 367 and go 0.5 mi to the parking area.

Molly's Rock Picnic Area has a shelter, sanitary facilities, nature study area, and hiking trails. From the shelter I followed the signs on a wood-chip loop trail around the lake to a mature mixed forest. At 0.2 mi I crossed a stream where there was elderberry, holly, dogwood, Hercules club (also called Devil's walking stick: *Aralia Spinosa*), sourwood, and ferns. At 0.3 mi there was a resting bench. The trail returned to the lake at 0.6 mi and crossed a bridge at the head of the lake to the picnic shelter. This is a peaceful area, and I saw or heard many birds—orioles, warblers, indigo buntings, nuthatches, blue jays, and meadowlarks.

Woods Ferry Recreation Area

Facilities at Woods Ferry Recreation Area are a campground, picnic area, nature trail, boat ramp, restrooms, and showers.

Access: From jct of SC 121 and SC 72 at SR 25 (12 mi SW of Chester and 2.7 mi E of the Broad River), go 2.1 mi on SR 25 to SR 49 at Leeds. Continue on SR 49 for 3.7 mi to SR 574, and turn L on SR 574. Woods Ferry is 3.5 mi ahead.

Woods Ferry Trail

Length: 1 mi (1.6 km); **easy;** USGS Map: Leeds; trailhead: parking area.

From the picnic area I walked to the bank of the quiet Broad River and went downstream to the uncleared forest, following the gray diamond blazes. The trail meandered through a dense hardwood forest of birch, oaks, gum, ash, poplar, and elm. Some dogwood and cedar were interspersed, and there were scattered loblolly pines. Mosquitoes ignored my insect repellent. After a 1-mi loop, I returned to the parking area.

Francis Marion National Forest

SECTION 4
Witherbee and Wambaw Ranger Districts
(Berkeley and Charleston Counties)

The Francis Marion National Forest was established in 1934 and has two adjoining ranger districts: Witherbee, with 129,755 acres, in the W half, which extends to Lake Moultrie; and Wambaw, with 120,734 acres, which extends to the Intracoastal Waterway. Its N border is the Santee River, and sections of its S border reach Wando River and the headwaters of the East Branch of the Cooper River. A network of about 600 mi of roads are maintained in the total 250,489 acres. Four wilderness areas have been designated by Congress: Wambaw Creek (1,825 acres); Wambaw Swamp (4,815 acres); Little Wambaw Swamp (5,047 acres); and Hell Hole Bay (2,125 acres). Wambaw Creek has a 9-mi canoe trail with access points at Still Landing (Mill Branch Road, FR 211) and Echaw Road (FR 202). The trail is a scenic blackwater passage among cypress and tupelo. Wildlife is prominent, and hunting, fishing, and camping are allowed. Dry places for camping are rare; permits are necessary.

Two major hiking trails are in the forest: **Swamp Fox Trail** (29 mi), a multi-use passage (in most sections) of the **Palmetto Trail** through both districts; and **Jericho Trail** (17.8 mi), an equestrian, biking, and hiking loop trail within Witherbee District. There are also short foot trails. **Huger Loop Trail** (1.8 mi) is a wide trail through a mixed forest of hardwoods and pines, wildflowers and dogwoods. The trailhead is at the corner of SC 402 and FR 159. **Sewee Shell Mound Interpretive Trail** (1 mi) features superb views of the salt marsh, tidal creek, and a prehistoric shell ring. Access is on Salt Pond Road (FR 243) 2.5 mi E of its jct with Doar Road (SR 432). Other interpretive trails are: **Ion Swamp Trail** (2-mi loop), which traverses embankments involved in rice production, has waterfowl, and has access off US 17 on Ion Swamp

Road (FR 228); and **Battery Warren Trail** (1 mi), a walk-in to a bluff on the Santee River for viewing the site of a Civil War blockade fort, and with access NE of Honey Hill off Echaw Road (FR 204) onto FR 204A. Although the forest does not officially list a trail at Guilliard Lake Recreation Area, visitors have created a riverside pathway (described later in this chapter). The forest has five recreation areas, but only Buck Hall has campground amenities. It is NE of Awendaw off US 17 on Buck Hall Landing Road (FR 242). Other recreational areas are Canal, 2 mi S of Bonneau on US 52; Huger, on SC 402, near the jct with Copperhead Road; and Elmwood, off Echaw Road (FR 205) onto Mill Branch Road (FR 211). The district offices have maps with descriptions on all the trails, recreation areas, and places of interest. You may also wish to inquire about areas for birdwatching, the Sewee Visitor and Environmental Education Center (on US 17 in Awendaw), the 40-mi **Wambaw Cycle Trail**, rifle ranges, hunting seasons, a 68-acre seed orchard, and unique visits to four Carolina bays.

Early on September 22, 1989, Hurricane Hugo devastated the forest, with winds of more than 135 mph. Considered one of the worst natural disasters in the history of national forests, Hugo destroyed more than 70 percent—at least 1 billion board ft—of Francis Marion's magnificent sawtimber. About 80 percent of the forest roads were blocked, and 90 percent of the red-cockaded woodpecker habitat was badly damaged or eliminated. (Before the hurricane the forest had the world's highest population density of red-cockaded woodpeckers.) Immediately after the storm passed, a wildlife-impact project was begun to save the endangered species. More than 530 artificial cavities and start holes were installed for those birds that survived. Visitors to the forest now will notice that the roads are clear, trails have been repaired and improved or extended, and there is an increase in the red-cockaded woodpecker population. But for many years to come, you will see reminders of the hurricane from standing but broken trees and trees cut to open the trails and roads.

Information: Witherbee Ranger District, 2421 Witherbee Rd.,

Cordesville, SC 29434; (843) 336–3248. Wambaw Ranger District, P.O. Box 788, McClellanville, SC 29458; (843) 887–3257.

Access: For Witherbee Ranger District from US 52 and SC 402 (N of Moncks Corner), drive E on SC 402 for 3.6 mi, turn L on Witherbee Rd. (SR 171), go 6.2 mi to a L turn on SR 125, and go 0.4 mi to office, R. For Wambaw Ranger District, at the jct of US 17 and SC 9 in McClellanville, take SC 9 to office, R.

Swamp Fox Trail

Length: Section I (older and more E): **29 mi** (46.4 km); **easy** to **moderate;** USGS Maps: Awendaw, Ocean Bay, Huger, Bethera. **Section II** (newer and more W): **17.2 mi** (27.5 km); **easy** to **moderate;** USGS Maps: Bethera, Cordesville, Bonneau SW.

Access for Section I: In Awendaw the E trailhead is at a parking area on the W side of US 17 (0.2 mi N of the jct with US 17 and Steed Creek Road [SR 133]). For the W trailhead drive from US 52 N of Monks Corner to Cross Cooper River bridge. After 0.7 mi turn E on SC 402. Go 3 mi to Witherbee Road, L, and drive 6.8 mi to the parking area at the Witherbee District Office, R. The trailhead is across the road. From Huger drive N on SC 402 for 2.7 mi, turn R on Copperhead Road for 2.2 mi, then R on Witherbee Road for 0.4 mi. If approaching S from Jamestown on SC 41, turn R on SR 125 and go 7.5 mi.

Designated a national recreation trail in 1979, **Section I** of the trail was severely damaged by Hurricane Hugo 10 years later. Since then parts of the trail have been relocated (one of which includes following 7.2 mi of **Jericho Trail,** mainly an equestrian route), and completely new sections—a total increase of more than 8 mi for **Section I** of the trail. The trail is named for General Francis Marion, the "Swamp Fox," whose brigade during the American Revolution would attack the British and then withdraw to the dense forests on Snow's Island. British colonel Banastre Tarleton called him an "old fox, the devil himself could not catch him."

The trail passes through pine barrens, low mossy grounds with hardwoods, and swamps and bays with cypress in still or flowing

dark waters. Almost everywhere you see the snapped barkless trees, sentinels of Hugo's fury. The slightest breeze provides a soughing sound among the longleaf and loblolly pines in open broomstraw savannahs, in contrast to the cloistered depths of the dense swamps and carpets of sphagnum moss. Wildlife you may see includes squirrel, deer, turkey, songbirds, quail, waterfowl, snakes, wildhog, and raccoon. Fire anthills are frequently seen along the trail. Wildflowers (including some insectivorous species) include blazing star, violet, lady lupine, hatpin, aster, and wild azalea. Dense shrubs are sweet pepper bush, pondberry, blueberry, gallberry, and fetterbush. Patches of ferns are prominent, sometimes the most beautiful in the spring, when fern croziers are uncoiling. Prominent hardwoods are oak, hickory, maple, poplar, elm, and sweetgum.

There are three primitive campsites (one with a water handpump) in this section. The trail has signage to indicate hiking only or parts for multiple usage by equestrians or bicyclists. The blaze is a white vertical bar with a square at the top.

I have been hiking the forest trails and timber tramways for more than 20 years, in all seasons, sometimes with hikers Eric Tang, Jeff Fleming, David Colclough, and Darrell Williams. My seasonal choice is late winter and early spring for temperature comfort and to avoid mosquitoes, ticks, and redbugs. It also does not conflict with the major fall hunting season.

To start the hike at the E trailhead, begin on an old railroad grade with pines, hardwoods, fragrant honeysuckle and jessamine, and ferns. Cross SR 217 at 0.7 mi and a bridge over Steed Creek at 0.9 mi. At 1.6 mi cross SR 133 to parallel S of FR 202, a road to cross for a parking area at 3.1 mi. Walk through a young pine forest on a smooth path to reach Cooter Creek Road (FR 224) at 3.5 mi. Turn R and follow the gravel road and bridge over a tributary of Wambaw Swamp. Leave the road and continue on the railroad grade. In open areas the sweet glue on sundews sparkles in the sun. (According to folk medicine, the sundew, a scopose herb with saponia, reduces coughing.) Cross other forest roads and arrive

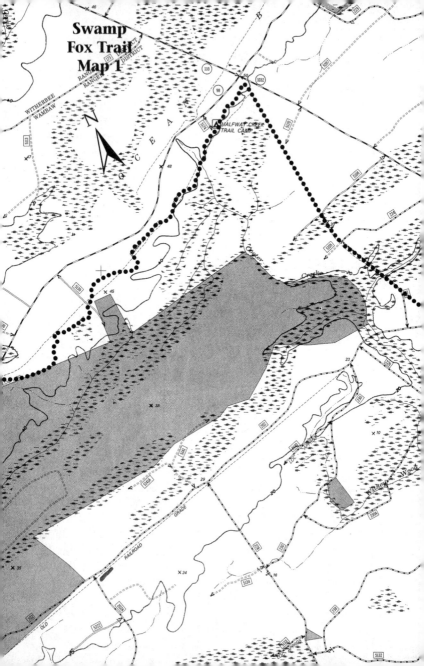

Swamp
Fox Trail
Map 1

HALFWAY CREEK
TRAIL CAMP

WITHERBEE
WAMBAW

RAILROAD GRADE

OLD

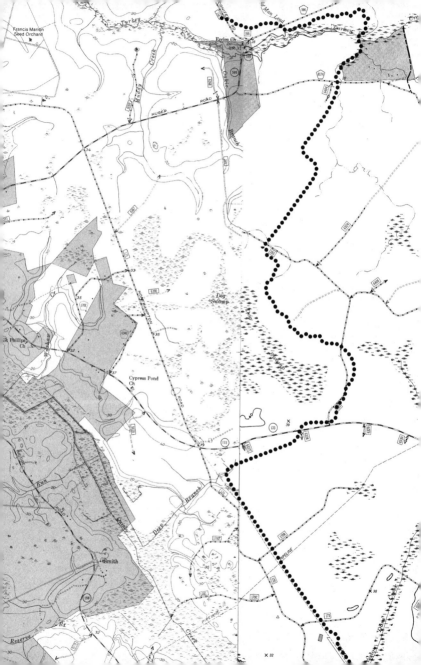

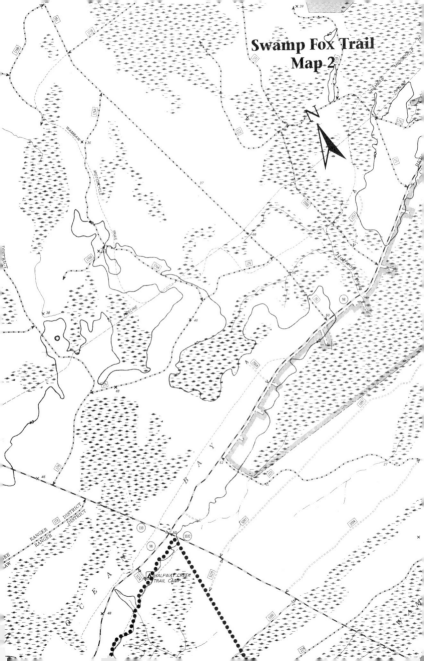

**Swamp Fox Trail
Map 2**

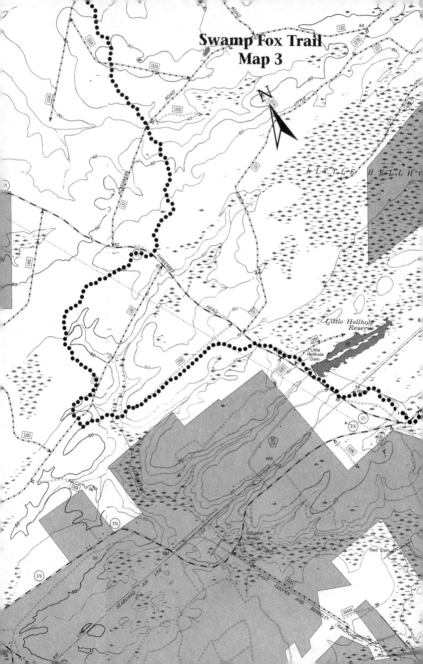

Swamp Fox Trail
Map 3

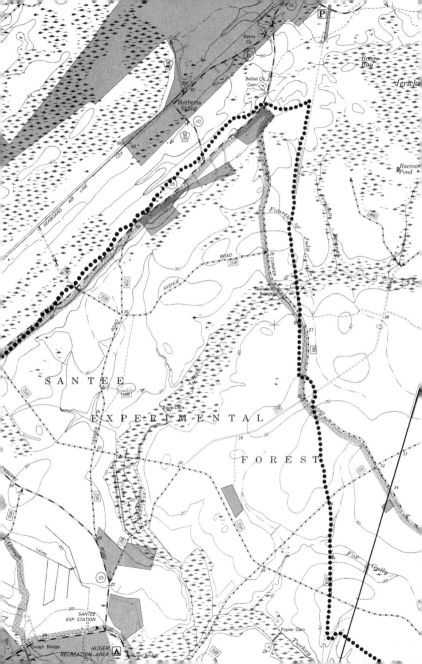

Swamp Fox Trail
Map 4

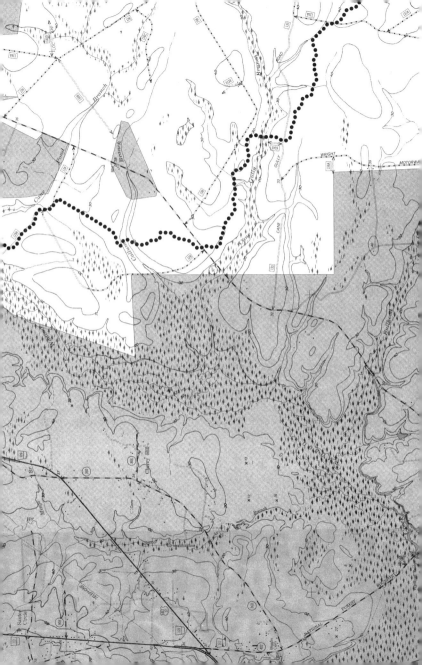

near the corner of SR 133 and SC 98 at 5.5 mi. At 6 mi pass through Halfway Creek Campground, where leaf beds lie under live oaks and drinking water is from a hand pump. (Here are a parking area and access road from SC 98). For the next 2.9 mi, follow a weaving white sand trail through one of the forest's most beautiful stands of longleaf pine. It can remind us of Paul Hamilton Hayne, a South Carolina poet, who wrote a number of poems about pines. A brief example is this excerpt from "Aspects of the Pines":

> A stillness, strange, divine, ineffable,
> Broods round and o'er them in the wind's surcease,
> And on each tinted copse and shimmering dell
> Rests the mute rapture of deep hearted peace.

Cross Halfway Creek Road (SC 98) and onto an old railroad grade. Pass the Harleston Dam Primitive Campsite, L, and at 10.2 mi cross a bridge over Harleston Dam Creek. At 10.9 mi cross FR 173, leaving the boundary of Wambaw Ranger District into Witherbee Ranger District. After passing under a powerline, cross FR 170B to enter a wet area and over a footbridge in a cypress grove. At 12.9 mi cross SC 133 (the highway between Huger and Awendaw). For the next mile the trail crisscrosses FR 265 to head NW along the edge of Dog Swamp. Hardly discernible now (unless you hiked the trail before Hurricane Hugo), the former **Swamp Fox Trail** turned L at 14.9 mi to terminate at a parking area on Irishtown Road (FR 251F) near a jct with SC 402. (Currently, the 1.8-mi **Huger Loop Trail** follows part of the former **Swamp Fox Trail** from the parking area.) Cross FR 265 again at 15.3 mi to follow a straight, old, and gated FR 610A through open pine forests to Huger Road (FR 174) at 17 mi, a popular hunting area.

Cross FR 174 to a wide trail and descent slightly to the wetlands of scenic Turkey Creek. Among cypress and palmetto, cross a footbridge at 17.5 mi. Continue N but soon curve W and parallel FR 166 before crossing it at 18.5 mi. After a 390-ft parallel with Old

Man Lead Branch, jct with the **Jericho Trail,** R. (Designated an equestrian trail, its loop also goes L to follow the **Swamp Fox Trail** for 7.2 mi.) Cross Conifer Road (FR 166) again at 19.1 mi. The trail parallels the wetlands of Turkey Creek with numerous log bridges before crossing Irishtown Road (FR 251F) at 21 mi, and busy SC 41 at 21.8 mi.

Across SC 41 the trail crosses a footbridge (honoring the Fleet Murphy family) and turns sharply N on an old railroad logging tram. Cross Yellowjacket Road (FR 159) at 23 mi. Cross Conifer Road again and then FR 158 to twice more cross Conifer Road, the last at 24.3 mi. At 24.5 mi a long gabian has been created with granite boulders to cross a swampy section of Nicholson Creek. This allows for passage of horses, bikers, and hikers. A bridge follows and at 24.6 mi is Nicholson Creek Primitive Camp, R. The straight trail parallels Jericho Branch and crosses Fourth of July Branch. At 25.8 mi the **Swamp Fox Trail** turns W, leaving the **Jericho Trail,** and arrives at the jct of Conifer Road and Witherbee Road (SR 125) at 26.2 mi. Cross the road, turn SW, and parallel Witherbee Road for the next 3 mi. It crosses SR 722 at 27.8 mi. At 29.2 mi reach the W end of **Section I** and the E trailhead of **Section II** across the road from a parking area at Witherbee Ranger Office.

Access for Section II: In addition to the E trailhead, the W trailhead is at Canal Picnic Area on US 52, N of Moncks Corner, 4 mi from US 52 and US 17A jct, or 2 mi S from Bonneau.

Continue SW from the Witherbee Ranger Office to parallel Witherbee Road (SC 171). At 0.4 mi curve R (W) and follow a wide forest road R of an old canal. Exit the woods to Witherbee Road, turn R, and cross the Seaboard Railroad at 1.1 mi. Reenter the forest and cross the dam Little Hellhole Dam, a haven for waterfowl, at 1.4 mi. Cross Witherbee Road at 1.9 mi into an open forest with sedges, grasses, bracken, and pitcher plants. After 0.2 mi turn L on an old forest road. Pass under a powerline at 2.2 mi. Enter a hardwood wet area and cross a 220-ft boardwalk over Alligator Creek. Gently ascend to cross FR 130 at 3.2 mi. Follow old roads through an open pine forest and broomstraw to cross Witherbee Road again at 4.4 mi.

In a grassy field with scattered longleaf pine are trumpet *(Sarracenia flava)* and hooded *(sarracenis minor)* pitcher-plants. After a grove of young hardwoods, cross a footbridge over the headwaters of Bullhead Run at 5.5 mi. Cross Ackerman Road (FR 132) at 5.6 mi. Pass a singular large longleaf pine at 5.8 mi, near the crossing of FR 132A at 6.1 mi. After passage through a young pine forest, cross FR 133A at 7 mi. There are a number of log bridges between here and Cane Gully Road (FR 133) at 8.2 mi. From here it is 290 yd on a wide pathway and dense pine forest to Cane Gully Primitive Camp near a pond. Cross a bridge, where the stream cascades underneath, to a high dike. Cypress is prominent. Turn L at 8.5 mi and follow old timber-cut roads graced with large dogwoods. At 9.8 mi cross SC 97 to FR 128, and immediately turn R into the forest. Through some wet areas cross a short bridge over Callum Branch at 10.6 mi among poplar, holly, and yaupon. Reach FR 128 again at 11.3 mi. Turn L and after 0.1 mi enter the forest at a road fork to parallel FR 128A. Pass a large sawdust pile at 11.7 mi; cross FR 128A at 11.8 mi, but notice a side trail L to the end of FR 128A at 12 mi.

For the next 0.7 mi, you will have perhaps the most spectacular scenery of the trail. There are large cypresses draped with Spanish moss, cypress knees rising from the sable water, and palmettos on the banks of an old canal. Fourteen bridges and boardwalks, skillfully crafted and environmentally friendly, make the journey possible through Wadboo Swamp. At 13.1 mi is a side trail, L, to access the cul-de-sac of Patts Road (FR 199). Pass under a powerline at 13.9 mi and arrive at US 17A and Patts Road at 14 mi. (It is 6 mi L [S] on US 17A to Moncks Corner.)

Cross US 17A into a pine forest with frequent log bridges bordered with switch cane and sweet pepper bush. Reach a crossing of paved SR 379 at 14.7 mi. At 15.3 mi leave the wood's path to avoid a swamp by turning R on FR 115. After 0.2-mi turn L off the road. Pass R of two swamps, cross FR 115A at 16 mi, then follow a long logwalk and bridge at 16.2 mi. The tannic-colored water flows L (S) to Canady Branch. Pass under a powerline at 16.4 mi, and exit the forest at a parking space beside highway US 52 at 16.8 mi. (It is 2 mi R [N] to the town of Bonneau.) Cross the highway to turn L in the forest.

At 17.2 mi is the W end of the **Swamp Fox Trail** and the connection (R) with the E end of Lake Moultrie Passage of the **Palmetto Trail.** (See the **Palmetto Trail** in Chapter VI.) Ahead is a bridge to the Canal Picnic Area, with picnic tables and shelter, vault toilets, hand pump water, and a vehicular access to US 52. The facility is for day use only and is 6 mi N of Moncks Corner.

Jericho Trail

Length: 17.8 mi (28.5 km); **easy** to **moderate;** USGS Maps: Huger, Bethera, Ocean Bay, Schulerville; trailhead: SC 41 parking area.

Access: From Huger at jct of SC 402 and SC 41, drive 7 mi N on SC 41 to parking area, L (1.8 mi S of Seaboard Railroad crossing).

Since Hurricane Hugo in 1989, this multi-use loop trail for horses, bikers, and hikers has been cleared of fallen trees, some bridges have been built or restored, and a number of trail miles have been relocated. The major change is the relocation N of Turkey Creek to avoid deep water and danger of flooding. I particularly appreciate the change after an unexpected flooding during a hike with Jeff Fleming, David Colclough, and Eric Tang in 1983. (The trip was described in the first three editions of this book.) Another major change is combining 7.2 mi with the rerouted **Swamp Fox Trail.** After a hike in 1997 I noticed that the trail was infrequently used and remains an equestrian preference. As on the **Swamp Fox Trail,** hunters are in the area during the hunting seasons. Summertime is not a recommended season for hiking because of biting insects, and the trail should be avoided during heavy rains and flooding. Primitive camping permits are provided by the ranger offices.

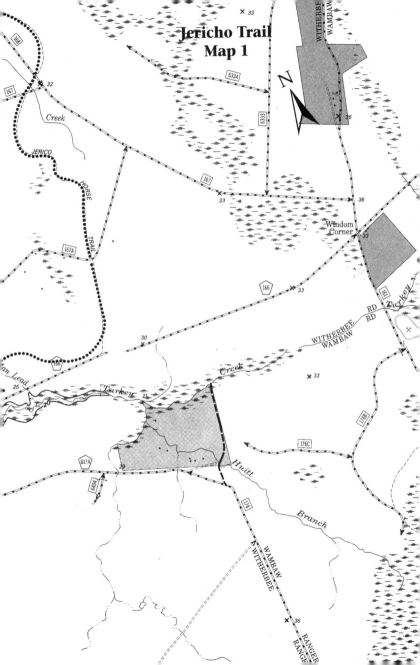

Jericho Trail
Map 1

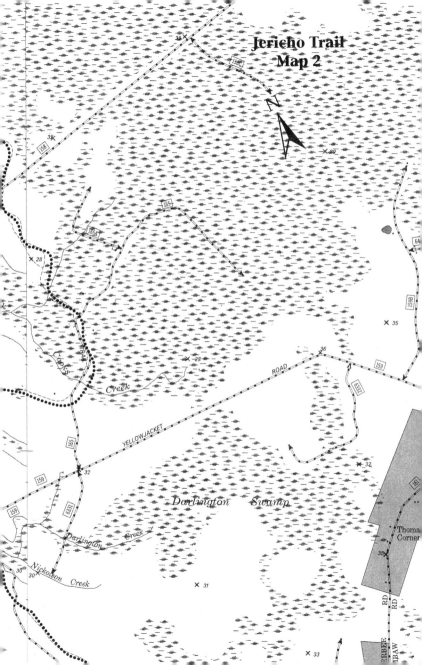

**Jericho Trail
Map 2**

Follow the trail clockwise, cross SC 41, and partially follow an old roadbed and dike, formerly Big Island Motorway. After 1.0 mi enter a pine forest with a ground cover of blueberries, then cross Hell Hole Road (FR 158). At 2.2 mi cross a tributary of Cook's Creek in a stand of hardwoods. Arrive at FR 165 at 2.4 mi, turn R and follow it over culverts that drain into Cook's Creek. Leave the road and walk into an open forest and grazing fields. Fire anthills, deer, wild turkeys, and chameleons are likely to be seen in this area. Enter a wildlife-management area at 3.4 mi, arrive at Yellow-jacket Road (FR 159) to cross a bridge over Nicholson Creek, then turn L on FR 168. Cross Burned Cane Rd (FR 167) at 6.5 mi, pass more grassy fields and open forests on the L, and enter a longleaf pine forest at 7.4 mi. After FR 167A, at 7.8 mi, cross Old Man Lead Branch to jct with the **Swamp Fox Trail** at 8.5 mi. (To the L on **Swamp Fox Trail** it is 390 ft to Conifer Road [FR 166]).

From here the trail is described in the **Swamp Fox Trail** entry (earlier in this chapter) for the next 7.2 mi. At 15.7 mi the trail turns L (0.4 mi W to Witherbee Road [SR 125]). Continue R (N) on the old tramway, cross a bridge over Boar Bay (part of Jericho Swamp), and veer R at 16.2 mi. Reach a parking area at SR 148 at 16.4 mi. (It is 0.4 mi L on SR 148 to a crossroads in the community of Bethera on SR 125.) At 16.8 mi turn R onto an old sawmill road and reach the site of Jericho Plantation. Large live oaks shade the vanished homestead. Skirt N of Jericho Swamp and return at 17.8 mi to the trailhead on SC 41.

Guilliard Lake Scenic Area

Guilliard Lake Trail
Length: 0.6 mi round-trip (1 km); **easy;** USGS Map: Jamestown; trailhead: parking area.

Located on the S side of the Santee River in the Wambaw Ranger District, this 1,000-acre forest was established to preserve some of the ancient trees, particularly cypress. Perforated limestone outcroppings are in the area on Dutant Creek. Camping is limited here to six sites; fresh water and activities such as picnicking, fishing, birding, and nature study are available. You can reach it from Jamestown by taking SC 45 SE for 3.6 mi to FR 150 and turning L. Go 1.6 mi on FR 150 and turn L on FR 150-G. Go another 1.7 mi to the picnic area.

When Scott Smith and I routinely checked the facilities at Guilliard Lake, the site of the former town of Jamestown, we were surprised at its natural beauty and mystique. The trail went upstream and crossed a small stream to follow the river's edge. Huge trees, some contorted and convoluted, grew around us. Ash, cedar, elm, loblolly, and live oaks were intertwined, seized by long, snakelike Alabama supplejack, coiling, curling, twisting, crawling, hanging over limbs, and dangling over the trail—a route out of *Raiders of the Lost Ark*. The vines were smooth, damp, and shiny from the junglelike moisture. The ferns and partridge berry were so thick that a moccasin could have slithered up my trouser legs before I could have untangled myself from the vines. Before we turned back we lowered ourselves into a floodplain where the dark earth was dry enough for us to see 8-ft-tall cypress knees. They were scaly, or glazed, but always damp, alive, ready to pulsate, like creatures from *Alien*. A base of what I think was an ash had ballooned to such proportions that five adults could stoop to walk inside. Some unfamiliar birds squawked raucously overhead where the trail ended at 0.3 mi. Back through the cypress, I thought of Beatrice Ravenel's words: Cypress roots "at the edge of the swamp as roughly fluted, age-wrinkled, have budded their rufous knobs like dim and reptilian eyes. That watch."

Chapter II
National Parks, Refuges, and U.S. Army Corps of Engineers Projects

SECTION 1
National Parks

Congaree Swamp National Monument (Richland County)

"That in order to preserve and protect for the education, inspiration and enjoyment of present and future generations an outstanding example of a near virgin southern hardwood forest situated in the Congaree River floodplain . . ." began Public Law 94-545, passed by the 94th Congress in October 1976. It was the result of 26 years of research and efforts by such groups as the Audubon Society and Sierra Club in Columbia and individuals such as Harry R. E. Hampton and Richard Pough, and of the formation of Congaree Action Now (CAN) to preserve this majestic natural heritage.

Comprising 22,200 acres, the monument is the largest natural area for floodplain study in the Southeast. More than 325 vascular flora have been identified here, including nine species of wild orchids and 16 species of ferns. National and state record-size trees have grown here for years. Wildlife is abundant, with 38 species of mammals, 33 species of reptiles, 170 species of birds (including one species that is endangered), and 50 species of fish. Poisonous snakes are the cottonmouth moccasin, copperhead, and canebreak rattler. Fishing is allowed, with the exception of Weston Lake, according to state laws. Permits, which are free, are necessary for camping.

Flooding occurs an average of 10 times per year, inundating up to 90 percent of the park at times. My first visit to the park was a March day when flooding had occurred. Ranger Fran Rametta was my guide, and we drove on a roadbed that was covered with water. Although a trailhead at an old hunting lodge was on high ground, the water surge prevented passage farther into the forest. On a subsequent visit when the floodplain was dry, Ranger Rametta led a group of us on an unforgettable hike to the heart of the swamp.

In addition to land trails, there is a marked canoe trail on Cedar Creek. Access is on SR 1288, off SR 734, from SC 48 at Gadsden. (You must furnish your own canoe and life-saving equipment.) A permit from the ranger station is required if you plan to camp overnight on a canoe trip. One advantage of canoeing is that you can explore areas of the swamp that are inaccessible by land trails.

Information: Congaree Swamp National Monument, 200 Caroline Sims Rd., Hopkins, SC 29061; (803) 776–4396.

Access: From downtown Columbia at the jct of I-77 (Exit 5) and SC 48, take SC 48 SE for 12.2 mi to a fork. Take the R fork, SR 734, which is Old Bluff Rd. (If you are on I-26, exit at 116 to SC 48 for the fastest route.) Follow Old Bluff Rd. 4.6 mi to the CONGAREE SWAMP sign. Turn R on Caroline Sims Rd., a dirt road, and go another 0.8 mi to the ranger station. (If arriving from the E, drive 11.3 mi from US 601 at Wateree on SC 48 to Gadsden, turn L on SR 1288 and R on SR 734 to the park entrance. Follow signs along SC 48 [Bluff Rd.] to the monument.)

Bluff Trail (1.6 mi), Boardwalk Loop Trail (2.5 mi), Weston Lake Trail (4.6 mi), Kingsnake Trail (11.1 mi), Oak Ridge Trail (7.5 mi), and River Trail (10.4 mi)

Length: 37.7 mi round-trip, combined (60.3 km); **easy** to **moderate**; USGS Map: Gadsden; trailhead: parking area.

The Congaree Swamp trails are multiple loops that extend from the ranger station to the Congaree River. Trails are color-coded with marks on trees. The routes provide a classic example of the range of tree heights—emergent, the highest; high canopy; second canopy; and the understory trees and shrubs.

The 1.6-mi **Bluff Trail** circles the ranger station and has a primitive campsite on the E section of the loop. From this trail and at the parking area is the elevated **Boardwalk Trail,** where you encounter a typical wet portion of the swamp. The **Boardwalk Trail** connects with the **Weston Lake Trail.** It was on the **Weston Lake Trail** that we saw an overcup oak, a monumental national champ rising 16 stories high and more than 22 ft in circumference near Cedar Creek. (This oak was later blown down by Hurricane Hugo.)

Nearby is a loblolly pine champ, about 300 years of age, which is more than 15 ft in circumference and 145 ft tall. Along the trail papaw grows in profusion during the summer months. A low boardwalk, built after Hurricane Hugo, is connected to the **Weston Lake Trail** loop and elevated boardwalk.

From the **Weston Lake Trail,** there are two footbridge crossings of Cedar Creek. The SE bridge is a route to the 11.1-mi **Kingsnake Trail** loop. At the SW bridge is a route to the 7.5-mi **Oak Ridge Trail** loop and the 10.4-mi **River Trail** loop.

We followed the **River Trail** counterclockwise and, after 3.3 mi, reached the N bank of the Congaree River. We turned L, downstream, and passed through a dense forest of giant sweet and black gum, cypress, sycamore, and ash. Among the understory plant life were scattered water elm, spicebush, ironwood, and switch cane. After leaving the riverside we turned L along Boggy Gut to complete the loop and return to the **Oak Ridge Trail** jct.

Cowpens National Battlefield (Cherokee County)

General Daniel Morgan, considered by military historians to be one of the superior battlefield tacticians in the American Revolution, hurriedly deployed his 900 men on a slope in Hannah's Cowpens. It was the afternoon of January 16, 1781. That morning their breakfast had been interrupted when they heard that "Benny (the British) is coming." Leaving their camp near Thicketty Creek, they would make a stand against Lt. Colonel Banastre Tarleton and his 1,100 infantry and cavalry on a frontier pasturing ground.

A pitched battle ensued about daybreak on January 17, 1781. In about an hour it was all over. The British suffered 110 dead, more than 200 wounded, and 500 captured. Rebel losses were 10 dead and 60 wounded. Illustrating the significance of this British defeat to Congress, a bill was passed on March 9, 1781, awarding three of the 12 Revolutionary War-hero medals to officers of Cowpens: Brig. General Daniel Morgan, Lt. Colonel William Washington, and Lt. Colonel John E. Howard.

The 842-acre park, established March 4, 1929, has an interpretive center, wayside exhibits on the trails and the tour road, a picnic area, the Robert Scruggs House, and a U.S. Memorial Monument.

Information: Cowpens National Battlefield, P.O. Box 308, Chesnee, SC 29323; (864) 461–2828/7077.

Access: From the jct of SC 11 and SC 110, go E on SC 11 0.2 mi to park entrance. It is 2 mi E from Chesnee on SC 11 and US 221A and 8.5 mi N of Gaffney on SC 11 from I-95.

Cowpens Battlefield Trail

Length: 1.2 mi (1.8 km); **easy;** USGS Map: Cowpens; trailhead: Visitor Center.

This loop trail with 10 exhibit stations is paved from the Visitor Center to the Green River Road, the site of the British formation march. (Another paved trail, 0.2 mi, also leads to this point from the tour road, Battlefield Overlook.) The other half of the trail follows the Green River Road, a well-maintained dirt route, to the lawn of the Visitor Center.

Among the vegetation on the trail is wild cherry, Virginia pine, maple, cedar, sweet gum, sourwood, oaks, dogwood, sumac, mulberry, New England tea, and elderberry. Wildflowers bloom in the open fields.

Fort Sumter National Monument
(Charleston County)

There are two short trails, each approximately 0.5 mi, where leaves and tree limbs never fall but whose historic paths receive the salty mist of Charleston Harbor. Each year thousands of visitors stroll the walkways and climb the stone steps at two national monuments: Fort Sumter, "where the Civil War began"; and Fort Moultrie, across the channel, site of the first decisive American victory in the Revolutionary War.

Fort Moultrie, on Sullivans Island, has undergone a number of stages of development and reconstruction. The first fort was built in 1776 to protect Charleston from the British. After the Revolution the second Fort Moultrie, a five-sided earth and wood battery, was built, but a hurricane destroyed it in 1804. A brick fort was built in 1809 and was used in the Civil War. After 1885 a new battery of concrete and steel was constructed. On your walk, which should include Cannon Walk and Battery Jasper, you will go back in time, from WW II Harbor Entrance Control to the site of the palmetto and sand fort of 1776.

The U.S. government began building Fort Sumter in 1829 and had almost completed the structure on a harbor shoal by 1860. Designed for a garrison of 650 men and 135 guns on three tiers, only 85 men and 60 cannon were there when, on August 12, 1861, a Confederate battery at Fort Johnson on the shoreline opened fire. The shelling lasted 34 hours, and on April 14 Major Robert Anderson, the fort's commanding officer, agreed to evacuate. On April 15 President Lincoln began mobilizing the U.S. militia. For four years, "the longest siege in warfare," the Confederates held the fort and never surrendered to Union attacks.

The two forts are administered jointly. Visitors' hours at Fort Moultrie are 8:00 A.M. to 5:00 P.M. (closed on Christmas Day). Access to Fort Moultrie is on W Middle Street on Sullivans Island. From US 17 take SC 703 and follow the signs. Hours for Fort Sumter change on a seasonal basis. Access is by boat only. While visitors can take personal boats to Fort Sumter, most visitors take tour boats. In Charleston turn onto Lockwood Drive from US 17 and go to the Municipal Marina (near the W end of Calhoun Street). In Mt. Pleasant boats depart from Patriots Point. For boat schedules contact Fort Sumter Tours.

Information: Fort Moultrie National Monument or Fort Sumter National Monument, 1214 Middle St., Sullivans Island, SC 29482; (843) 883–3123. Fort Sumter Tours, Box 59, Charleston, SC 29402, (843) 722–1691.

Kings Mountain National Military Park (Cherokee and York Counties)

Established in 1931 by the U.S. War Department and transferred to the National Park Service in 1933, Kings Mountain National Military Park has 3,945 acres of rocky clay soil, on which an oak and hickory forest and scattered pines grow. Named after an early settler, the area was farmland, grazing fields, and timberland. A small, outlying spur of the Blue Ridge Mountains, its highest elevation is 1,045 ft, at Browns Mountain. An exceptionally significant war shrine of the American Revolution, it commemorates a band of 910 frontiersmen whose speed, courage, and marksmanship defeated 1,104 Loyalists, led by British major Patrick Ferguson, on October 7, 1780. "It was the greatest victory of the Southern militia," wrote historian Wilma Dykeman in *With Fire and Sword*. (See **Overmountain Victory Trail** later in this chapter for more information.)

The Visitor Center has considerable exhibit material for interpreting the history of the area and the battleground. An interpretive **Battlefield Trail** with visual displays begins at the Visitor Center and circles the ridge crest. The park has 4.8 mi of the 15-mi Kings Mountain National Recreation Trail, which loops through the Kings Mountain State Park. Another significant trail (mainly a tour-road trail) is the **Overmountain Victory Trail,** which has its S terminus here. The park is open daily 9:00 A.M. to 5:00 P.M., except Thanksgiving Day, Christmas Day, and New Year's Day. Each year at 3:00 P.M. on October 7, the park has a simple ceremony after the **Overmountain Victory Trail** marchers arrive.

Information: Superintendent, Kings Mountain National Military Park, P.O. Box 40, Kings Mountain, NC 28086; (864) 936–7921.

Access: From I-85 near the North Carolina state line, turn at park sign on SC 216 to the park entrance.

Kings Mountain Battlefield Trail

Length: 1.5 mi (2.4 km); **easy;** USGS Map: Grover; trailhead: Visitor Center terrace.

To get the most out of the trail, first see the interpretive film and displays in the Visitor Center. Then exit on the terrace and go R. The entire loop is paved with asphalt to aid the physically handicapped. Visual displays are along the route.

After 0.3 mi we passed a small stream on the R where button bush, ostrich fern, mountain laurel, wild ginger, and trailing arbutus grew. At 0.5 mi we passed a spring on the L, the spot where the frontiersmen tended to their wounded. At 0.7 mi on the R is a spur trail to the place where President Hoover spoke to 75,000 people on October 7, 1930, in celebration of the sesquicentennial of the Battle of Kings Mountain. At 1 mi we passed the centennial monument in honor of the "officers and others," and at 1.2 mi we passed an obelisk, erected in 1909, which lists all the Patriots who died or were wounded in the battle. Descending from the ridge we passed the rock cairn where Major Ferguson was buried in a raw cowhide. Some historians believe that Virginia Sal, one of two women with Major Ferguson during the battle, was buried beside him. The battle, which was fought from 3:00 to 4:00 P.M. on a Saturday, pitted Americans against Americans—Patriots against Loyalists. The only Englishman was Major Ferguson. The Patriots' desire for revenge led them to murder some Loyalists after they had surrendered. Patriot losses were 28 killed and 62 wounded; and Loyalist losses were 225 slain, 163 wounded, and 716 taken prisoner. Major Ferguson's decision to ensconce his troops on a hilltop where he could be surrounded proved to be a deadly mistake, even though he had said that "God could not drive him from it." The trail returns to the Visitor Center at 1.5 mi.

Kings Mountain Hiking Trail

Designated a national recreation trail in 1981, this excellent trail for hiking and camping is 15 mi long, with 4.8 mi in Kings Mountain National Military Park and the other 10.2 mi in Kings Mountain State Park. (See Kings Mountain State Park in Chapter III.)

Please observe park regulations if you plan to camp on the **Kings Mountain Hiking Trail.** Hikers must use only the Garner Branch campsite in the park, must register at the Visitor Center, and must register any vehicle left overnight in the parking area. No pets, horses, or ORVs are allowed on the trail. Firearms and fireworks are prohibited. Basic trail courtesy requires that you pack out what you pack in. (Other campsites are available in Kings Mountain State Park; 803–222–3209.)

Overmountain Victory Trail (Park Section)

Length: 2.3 mi (3.7 km); **easy;** USGS Map: Grover; trailhead: Kings Creek.

The **Overmountain Victory Trail,** also called the **Overmountain Victory National Historic Trail** (as amended by the National Trail System Act of 1978 and 1980), is a 313-mi motor route from Craig's Meadows in Abingdon, Virginia, to Kings Mountain National Military Park battlefield in South Carolina. Short segments—totaling about 12 mi—of the route are on federal lands in Cherokee National Forest in Tennessee; Pisgah National Forest, Blue Ridge Parkway, and W. Kerr Scott Reservoir in North Carolina; and Cowpens and Kings Mountain battlefields in South Carolina.

The trail simulates as closely as possible the route taken by the overmountain frontiersmen in September and October 1780 to accept the challenge made by Major Ferguson. He had threatened that, if they continued to oppose British rule and arms, he would march into the mountains, "hang their leaders, and lay their country waste with fire and sword."

For a number of years, members of the Overmountain Victory Trail Association have been traversing the route. They and thousands of other hikers, equestrians, and motorists celebrated the 1980 bicentennial with a march from Abingdon to Kings Mountain. The organization strives to identify and protect the "historic route and its historic remnants and artifacts for public use and enjoyment." Three major publications on the history, management, and mapping of this trail are published by the National Park Service, Southeast Regional Office, 1924 Bldg., 100 Alabama St. SW, Atlanta, GA 30303; (404) 562–3124.

Chris Revels, (now chief ranger) at Kings Mountain, showed me the trail route for my first hike. I drove W from the Visitor Center to the park boundary and turned L on paved SR 86. After 1.7 mi I reached a jct with SR 85, first on the R and ahead on the L. I parked on the L and began hiking L, almost parallel with SR 86, for 0.4 mi back to Kings Creek, the beginning of the trail into the park. After wading the shallow stream, I followed Houser Road to the Henry Houser homestead (1803) on the L.

Continuing ahead to a powerline jct, I turned R at 0.4 mi, ascending and descending to a power-line jct at 0.6 mi. I turned L, then R into a hardwood and scattered-pine forest. Leaving the old forest road at 1.4 mi, I turned R on the graveled park road, Yorkville Road, and approached SC 216 at 1.8 mi.

Across the highway I took graveled Shelbyville Road and went 0.2 mi to a gated fireroad. I turned R on the fireroad, which has first a R and then a L jct with the **Kings Mountain Hiking Trail.** The trail continues straight ahead at both jcts and reaches the **Battlefield Trail** at 2.3 mi. I stopped in the area where young Major William Chronicle died while leading his men up the hill. Nearby there was a sign: WITHIN THE HOUR A BLOW WILL BE STRUCK FOR LIBERTY.

Ninety Six National Historic Site
(Greenwood County)

Several romantic legends explain how Ninety Six got its name. One tells of a Cherokee maiden, Cateechee, who rode 96 mi on horseback from Keowee to save the English trader she loved from an impending Cherokee attack at the British fort. A more prosaic story is that Ninety Six first appeared as a name in George Hunter's map of the Cherokee Path, a trade route from Charleston to the Cherokee village of Keowee, 96 mi ahead.

Designated a historic site in 1976, the 989 acres of colonial settlement, fort, and battlefield ruins are on the S edge of the town of Ninety Six—a town with a number in its name and its name in its zip-code number and in its post-office-box number. The name was changed in 1785 to Cambridge. Many settlers objected, however, and local inhabitants supported the change back to Ninety Six in 1852. Between Greenwood, the "Emerald City," and beautiful Lake Greenwood, the town and the park are in the heart of the Old Ninety Six District. The park is open daily except Christmas Day and New Year's Day. There is a visitor center, videotapes with historical information, and a short nature trail with 20 plant markers. No camping is allowed in the park.

Information: Ninety Six National Historic Site, P.O. Box 496, Ninety Six, SC 29666; (864) 543–4068.

Access: From downtown Ninety Six at the jct of SR 248 and SC 34, go S 1.7 mi on SR 248 to the park entrance on the L.

Ninety Six History Trail

Length: 1 mi (1.6 km); **easy;** USGS Map: Ninety Six; trailhead: parking area.

"The greatest thing about this park is the Star Fort," Park Superintendent Robert Armstrong will tell you. I entered on a wide paved trail with a border of honeysuckle and periwinkle in a young mixed forest, crossed the Island Ford Road, and made a loop around the siegeworks of the British Star Redoubt. Along the trail are exhibit signs that fully explain the Revolutionary War battle that took place here. University of South Carolina archaeologists have made extensive study of the earthworks where General Nathanael Greene ordered an assault on the fort on June 18, 1781. His troops were repulsed by the Loyalists defending Ninety Six. After the attack failed the impending arrival of 2,000 British regulars commanded by Lord Francis Rawdon forced General Greene to withdraw. But soon afterward Lord Rawdon ordered the post burned and abandoned. After the earthworks at 0.5 mi, I passed in a grassy field "a real country town" (c. 1769–1781), where, signs explain, there once were "12 dwellings, courthouse, and jail." I examined the stockade fort and the area nearby, where a sign read:

JAMES BIRMINGHAM
VOLUNTEER
LONG CANE MILITIA
KILLED HERE
ON NOVEMBER 19-21-1775
THE FIRST SOUTH CAROLINIAN TO GIVE
HIS LIFE IN THE CAUSE OF FREEDOM.

SECTION 2
Wildlife Refuges

Cape Romain National Wildlife Refuge (Charleston County)

The Cape Romain National Wildlife Refuge is among the four wholly in South Carolina and more than 500 in the nation. Created by Congress, they are administered by the U.S. Fish and Wildlife Service of the Department of the Interior.

The refuges provide a natural environment for the protection of all species of wildlife, including those species that are endangered or threatened, and recreational facilities that are environment- or wildlife-oriented.

Poet laureate James Dickey has said that the "prettiest beach" he has seen anywhere in his travels is Pawley's Island, "except perhaps for the eastern beach of Bull's Island . . . a landscape out of Rimbaud."

Bull's Island is wild, free of people, and, as restless French poet Arthur Rimbaud wrote in "Le Bateau Ivre," "I have bathed in the poem of the sea . . . devouring the green azures."

This island is indeed a refuge from the noise and stress of highways and offices. But you can retreat there only for a day now; camping has been forbidden since 1978. And well it should be, because Bull's Island (named in honor of Stephen Bull, a colonial leader) is part of the Cape Romain National Wildlife Refuge. This refuge is recognized by many naturalists as the most significant wildlife area on the East Coast and is known for its wide range of waterfowl. More than 270 species of birds, some extremely rare, have been recorded there. Ornithological studies indicate that 107 of the general species nest on the refuge.

More than 35 mammal species have been identified in the refuge as well. On Bull's Island there are fewer species, but among them are white-tailed deer, raccoon, otter, southern fox squirrel, marsh rabbit, and a number of bat and mice species. Dolphin are found in salt marshes W of the island.

Among the amphibians are green tree frog, spring peeper, squirrel tree frog, and southern leopard frog. Reptiles include eastern mud turtle, yellow-bellied turtle, diamondback terrapin, Atlantic loggerhead turtle (an endangered species), Kemp's Ridley turtle, and alligator. Although both the southern copperhead and the eastern cottonmouth are in the refuge, the cottonmouth is the only poisonous snake identified on Bull's Island. At least eight other species of snakes have been catalogued within the refuge.

A treasure in the coastal environment, this 64,229-acre refuge has 34,229 acres of land, salt marshes, tidal creeks, and barrier islands. An additional 30,000 acres of open water provide a sanctuary for migratory waterfowl. Established in 1932, the refuge includes four major barrier islands: Cape Island; Raccoon Key; Lighthouse Island; and Bull's Island, called "gem of the Barriers" by Alexander Sprunt, Jr.

Bull's Island, the largest of the four, has 5,108 acres, of which 900 comprise eight impoundments of fresh water. It is approximately 6 mi long and 2 mi wide. In the interior are 1,500 acres of maritime forest. Hurricane Hugo destroyed 98 percent of the loblolly pine and 45 percent of the hardwoods, such as live oak, in 1989. Botany-oriented hikers will see an understory of red bay, yaupon, wax myrtle, holly, jessamine, muscadine, supplejack, and peppervine. Ferns and wildflowers complete the landscape. Aquatic plants include banana waterlily, sago pondweed, bulrush, giant foxtail, wild millet, and spike rush.

In January and February oystering and clamming peak, and ducks such as scaup and scoters are abundant in the open water before they move into the tidal creeks. Pelicans return in February. Saltwater fishing for channel bass is at its best in March. In April loggerhead sea turtles mate in the bays and tidal creeks. Alligators and loggerheads begin nesting on Bull's Island in May. July brings pelicans, herons, egrets, and shorebird fledglings; they begin flying in August. Wood ibis and black-crowned and yellow-crowned night herons are plentiful on Bull's Island in July. Dowitchers and herring gulls arrive and blue-winged teals leave in September. Migrating waterfowl arrive in large numbers for wintering in October. The fall channel-bass run peaks in November, and the local Audubon Society conducts its annual Christmas Bird Count on Bull's Island in December.

Travel to Bull's Island is by boat; once there you travel on foot. A charter boat is operated by Coastal Expeditions (843–881–4582).

You should go first to the Sewee Visitor Center on Highway 17 N, approximately 20 mi N of Charleston, for information on changes in restrictions, fishing regulations, or other visitor information. At Moore's Landing are restrooms and a boat ramp (usable only at high tide). Other boat ramps are at Buck Hall and McClel-

lanville, both NE of Moore's Landing (off US 17). Water distance to the island is about 3 mi. Headquarters hours are weekdays only, 8:30 A.M. to 4:30 P.M.

Take everything you will need for a day hike: food, hiking shoes, rain gear, sun protection, and insect repellent. Near the information exhibit on the island are a rain shelter, restrooms, picnic tables, and drinking water.

In addition to the three trails described below, other hikes are on the beach, going NE for 4 mi to Boneyard Beach or SW to the S end (4 mi from the shelter). As no camping is allowed in the refuge, hikers may wish to consult the South Carolina Wildlife and Marine Resources Department about camping on Capers Island, which adjoins Bull's Island. A permit is required. For information call (843) 795–6350.

Information: Sewee Visitor Center, 5821 Hwy 17 N, Awendaw, SC 29429; (843) 928–3368.

Access: Leave US 17 (15 mi N of Mt. Pleasant and 3.8 mi S of Awendaw) on Sewee Rd. Go 3.5 mi and turn R on Bull's Island Rd.; go 1.6 mi to Moore's Landing, the Intracoastal Waterway, and the refuge hq.

Support Facilities: Buck Hall Campground (Francis Marion National Forest) is approximately 10 mi N of Moore's Landing. Access is off US 17 (7 mi S of McClellanville), E on FR 236 for 0.2 mi. No hook-ups or showers, but flush toilets, picnic tables, and grills. Open all year. Telephone Wambaw Ranger District at (843) 887–3257.

Bull's Island Wildlife Trail

Length: 2 mi (3.2 km); **easy;** USGS Maps: Sewee Bay, Bull Island; trailhead: near information exhibit on Bull's Island.

From the dock follow the service road for 0.4 mi to the information exhibit and trail sign. Made a national recreation trail in February 1982, the trail is designed to show a cross section of the various wildlife habitats and flora representative of the southern barrier islands.

With me on this late-March hike were David Colclough, Jeff Fleming, Eric Tang, and our boatsman, Henry Kerr. At 0.5 mi we crossed a service road in the forest and followed a levee between Upper Summerhouse Pond on the R and Lower Summerhouse Pond on the L. Alligators often sun on the grassy banks. "This is sago pondweed and this is widgeon grass," Henry said, pointing his finger at the marsh. Coots were swimming nearby. "They bob their heads like a cork most all the time," he said.

The Fish and Wildlife Service had been clearing out some of the marshes, leaving mud that looked like ebony clay. "Now, to get rid of sand gnats," Henry said, "you mix rubbing alcohol and Avon's Skin-so-Soft." At 1.4 mi we turned L on a service road, where a fox squirrel and a raccoon, busy with their daily chores, ignored us. We reached Beach Road, turned R, passed the refuge personnel building, and returned to the trailhead.

Sheepshead Ridge Loop Trail

Length: 3.7 mi (5.9 mi); **easy;** USGS Maps: Sewee Bay, Bull Island; trailhead: near information exhibit.

We set out on the Sheepshead Ridge Road (on which passage is difficult after a heavy rain) through pines, palms, wax myrtle, and bullis vines. At 1.3 mi we turned R to cross a levee in Jack's Creek Pool and a short mound in an open area. Canvasback ducks were numerous. We returned to Beach Road at 2.6 mi and turned L to hike 0.2 mi to the beach. Sand dollars were prominent on the wide beach. Huge banks of logs looked as if a tidal wave from the movie *Green Dolphin Street* had hit the refuge. We returned on Beach Road to the shelter for a loop of 3.7 mi.

Old Fort Loop Trail

Length: 6.6 mi (10.6 km); **easy;** USGS Maps: Sewee Bay, Bull Island; trailhead: near information exhibit.

We turned L on Old Fort Road in front of the refuge personnel building and hiked through the forest to the remains of the old tabby wall, thought to be a fort or lookout for pirate ships in Bull's

Bay, at 2.2 mi. After a clockwise loop around Jack's Creek Pool, we reached Lighthouse Road again at 4.9 mi. We followed the road back to Beach Road, turning R, and completed the loop at 6.6 mi.

Carolina Sandhills National Wildlife Refuge (Chesterfield County)

An example of what 50 years of excellent natural-resources management can do for 45,348 acres of destroyed forest, impoverished soil, and vanished wildlife is the Carolina Sandhills National Wildlife Refuge. Established in 1939 as a wildlife-management demonstration area, it has become a diversified environment of restored forest with timber management, containing 30 ponds (335 acres) and 1,100 acres of open field habitats. Deer and beaver have returned. Other mammals are raccoon, mink, otter, skunk, red and gray fox, bobcat, fox squirrel, gray and flying squirrels, muskrat, and rabbit. More than 190 species of birds, 40 of which are rare, have been cataloged. Migratory ducks, including mallards, black ducks, widgeons, pintails, and ringnecks, as well as Canada geese, take refuge here in the winter months. This refuge has one of the nation's largest populations of the endangered red-cockaded woodpecker.

The refuge is on the Fall Line, with gently rolling sandhills between the piedmont plateau and the coastal plain. Its forest is chiefly longleaf pine and turkey oak. Scattered hardwoods are more prominent near streams. Open for daytime use only, the refuge has auto-tour routes to observation decks and nature study, picnicking, and hiking. Hunting and fishing are allowed according to refuge regulations.

Information: Refuge Manager, Carolina Sandhills National Wildlife Refuge, Route 2, Box 100, McBee, SC 29101; (843) 333–8401.

Access: On US 1, 11.5 mi S of Patrick and 3.5 mi N of McBee, enter at the refuge entrance sign. The refuge hq is on the L.

Support Facilities: The nearest campground is Cheraw State Park, 18.5 mi N on US 1.

Woodland Pond Trail

Length: 0.9 mi (1.4 km); **easy;** USGS Maps: Angelus, Middendorf; trailhead: parking area.

From the refuge headquarters on US 1, go 1 mi on the refuge road to Pool A, on the L, on the N side of Little Alligator Creek to the parking area. Follow the sign at the woods edge, and at 0.1 mi cross a footbridge over the edge of the lake. Some evidence of past beaver activity is here. At 0.5 mi cross a footbridge over a stream, then take a boardwalk, and return to the paved road. Turn L by the dam, and return to the parking area. Vegetation includes pines, poplar, oaks, and red bay.

Tate's Trail

Length: 4 mi (6.4 km); **easy;** USGS Maps: Angelus, Middendorf; trailhead: Martin's Lake boat ramp.

From **Woodland Pond Trail** go another 3.2 mi N on the paved refuge road to a sign at Martin's Lake on the R. Follow the gravel road for 1 mi, passing a parking area on the L at 0.6 mi on the way to the boat ramp.

Scott Smith let me out at the boat ramp so I would not have to backtrack. From the boat ramp I entered the trail and saw Carolina buckthorn, witch hazel, trailing chinquapin, pineweed, juniper, pines, bayberry, mosses, and ferns. At 0.5 mi I reached the observation deck, from which I could see across the lake to fields of grain for the migratory birds. After another 0.4 mi I reached the wildfowl photography blind; then the blazed trail continued to a deer crossing at 1.3 mi. Deer tracks were numerous. I crossed the refuge paved road to the SW side of Pool D. Plants in the area included rattlebox, dwarf papaw, false indigo, sumac, camphorweed, wooly mullein, snakeroot, titi, pink spiderwort, bonamia, and alder. Here as elsewhere the state flower, yellow jessamine (*Gelsemium sempervirens*), grew in profusion. More than 125 species of plants grow in the trail area.

I entered the woods again at 1.8 mi on an old logging road, turned R at 2 mi, and crossed a wood bridge over a creek. On an old road at 2.9 mi I reached a jct with a loop trail around Lake 12, but I noticed another jct with the loop trail at 3.2 mi after crossing a footbridge over a creek. The trail now entered a partial hardwood area before its exit at 3.4 mi on SC 145 (from here it is 6 mi S to US 1 on SR 145). I continued across the road to the Lake Bee dam and at the other side turned R on a trail without blazes. Pool H and a refuge road were at 4 mi, where Scott was waiting to pick me up.

Santee National Wildlife Refuge
(Clarendon County)

Established in 1942, the Santee National Wildlife Refuge has four management units—Bluff, Dingle Pond, Pine Island, and Cuddo—bordering on Lake Marion, a hydroelectric reservoir. The refuge has 15,095 acres (1,425 acres of cropland; 2,350 acres of forest; 9,000 acres of open water; and 2,320 acres of shallow impoundments, ponds, marsh, and swamp), with 25 mi of canals.

Approximately 30,000 ducks and 1,500 Canada geese winter at the refuge, and more than 200 species of other birds live there or visit. Mammals include bobcat, deer, raccoon, squirrel, mink, otter, and fox. The more than 100 species of fish there include chub, shiner, sucker, sunfish, largemouth bass, perch, sturgeon, gar, shad, pike, catfish, silverside, crappie, mullet, bowfin, striped bass, white bass, and carp.

January is the peak month for Canada geese and mallards. In February there is an increase of wood ducks, purple martins, and bluebirds. Alligators have been seen sunning on some of the canal edges in March. April and May are excellent months for fishing. In August the summer warblers begin to migrate south, but September is the peak month for migratory songbirds. Ruby-crowned kinglets, white-throated sparrows, finches, cormorants, hawks, and bald eagles are seen in October and November. February is good to fish for largemouth bass, catfish, and striped bass. Sport fishing is permitted year-round, but specific waters are closed from November 1 through February 28. (Check with the refuge manager for fishing regulations.) Camping, overnight mooring of boats, swimming, open fires, and firearms are not allowed in the refuge.

The trails are in the Bluff, Dingle Pond, and Cuddo units. (Consult the refuge manager before hiking the 12-mi dike road in the Cuddo unit.)

Information: Refuge Manager, Route 2, Box 370, Summerton, SC 29148; (803) 478–2217.

Bluff Unit

The Visitor Center, open Monday through Friday, is located here, as are the maintenance complex, observation tower, a wildlife foot trail, and Fort Watson, the first post in South Carolina retaken from the British on April 15, 1781.

Access: From I-95 (exit 102) and jct with US 15-301, follow the signs N on US 15-301 for 0.3 mi, and turn L on SR 803. Go 0.3 mi on SR 803 to the Visitor Center on L, and another 0.7 mi to Fort Watson.

Santee Wildlife Trail
Length: 1.1 mi (1.8 km); **easy;** USGS Maps: Summerton, Vance; trailhead: parking area.

This trail is also called **Wrights Bluff Nature Trail.** From the parking area, Clive and Sonyie Rassow and I entered the forest to cross a boardwalk at 0.1 mi. The trail was wide and covered with pine straw; it was surrounded by pine, wax myrtle, grapevine, poison ivy, sweet gum, devil's walking cane, sensitive fern, and the unisexual perennial herb with fragrant nonpetaled soft white flowers, the stinging nettle (*Cnidoscolus stimulosus,* not to be confused with another stinging nettle, the *Urtica dioica).* At 0.4 mi we entered a young hardwood forest with Spanish moss hanging from the oaks.

After crossing another boardwalk we turned R to an observation deck at 0.6 mi.

As we neared a gravel service road, we heard dozens of doves. They were in such abundance and cooing so loudly we stopped to listen. "Perhaps they are making love," Clive said. "St. Augustine said that 'doves show love when they quarrel with each other,' " Sonyie added.

At 0.8 mi we passed over an elevated boardwalk with a view of a lake. Pickerel weed and sweet-scented water lilies loomed over their watery foundation. We reentered a pine forest before taking an exit in an old field near the parking lot.

Dingle Pond Unit

Southeast of the Bluff Unit is the Dingle Pond Unit, which allows fishing, nature study, canoeing, and hiking.

Access: From I-95 (exit 102) and SR 400 jct, go E by the Howard Johnson Motel for 0.3 mi and turn L (R is SR 390). Follow SR 400 for 1.7 mi to gated road on R.

Dingle Pond Trail

Length: 1.8 mi round-trip (2.9 km); **easy;** USGS Maps: Summerton, Vance; trailhead: gated woods road.

Along the woods roadbed we heard ducks and frogs before we saw the swamp and lakes area. On each side of the trail were wax myrtle, pine, and devil's walking cane.

At 0.3 mi water from the W lake flowed into the more E lake. Water lilies and cattails grew thick with other marsh plants. Ferns bordered the banks. We continued on the old roadbed through a pine forest with Spanish moss. We heard or saw catbirds, cardinals, towhees, and mockingbirds. At 0.7 mi we reached the end of the gated road, but another 0.2 mi led us to SR 390 (the KOA road from the fork with SR 400). We backtracked, seeing much we had missed on the way in.

Savannah Coastal Refuges (Jasper County)

The seven Savannah Coastal Refuges span 100 miles of coastline with a total of 53,340 acres (600 more acres are in negotiation). Five of the refuges are in Georgia—Blackbeard Island, Harris Neck, Tybee Island, Wassaw, and Wolf Island. Pinckney Island is located entirely within South Carolina; Savannah Refuge, the largest of the coastal refuges, lies in both Georgia and South Carolina.

In this low country, and especially on the barrier islands, which the Spanish called "Golden Isles," the diversity of fauna and flora has attracted such naturalists as Alexander Wilson, Mark Catesby, John James Audubon, and William Bartram. Contemporary naturalists and the public in general continue to find this area appealing for the same reasons. Here you will see freshwater marshes, tidal rivers and creeks, and river-bottom hardwood swamps. The former rice fields of the colonial period have been impounded for waterfowl and wading bird management. Each year thousands of migratory ducks, representing 12 or more species, winter on Savannah Refuge from November through February. Wood ducks, purple gallinules, and king rails are regular nesters. You will see alligators from March through October, and bird-watching for the more than 200 species is at its best from October through April. Fishing is permitted in the freshwater pools from March 15 to October 25. Group tours can be arranged by contacting the refuge headquarters in Savannah at (912) 652–4415.

Information: Refuge Manager, Savannah Coastal Refuges, P.O. Box 8487, Savannah, GA 31412; (912) 652–4415.

Access: From the jct of I-95 (Exit 5) and US 17 in Hardeeville, go S on US 17 for 8 mi to refuge entrance.

Laurel Hill Wildlife Drive and Cistern Trail

Length: 6.3 mi round-trip, combined (10 km); **easy;** USGS Maps: Limehouse, Savannah; trailhead: parking area.

At the wildlife-drive entrance sign on US 17, Scott Smith and I turned at the refuge gate to the parking area. A large sign indicated that we were permitted to observe the wildlife for photography or nature study; to hike, picnic, and fish (in season and if using boats with electric motors only). Camping, swimming, the use of firearms, fireworks, open fires, and the collection of plants or animals were prohibited.

We had a choice of walking the Laurel Hill Wildlife Drive (open from sunrise to sunset) or driving around the loop route. We chose the walk because it was January, and we could see more of the migratory waterfowl. The earthen dikes separate management pools (formerly rice fields tended by slaves) from old hardwood hammocks. At 1.1 mi we reached the Cistern Trail, a short, 0.2-mi loop that passed an old cistern. Vegetation here includes live oaks, cabbage palmetto, hackberry, and mulberry. There was a dike at 3.4 mi on the L and another at 3.6 mi. We photographed mallards, pintails, ring-necked ducks, and a few herons and egrets. At one point, near a dike on the L at 4 mi, we had an excellent view of a great blue heron. We reached US 17 and were back at the parking area at 6.1 mi.

SECTION 3
U.S. Army Corps of Engineers Projects

Thurmond Lake (McCormick County)

Formerly Clarks Hill Lake, Thurmond Lake (named for Senator Strom Thurmond) is the nation's largest U.S. Army Corps of Engineers project east of the Mississippi River. Completed in 1954 as part of a comprehensive development plan for the Savannah River Basin, it serves more than 8 million visitors annually. Nine Corps recreation areas (five in South Carolina and four in Georgia) and 13 campgrounds (four in South Carolina and nine in Georgia) are provided. Six state parks are also located on Thurmond Lake (three in each state).

The lake is 39 mi long with 1,200 mi of shoreline and 70,000 acres of water. Fishermen enjoy catching largemouth bass, crappie, catfish, hybrids, stripers, and bluegill. The large expanses of water offer excellent opportunities for sailing, skiing, boating, and swimming.

Hydroelectric energy is one of the Corps's commitments to the public. At Thurmond Lake seven generators can each produce 40,000 kilowatts of power at any given time. Visitors are welcome to tour the power plant and other facilities, but should first visit the Visitor Center on US 211 near the dam on the South Carolina side.

(On the Georgia side of the lake, at the edge of the dam, is where the yellow-blazed **Bartram Trail** begins. It meanders through wooded bottomland and gentle slopes around the lakeshore for 22.9 mi in trail Section I and 14.7 mi in trail Section II to the Little River bridge on GA 47. Picnic and camping areas are available along the way.)

Information: Resource Manager's Office, P.O. Box 10, Clarks Hill, SC 29821; (864) 333–1100 or (404) 722–3770.

Below Dam Fishing Pier

This recreation area has a boat ramp, picnic grounds, and a Vita-course exercise and hiking trail.

Access: Near the Thurmond Lake Visitor Center on US 221, take the driveway across from the center to the parking area at the fishing pier.

Clarks Hill Trail
Length: 1 mi (1.6 km); **easy;** USGS Map: Clarks Hill; trail-head: parking area.

Begin in an open field and follow a former exercise loop trail. There is an old tramway bed that serves as an additional route for a nature trail to the Savannah River. Tall gum, oaks, sycamore, poplar, locust, ash, and river birch are part of the forest on this trail.

Modoc Campground

Facilities here consist of a campground with or without hook-ups, group campground, boat ramp, picnic ground, comfort station, drinking water, amphitheater, playground, showers, and two hiking trails. There is a year-round campground caretaker.

Access: Campground entrance is located 0.5 mi S of Modoc on US 221.

Modoc Nature Trail

Length: 1.5 mi (2.4 km); **easy;** USGS Map: Clarks Hill; trailhead: parking area.

We began the trail across from the main shower house and meandered through loblolly pine, sweet gum, oaks, dwarf palmetto, and ferns. Muscadine grapevines and jessamine shared space with wisteria. We read interpretive markers along the way. Boy Scouts had been maintaining the trail. A loop brought us back to the point of origin.

Modoc Walking Trail

Length: 0.8 mi (1.3 km); **easy;** USGS Map: Clarks Hill; trailhead: parking area.

We began this hike behind the main shower house and roughly followed the shoreline. The high bluffs overlooking the lake provided excellent views.

Hiking clockwise, halfway through the trail we crossed two gravel roads. At 0.5 mi the view of the lake was magnificent. Boy Scouts help maintain this trail, too.

Hartwell Lake
(Anderson, Oconee, and Pickens Counties)

Hartwell Lake, with 56,000 acres of water and a shoreline of 962 mi, was constructed by the U.S. Army Corps of Engineers between 1955 and 1963 as a hydropower and flood-control project on the Tugaloo, Seneca, and Savannah Rivers. The dam was built across the Savannah River from Hartwell, Georgia, and rises 204 ft from the riverbed. Much of the area's history is now under water, but the stories and legends of the Cherokee Indians, William Bartram, Andrew Pickens, John C. Calhoun, and Revolutionary War heroine Nancy Hart (for whom Hartwell is named) will always be above water.

The recreational areas for this massive impoundment (ranked among the 10 most-visited Corps of Engineers projects in the nation), where clean power produces more than half a billion kilowatt-hours annually, are expansive: 31 in Georgia and 50 in South Carolina. Six of the 11 campgrounds are in South Carolina. Other facilities include more than 46 commercial marinas, state and municipal parks, and accesses. The Visitor Center on the Georgia side provides living history, tours, nature study, energy interpretation, and safety projects. The **Hartwell Lake Beaver Trail** is closed.

Information: Resource Manager, Natural Resources Management Center, Lake Hartwell, P.O. Box 278, Hartwell, GA 30643; (404) 376–4788.

Chapter III
State Parks, Forests, Historic Sites, and Wildlife Management Areas

And in each tinted copse and shimmering dell
Rests the mute rapture of deep hearted peace.
Paul Hamilton Hayne, "Aspects of the Pines"

There are more trails in the 81,000 acres of the South Carolina state parks than in any other system in the state. Of the 60 properties, 48 (plus five historic sites) are operational parks. Only four (Goodale, Hamilton Branch, Old Dorchester, and Sergeant Jasper) do not have designated foot trails. From the beginning of the parks in 1934, when the state legislature passed a bill to give the responsibility for the system to the Commission of Forestry, a "Nature Trail" was considered a standard element in the planning and development of a park. Currently there are 80 named foot trails covering more than 200 miles. Camping facilities are provided in 35 of the parks; fishing in 44 of the parks; horseback riding in Croft, Kings Mountain, Lee, McCalla, and Poinsett; and bicycling in Charles Towne Landing, Hunting Island, Paris Mountain, Santee and Sesquicentennial.

The state park system developed from a grassroots desire on the part of citizens to have more recreational facilities. Acting on this desire, a group of citizens in the Cheraw area donated 706 acres to the state in early 1934. Myrtle Beach donated 1,067 acres. Then Sumter County donated 1,000 acres for Poinsett State Park, followed by 1,235 acres from the Charleston Water Works for Givhans Ferry State Park. Kings Mountain State Park, with 6,141 acres, came from federal donations in the fall of 1934. In 1935 there were donations of land for five more state parks—Edisto

Beach, Paris Mountain, Table Rock, Lee, and Oconee. That same year the Sesqui-Centennial Commission in Columbia donated land for the Sesquicentennial State Park. It was a chain reaction across the state, and on July 1, 1936, Myrtle Beach State Park opened to the public as South Carolina's first state park. Since then the public's demand for recreational facilities has resulted in one of the best state-park systems in the Southeast. Annual total attendance at the parks is more than 10 million.

During the late 1950s and early 1960s, the state park system went through a delay in growth while making an effort to avoid racially integrated state parks, but in 1996 all parks were open in obeyance of the 1954 Civil Rights Act.

The park system then continued to grow and eventually became too large for supervision by the Forestry Commission. In 1967 responsibility was transferred to the Division of State Parks and Recreation under the newly created Department of Parks, Recreation and Tourism (PRT). Attendance soared, and by 1968 the General Assembly provided new life for the parks with a $6-million bond issue.

Since then the park system, through its plans, development, and expansion, has become one of the state's major attractions for local citizens and tourists. It is "the major provider of outdoor and cultural history education programs in our state," stated Dan Turpin, chief of education and information. This has required outstanding leadership, and Ray M. Sisk, retired director, and Charles Harrison, current director of the Division of State Parks, have been there to provide it. The parks staff have been exceptionally committed to repair and reconstruction of park facilities destroyed or damaged by Hurricane Hugo on September 22, 1989, and the "Storm of the Century" on March 13, 1993. Reports of their work have been publicized in *Park Lites,* the official publication of PRT; in *Parkview,* a seasonal newsletter on growth and advancement of the parks; and in the state news media.

To receive *Parkview,* a state park guide to outdoor adventures with a detailed listing of activities and educational programs; *South Carolina Travel Guide,* "It's Your Life. Fill It Up"; South Carolina State Parks brochure; and individual park brochures, contact South Carolina State Parks, 1205 Pendleton St., Columbia, SC 29201; (803) 734–0156, toll-free (888) 88–PARKS.

SECTION 1
Upcountry and Mountains

Spectacular attractions in the Appalachian Mountains and foothills include wild and scenic rivers, high waterfalls, large lakes, and rocky mountain peaks such as Table Rock and Caesars Head—both over 3,000 ft in altitude. The **Foothills Trail,** has termini at Oconee and Table Rock State Parks, and an extension to the Jones Gap Station of the Mountain Bridge State Natural Area. Some of the 12 parks in this region have historic sites, excellent equestrian facilities, cabins and campgrounds, and stocked lakes for fishermen. Through the region run I-26 (N–S) and I-85 (SW–NE), which connect with the 115-mi Cherokee Foothills Scenic Highway, SC 11.

Croft State Park (Spartanburg County)

In 1949 Croft State Park, with 7,088 acres, became the state's second-largest park. With this acreage the facilities can be expanded as urban development in the vicinity increases. Among the current facilities are an Olympic-size swimming pool, a boat dock for fishing, paddle boats, a 50-site campground, picnic areas, a horse arena (the home of the Spartanburg Horseman's Association), and multiple-use trails. Maps are available for the following horse trails: Rocky Ridge (3.5 mi), Foster's Mill Loop (6.5 mi), Lake Johnson Loop (2.4 mi), Lake Johnson/Fairforest Creek Loop (4.5 mi), Fairforest Creek (3.5 mi), and Craig (1.0 mi).

The park is rich in history; there are Cherokee Indian mounds, old Antioch Church gravesites and other graveyards, and foundation sites of early settlers' homes. During World War II this area and properties adjoining the park were used as Camp Croft for nearly 200,000 troops and as a recruiting and induction station for selectees from W North Carolina. The park was named in honor of Maj. General Edward Croft, chief of the U.S. Infantry in the 1930s.

Information: Croft State Park, 450 Croft State Park Rd., Spartanburg, SC 29302; (864) 585–1283.

Croft Jogging Trail

Length: 0.5 mi (0.8 km); **easy;** USGS Map: Spartanburg; trailhead: opposite the campground entrance.

From the corner of the campground and boathouse roads, I followed the signs. This was a good jogging trail, and the 10 physical-fitness stations make it an exercise trail. The trail was smooth and wide, a good place for observing wildlife and plant life. It was in a mixed forest, and wisteria and silverberry were prominent.

Lake Johnson Trail

Length: 5.5 mi (8.8 km); **moderate;** USGS Map: Spartanburg; trailhead: parking area at horse stables.

The park lists this as a "horse trail," but the park superintendent said that hikers also use the trail. He said that the trail can be made into a 25-mi loop bordering Edwin Johnson Lake.

Jeff Fleming and I drove 0.5 mi from the campground to the trail entrance on the road by the horse arena to the horse stables and parked. We entered the posted roadbed on the R. As the park map is not clear on this trail, we assumed that we were right because of numerous horse tracks. Silverberry fringed the old road as we hiked through a mixed forest. After 0.4 mi of gentle terrain, we came to a jct, where we turned R and crossed a steel bridge over Kelsey Creek. Ahead was a gradual climb on an old roadbed in a mixed forest. At 1.7 mi we reached the ridge top in a pine forest. Here the park boundary extended E, where an old road showed horse and ORV use. (From here on the E route, a rider or hiker could have another 1.5 mi to SR 681 and on other private roads.) Ahead the forest changed to a mixture of pine, oak, hickory, mulberry, cedar, dogwood, and redbud. White asters and purple-blossom sensitive briar patches were on the road banks of red and yellow clay. A huge stand of poplar was on each side of the road at 2.8 mi, a few yards before our ascent on a treadway of silver-brown dirt.

Suddenly, out of the trees rose the WRET-TV tower of the South Carolina Education TV Network, which the park superintendent had told us was on the trail. We had climbed 3 mi. After 0.1 mi we passed a locked firetower, its metal rusting, its wood steps feeble, its window panes shattered. Like so many of these sentinels of the past, it is no longer needed, replaced by scheduled surveillance from helicopters. Twelve horseback riders and a lone hiker approached us. They assured us that our loop needed to be on the paved SR 295 for a short distance before we could reach the return route. After hiking 0.3 mi to a rusty gate at the park boundary, we turned L onto an old roadbed bordered with periwinkle and draped with wisteria. A deer bounded away to our L. At 4.9 mi we passed a long, open shelter and then descended to an open clay embankment. Reentering the woods, we noticed that the Foster cemetery had been restored by Boy Scout Troop 102. Did this troop have relatives here, we wondered, or did it see the need to preserve the memory of those whose gravestones were being covered by nature's forest blanket?

At 5.4 mi we crossed the dam of Lake Johnson, and at 5.5 mi we returned to the horse stables parking area.

Devils Fork State Park (Oconee County)

Devils Fork State Park, 622 acres, is on the SW shore of Lake Jocassee. It received its name from Devils Fork Creek and was developed in cooperation with Duke Power Company. It is leased to the

Division of State Parks for operations and management. Major features of the park are its outstanding beauty and its access to the 7,565-acre Lake Jocassee at the foothills of the Blue Ridge Mountains. Excellent for fishing, the lake has brown and rainbow trout; white, small, and largemouth bass; bluegill; and black crappie. Other park features are 20 mountain villas by the lake, full-service campground, park store, picnic area with shelters, bathhouse, and swimming area.

Information: Devils Fork State Park, 161 Holcombe Circle, Salem, SC 29676; (864) 944–2639.

Access: From the jct of SC 11 and SC 130, N of Salem, go NE on SC 11 3 mi and turn N on SR 25 to the park entrance.

Oconee Bells Nature Trail

Length: 1.0 mi (1.6 km); **easy;** USGS Map: Salem; trailhead: boat-ramp parking lot.

From the R corner of the boat ramp parking lot, the trail descends on steps to a loop jct. Turn R and it passes near a stream and through beds of oconee bells (*Shortia galacifolia*), a low, glaborous, waxy-green herb that grows only in a few mountain counties of the Carolinas. Oconee bells bloom in March and April with white apex-toothed petals. Other wildflowers are violets, crested dwarf iris, and galax. Among the flowering shrubs are rhododendron, flame azalea, and horse sugar (*Symplocos tinctoria*). The trail passes an old farm pond and goes through a hardwood and pine forest.

Keowee Toxaway State Park (Pickens County)

Keowee Toxaway State Park, which opened in 1970, has one of the state's most unique features—an emphasis on the heritage of the Cherokee Indians. Displays are in the Interpretive Center, orientation building, and four kiosks.

Highways 11 and 133 intersect in the center of the 1,000-acre park, and Keowee Lake is on the N boundary. Facilities include a 24-site campground, backpack camping on **Raven Rock Hiking Trail,** a picnic area, Lake Keowee for boating and fishing, trails, and a meeting house.

Information: Keowee Toxaway State Park, 108 Residence Dr., Sunset, SC 29685; (864) 868–2605.

Access: Park entrance is on SC 11, 7.1 mi W from the jct of SC 11 and US 178. The entrance is 1.2 mi E from the Keowee Lake bridge on SC 11.

Cherokee Interpretive Trail

Length: 0.3 mi (0.5 km); **easy;** USGS Map: Salem; trailhead: Interpretive Center.

From the parking area S of SC 11, I went up to the Interpretive Center and Museum for information on the trail, then followed the sign to the orientation building, where "Prehistory to 1500" told about the environment and the archaic Indians and ancestors of the Cherokee.

At the first kiosk, "Cherokee Culture 1500–1700" told of Cherokee dress, agriculture, games and dances, medicines, structures, and social and political systems. "The Coming of the Traders 1700–1745," at the second kiosk, emphasized the impact of English goods and trade problems. At the third kiosk, the theme was the "Cherokee War, 1745–1761"; subthemes were trade problems, the Creek War, conferences and treaties, and Fort Prince George. Near the end of the loop trail was the fourth kiosk, "End of an Era, 1761–1816," about the Treaty of 1761, the coming of the settlers, the Revolutionary War, the Hopewell Treaty of 1785, and the "Trail of Tears" in 1816.

Writing about the "Trail of Tears," the removal of the Cherokee from South Carolina, Reverend Evan Jones described the exodus firsthand. "Multitudes were allowed no time to take anything with them, except the clothes on their backs. Well-furnished houses were left prey to plunder . . . stripping the helpless of all they have on earth."

Raven Rock Hiking Trail
and Natural Bridge Nature Trail

Length: 4.2 mi round-trip, combined (6.7 km); **moderate** to **strenuous;** USGS Map: Salem; trailhead: parking area by the chapel.

Across SC 11 from the Interpretive Center is a parking area near the chapel. We began our hike here, to the R of the chapel, and followed a narrow blue-blazed trail through an oak forest. Blueberries, Bowman's root, and mountain laurel were part of the understory and ground cover. At 0.3 mi we went L on an old farm road with profuse bracken and Indian plaintain. After descending 0.6 mi into a mature forest, we crossed an underground stream in a rocky scenic area.

To the L, at a sign, is the **Natural Bridge Nature Trail.** It is a short, scenic connector trail, about 100 yd through mature rhododendron, to the return route of the **Raven Rock Hiking Trail.** (The connector provides the option of a loop to the L for another 0.5 mi back to the parking area.) Rosebay rhododendron and phlox were near a cascade and pool. From here we followed a steep, twisting trail among large boulders with scattered pines and mountain laurel. Occasionally we saw a light blue or white blaze. For the next mile the trail ascended and descended among ridges and ravines, twisting as if planned for an obstacle course. At 1.8 mi on McKinney Mountain (1,182 ft) the trail made a sharp turn L for the loop, but we continued ahead to reach the campsite. We descended steeply on a blue-blazed trail to an excellent campground on a peninsula of pines in Keowee Lake at 2.2 mi.

On the return we followed a blue-blazed trail R, along the lake to a fine view from a rocky bluff. Beyond this point we found the remnants of an old whiskey still and a small stream. (The blue blaze may be confusing here; turn back to the bluff and hike up the ridge to regain the main trail.) After we returned to the bluff and followed the ridge to rejoin the main trail, we descended steeply on a ridge to reach a cascading stream at 3.3 mi. Wake robins, wild geraniums, ferns, and hemlocks made this a most attractive area. We were so attentive to the plants that Steve Harris, my hiking companion, nearly ran the measuring wheel over a copperhead coiled in a sunny spot on the trail. At 3.6 mi we ascended away from the stream; the trail switched back and forth on an old logging road to connect with the **Natural Bridge Nature Trail,** at L. We crossed another stream a number of times and began our final ascent on an old logging road at 4 mi. At 4.1 mi we turned R off the road and reached the parking area. (Primitive camping is allowed on this trail for a small fee.)

Kings Mountain State Park
(York and Cherokee Counties)

In 1934 the U.S. government donated to the state of South Carolina 6,141 acres for the development of a state park with recreational facilities adjacent to the Kings Mountain National Military Park. As part of the Kings Mountain range of low foothills, the park is an oak and hickory hardwood forest with scattered pines. Numerous springs and clear streams are between the slopes of clay and quartz. Lake Crawford, an 8.3-acre impoundment with swimming and pedal boating, is the center of the park's activities. Adjacent is a campground with 119 sites, and nearby are group camps and primitive camping areas. A trading post with a display of pioneer artifacts has basic groceries and camping supplies. Other facilities are a laundry, a recreational building, carpet golf, a playground, and picnic areas. York Lake is S of SC 216 and the main campground.

Of historical significance is the "Living Farm," a replica of an 1846 South Carolina frontier farm. The "Homeplace," constructed of pine and chestnut, is a two-story log farmhouse and the site of a crafts demonstration and other household activities. The farm also includes a barn, a smokehouse, a blacksmith/carpenter shop, a sorghum mill and cooker, a corn crib, a cotton gin, small outbuildings, an herb garden, livestock and chickens, and a pioneer vegetable garden. I found Park Superintendent Lew Cato in the vegetable garden with a Rototiller on a hot summer day. "With only eight of us in a park this size," he said, "we have to be able to do everything." Each September the park has a two-day festival of pioneer games, country cooking, arts and crafts, and authentic folk music.

The park maintains 10.2 mi of the 15-mi **Kings Mountain Hiking Trail,** a joint project with Kings Mountain National Military Park.

Information: Kings Mountain State Park, 1277 Park Rd., Blacksburg, SC 29702; (864) 222–3209.

Access: From the jct of SC 161 and SR 216 near the North Carolina state line, drive W on SC 216 to the park entrance. From the W turn E on SC 216 at I-85.

Kings Mountain Hiking Trail

Length: 15 mi round-trip (24 km); **moderate;** USGS Maps: Filbert, Kings Mountain, Kings Creek, Grover; trailhead: campground main parking area.

Designated a national recreational trail in June 1981, the **Kings Mountain Hiking Trail** traverses low foothill country in Kings Mountain State Park and Kings Mountain National Military Park. It is an extension of a trail formerly called **Clark's Creek Trail.** Although entrance to the trail is at a number of crossroads and at the Visitor Center of the military park, I will describe it from the state-park campground so the trailhead is at a full-service campsite.

Ray Matthews and I began the trail from the group picnic area with shelters at the parking area; we descended for 0.2 mi to cross a tributary of Clark Fork and intersect with the **Gold Nugget Trail.** We ascended gradually on a wide trailway with white blazes and crossed the primitive campground road at 0.4 mi. At 1.1 mi we reached the national-park boundary, and at 1.2 mi we passed a stream on the R. Around us were mountain laurel, yellow root, rattlesnake orchids, club moss, wild ginger, fetterbush, and wood betony. We approached another stream on the L at 1.3 mi and followed it upstream to a stretch of false downy foxglove. At 1.7 mi we crossed a larger stream of the Long Branch tributaries, heading upstream on an even grade. After crossing the stream again at 2 mi, we ascended gradually to the summit of a hill at 2.3 mi. Sticky foxglove bordered the trail in a young oak forest. At 2.4 mi we reached a trail jct. To the L it was 0.2 mi to the Visitor Center of the national park. We heard the firing of a musket in that direction: The park was having a 1780-era demonstration of cooking a pot of beef stew. "It's kinda in honor of the overmountain men who had beef for a meal here at the battle," said Steve Marlowe, a park staff member.

Because we had already hiked the **Battlefield Trail** and seen the Visitor Center, Ray and I continued on the main trail to descend steeply and reach a small stream at 2.5 mi. This stream flows out of the battlefield summit where the patriots bathed their wounded on October 7 and 8, 1780. We ascended to an old fire road, which is the **Overmountain Victory Trail** route, and went 0.1 mi, turning L at 2.9 mi. (The gated fire road and the **Overmountain Victory Trail** continued straight.) After climbing a gentle grade, we crossed SC 216 at 3.2 mi. We continued ahead on an exceptionally well-maintained trail in an open oak forest. We soon descended in a rocky section to cross Stonehouse Branch on an old bridge at 3.6 mi. Although pine beetles have destroyed most of the pine forests in the area, we saw a few living pines in this section. Ferns, fetterbush, yellow root, and wild azaleas were prominent before we began to ascend at 4.5 mi. At 4.7 mi we reached a ridge crest, which led to the jct of the firetower spur trail. We hiked the 0.5-mi spur over a hill, down to a saddle, and up to the firetower on Browns Mountain (1,045 ft) where the view was the best we would see anywhere on the trail. Returning to the main trail, we descended through a beautiful open forest with occasional slate formations. At 5.4 mi we reached Garner Branch and a park service–designated campsite. We ascended to the boundary line between the parks and crossed over an open space into the state park at 5.9 mi. (L on the open boundary line it is 0.5 mi to Piedmont Road.)

We passed through a lumbered area, entered a mature hard-wood forest with undulating trailway, and reached a stream at 6.4 mi. Growing here were wild azaleas, switchcane, and ferns. At 6.6 mi we reached the Piedmont Road, SR 731, a graveled extension from SC 55. (To the L it is 1.6 mi to SC 216.) At this jct Sammy Gooding picked up Ray, and Bob Brueckner took Ray's place. Mountain laurel, borders of galax, wild ginger, Christmas fern, royal fern, black cohosh, strawberry bush, fetterbush, and yellow root grew near the clear stream. We went downstream and as-cended over a ridge and down to another stream with more moun-tain laurel at 7.3 mi. The trail curved up and around a ravine for 0.2 mi before descending back to the stream. We ascended over a ridge into a spacious deciduous forest at 7.8 mi. At 8 mi we noticed damage to the trail by horseback riders, damage that continued sporadically for the next 5 mi. At an old logging-road crossing at 8.2 mi, we saw a magnificent display of monarch, pipevine, swal-lowtail, and fritillary butterflies at a bank of goldenrod and rose pink. A grist of honeybees and yellow jackets were in the area. We reentered the woods, downstream. This section of the trail, at 8.7 mi, could be a good campsite. Huge poplar, beech, gum, oak, hick-ory, and ironwood on the hillsides and bottomland gave a fine shady location. Fragrant spicebush and crested dwarf iris were along the trail.

At 9.3 mi we crossed a service road and entered a bottomland. Here was a stand of walnut, the most we had seen in the park. Poplar and mulberry were scattered over dense woodland sunflow-ers, thistle, and ironweed (*Vernonia noveborarensis*). We crossed a wood footbridge over a tributary of Long Branch at 9.7 mi, turned L on a park service road, and followed it for 0.1 mi before turning R, into the forest. Abruptly we entered an old field with piles of quartz rock, reindeer moss, purple blooming liatris, scrubby pines, and dead pines. I expected to see a copperhead, but only a small black snake showed up. We crossed another service road at 10.5 mi and reached a tributary of Long Branch at 10.7 mi. Here is another good campsite with ferns and cascades above a pool. At 11.2 mi we

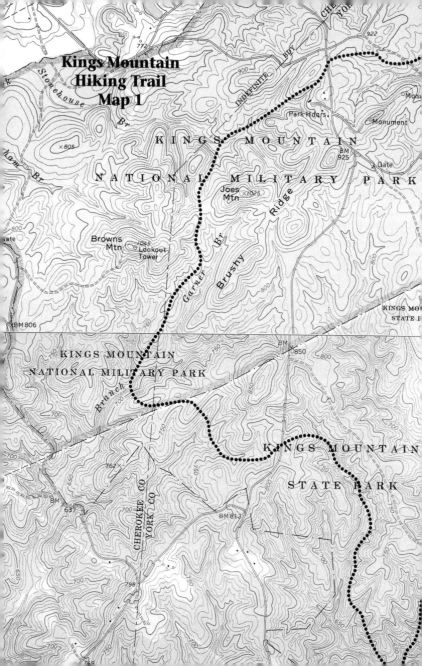

Kings Mountain
Hiking Trail
Map 1

KINGS MOUNTAIN

NATIONAL MILITARY PARK

Park Hdqrs.

Monument

BM 925

Gate

Joes Mtn

×1025

Ridge

Browns Mtn

1045 Lookout Tower

Garner Br

Blushy Br

800

800

KINGS MO
STATE F

BM 806

KINGS MOUNTAIN
NATIONAL MILITARY PARK

BM 850

800

Branch

700

700

750

650

KINGS MOUNTAIN

STATE PARK

762 ×

CHEROKEE CO
YORK CO

BM 637

700

BM 813

798

Stonehouse Br

× 805

772

900

922

INGS MOUNTAIN
NAL MILITARY PARK

KINGS MOUNTAIN
STATE PARK

Long

Branch

Clark

Cem

Lake York

Lake
York
666

Branch

Fk

KINGS MOUNTAIN STATE PARK

Long

Clark

Fork

**Kings Mountain
Hiking Trail
Map 2**

turned R, on a logging road. After 0.2 mi we turned R, off the road into the woods. At the confluence of the tributary with Long Branch, we turned L upstream and followed the branch banks, sometimes up on the slopes. At 11.7 mi the branch had cascades. The horse trail crossed the hikers trail at 12.3 mi and again at 12.5 mi. Although the horse trail was marked with a horseshoe label, hooves had churned the hiking trail to a thick porridge. This spot has space for camping near cascades. "It is a good place to cool your feet," said Bob, as we looked at a perfect rock bench in the middle of the stream. We rock-hopped across the stream and saw a patch of crane-fly orchids. Leafless in summer, the stalk and flowers of the orchids are almost the color of the brown forest duff. After crossing two more small streams, we passed under a power line at 12.8 mi and reached Apple Road at 13.3 mi. (From here, L, it is 0.25 mi to SC 216.) Across Apple Road was a grove of cedars and an old cemetery at 13.6 mi. From here to the SC 216 crossing, the trail undulated through an open deciduous forest. We crossed SC 216 at 14.6 mi and entered a young pine grove, which changed to hardwood on a slope. Quartz glistened. We descended to the stream and completed our loop. We turned R and reached the campground parking area at 15 mi. (If you include the hiking distance to the firetower, 1 mi, and the hike to and from the Visitor Center, 0.4 mi, this route is 16.4 mi.)

If you plan to camp out on the trail, and I hope that you will, be sure to register and camp only at Garner Branch in the Kings Mountain National Military Park. (See Chapter II, Section 1.) Also, if you camp in the state park, let the park headquarters know who you are and where you will be camping.

Lake Hartwell State Park (Oconee County)

Lake Hartwell State Park has 680 acres with a large family campground, laundry equipment, a trading post–tackle shop, two boat ramps, and a community recreation building, as well as picnic areas, a nature trail, and playground equipment. Fishing for bass, crappie, walleye, catfish, and bream is the major sports activity, but there are additional water sports: boating, sailing, windsurfing, and skiing.

Information: Lake Hartwell State Park, 19138-A SC 11, Fair Play, SC 29643; (864) 972–3352.

Access: On I-85, on the E side of the Hartwell Lake, take exit 1 to SC 11; proceed 0.5 mi N to the park entrance, L.

Beech Ridge Trail

Length: 1.4 mi round-trip (2.2 km); **easy;** USGS Map: Flint Hill; trailhead: trading-post parking area (maps are available).

On a route of low hills and lake edges, we followed the interpretive markers between the trading post and the entrance to the campground. Along the trail we saw regenerating loblolly pine, beech, dogwood, oak, holly, maple, and ferns. We also saw evidence of former clear-cutting and former pastures and farmland.

Mountain Bridge State Natural Area

Caesars Head and Jones Gap Stations (Greenville County)

Former Caesars Head State Park (7,467 acres) and Jones Gap State Park (3,346 acres) adjoin and have a total of 10,813 acres. They are now the Mountain Bridge State Natural Area, in the heart of what has also been called the Mountain Bridge Recreation and Wilderness Area. Within the stations are nearly 100 mi of connecting hiking trails. One of the most recent trails, #8, was opened in 1998 as a connector between **Jones Gap Trail** and **Rim of the Gap Trail.** The many interconnecting trails make excellent options for a day hike or overnight backpacking trips. With financial help and labor for trail construction by Naturaland Trust, the stations have a labyrinth of color-coded and numbered foot trails. (Naturaland Trust is a private, nonprofit conservation organization headquartered in Greenville.) Naturaland Trust has also installed trail-post signs at trailheads and intersections, has placed logo blazes on trail routes, and provides maintenance. All trails are numbered.

In this section are descriptions of how short or long adventurous loops can be formed within the two stations—loops that climb to spectacular views from rock outcrops, beside impenetrable granite slopes and walls, near and over cascades and waterfalls, through dark tunnels of evergreens, and deep into chasms of resplendent beauty. There are wildlife, trout, warblers, and rare wildflowers and ferns.

Commercial facilities are limited. There is not a campground, only primitive walk-in campsites that require reservations. At the Caesars Head Visitor Center, there are interpretive displays and a gift shop, classroom, vending area, and large picnic shelter. Programs on nature, mountain music, and arts and crafts are provided at the top of Caesars Head (3,266 ft), a rock cliff from which you can see Table Rock, the Dismal (a gorge with Matthews Creek between the mountain ridges), and other scenic locations. At Jones Gap Visitor Center there are interpretive displays, a store, a gift and tackle shop, picnic areas and shelters, and facilities for meetings and recreation. Here, as with Caesars Head, are general facilities for those with physical disabilities.

Information: Mountain Bridge State Natural Area, Caesars Head Station, 8155 Geer Hwy, Cleveland, SC 29635; (864) 836–6115. Jones Gap Station, 303 Jones Gap Rd., Marietta, SC 29661; (864) 836–3647. See *Mountain Bridge Trails* by Greg Lucas for Naturaland Trust, Box 728, Greenville, SC 29602; (864) 242–8213. This 250-page guidebook has detailed trail information, with maps.

Access: Caesars Head: From the jct of SC 11 and US 276, take US 276 and ascend 6.3 mi to the Visitor Center and parking area, L. From Brevard, North Carolina, take US 276 S and, at the state line, go 2.8 mi, R. From Jones Gap: On US 276/SC 11 (1 mi W of

Cleveland near the K-Mart), go 5.8 mi on SR 97, River Falls Rd., which become Jones Gap Rd., to the station entrance, and 0.2 mi farther to the parking area.

Caesars Head Trail

Length: 130 yd round-trip (0.6 km); **easy;** USGS Map: Table Rock; trailhead: Caesars Head Station parking area.

From the parking area walk to the overlook beside the water tower. Here are superb vistas of the Matthews Creek Gorge below, the Greenville Lake, Table Rock, smaller foothills toward the piedmont, and high mountains W, such as the Pinnacle and Hickory Nut Mountain. A brief section of trail descends from the overlook through a deep rock fracture named "Devil's Kitchen" and winds around to an excellent view of the Caesars Head profile.

One explanation of how Caesars Head got its name is that the cliff looked like Julius Caesar (students of Roman sculpture would have to use considerable imagination for this); another is that a hunter's dog named Caesar plunged to its death in a fox-chase accident. Some visitors say that the cliff looks like a sheep's or ram's head.

First Loop

Raven Cliff Falls Trail (#11) (2.4 mi); Gum Gap Trail (#13) (1.2-mi part of 3.3 mi); Naturaland Trust Trail (#14) (1.4-mi part of 5.8 mi); The Dismal Trail (#12) (1.4 mi)

Length: 8.5 mi, round-trip, combined (13.6 km); **moderate** to **strenuous;** USGS Maps: Table Rock, Cleveland; trailhead: parking area B on US 276.

Besides the **Caesars Head Trail, Raven Cliff Falls Trail** is the station's most used—and it has been since its days at the turn of the century, when visitors could use a carriage road from a resort hotel to see the 420-ft waterfalls and cascades. The trail can form part of an exhilarating loop that provides a swinging bridge over the top of the falls, pass the wall of Raven Cliff, and cross the splashing waters of Matthews Creek on cables.

From Caesars Head Visitor Center we drove N 1.1 mi on US 276 to a parking area, R, but walked across the road to the trailhead. (The blue-blazed **Foothills Trail** extension follows part of **Raven Cliff Falls Trail, Gum Gap Trail** W, and E on **Tom Miller Trail** and **Jones Gap Trail** to its E terminus at Jones Gap Station. See Chapter I.) We walked across US 276 to the red-blazed entrance and descended on a wide roadbed. The forest floor was covered with New York fern and blueberry.

After passing the site of an old dam, we ascended gradually on an S slope to the end of the roadbed at 0.6 mi. We curved across a ridge with rock outcroppings and views L of Table Rock and adjoining mountains at 0.8 mi. A descent into a ravine followed. At 1.7 mi **Raven Cliff Falls Trail** continued ahead, but we turned R on an old woods road, the route of **Gum Gap Trail.** We followed it on moderate terrain to a jct at 2.9 mi L with the pink-blazed **Naturaland Trust Trail.**

We descended on a foot trail among hemlock, rhododendron, birch, elm, fetterbush, and galax at 3.3 mi to a swinging bridge. It spans the upper falls for breathtaking views, unequalled anywhere in the state. At 3.4 mi we descended on a wood and metal ladder beside cliffs and overhangs. (To our L at 3.5 mi was a side trail with cables, a precipitous and dangerous passage, for viewing the falls and their base in The Dismal.) In the winter there are views of Caesars Head. Another ladder and stone steps provide a descent at 3.7 mi to The Cathedral, a high, massive rock face with layers of orange, tan, and steel-blue granite. At 3.9 mi we saw raven nests in high rock crevices. Descending on switchbacks to cascading Matthews Creek, we crossed on cables between hemlocks at 4.3 mi.

After a respite on the huge boulders, we passed through a forest of large oaks and maples to a turn L at 4.6 mi on **The Dismal Trail.** (The **Naturaland Trust Trail** continues E. See **Second** and **Third Loop** descriptions ahead.) In an open forest of hardwoods and scattered hemlock, we ascended on the blue/purple-blazed trail, partly on old roads. The ascent has 1,220 ft in elevation, with at least 24 switchbacks. At 5.9 mi is a partial view,

L, of Raven Cliff Falls, and at 6 mi is a jct with **Raven Cliff Falls Trail.** We turned L and descended 0.3 mi to an observation deck for viewing the state's highest series of cascades and waterfalls. We returned by following **Raven Cliff Falls Trail** to parking area B at US 276.

Second Loop

Raven Cliff Falls Trail (#11) (2.4 mi); The Dismal Trail (#12) (1.4 mi); Naturaland Trust Trail (#14) (4.1 mi of 5.8 mi); Frank Coggins Trail (#15) (0.3 mi of 0.8 mi); Coldspring Connector Trail (#7) (0.5 mi); Coldspring Branch Trail (#3) (1.0 mi of 2.6 mi)

Length: 10 mi round-trip, combined (16 km); **moderate** to **strenuous;** USGS Map: Table Rock, Brevard; trailhead: parking lot B on US-276.

Follow **Raven Cliff Falls Trail** (described in the **First Loop)** to its terminus at the observation deck. Backtrack 0.3 mi to turn R on **The Dismal Trail** and descend to jct with **Naturaland Trust Trail** at 4.1 mi. Turn L. You will pass through a section of property of the Asbury United Methodist Church Camp, but there may not be any signs. At 5.1 mi turn L at an old road jct; ascend steeply among large rocks and reach a ridgeline at 5.9 mi. To the N (L) is Caesars Head and sheer granite cliffs. Turn E to follow a ridge. Arrive at **Pinnacle Pass Trail** (#20) at 6.7 mi in a wide gap. **(Pinnacle Pass Trail** goes E 0.6 mi to cross US-276 on its way for another 9 mi to Jones Gap Station. See **Loop Three.)**

Continuing on **Naturaland Trust Trail,** arrive at a ridge and into an open forest of hardwoods at 6.9 mi. To the L are large boulders. At 7.3 mi ascend on switchbacks with sheer rock faces, L. Among hemlock and rhododendron, reach Rock Cliff Falls (flume) at 7.4 mi. Cross a private residential road to parallel US 276. At 7.7 mi cross US 276 to an old abandoned road. There is an 0.4 mi, white-blazed connector trail, L, at 7.9 mi. (It goes through a damp flat area with rhododendron to join an old road for connecting with **Frank Coggins Trail** and **Coldspring Branch Trail.)**

163

On the **Naturaland Trust Trail,** pass R of small Firewater Falls and cave at 8.0 mi. To the R is a private home, built in 1996. Descend and reach the E end of **Naturaland Trust Trail** at Cliff Fall at 8.2 mi. To the R is **Rim of the Gap Trail** (#6). (This scenic and rugged trail hugs the rock face on the N side of the ridge before switchbacking down the side of Little Pinnacle Mountain for 4.3 mi to **Jones Gap Trail** [#1]).

Turn L on **Frank Coggins Trail;** go 0.3 mi for a turn R on **Coldspring Connector Trail** (#7). (To the L the **Frank Coggins Trail** easily ascends, partly on a gravel road, for nearly 0.5 mi to US 276 and parking area A at Caesars Head Station.) On the blue-blazed **Coldspring Connector Trail,** descend in a ravine of rhododendron and galax. In a flat area pass large oak and cucumber trees before descending on 10 switchbacks. Near a cascading stream are patches of fetterbush and partridge berry. After 0.5 mi connect with orange-blazed **Coldspring Branch Trail** (#3). (To the R it descends 1.6 mi to jct with **Jones Gap Trail** [#1]).

Continue L for 0.4 mi on the **Coldspring Branch Trail** to jct with **Bill Kimball Trail** (#5), R. (It follows a ridge before a descent on switchbacks to join **Coldspring Branch Trail.)** Stay L on a ridge to end the loop at US 276 parking area B for a total of 10 mi.

Third Loop

Frank Coggins Trail (#15) (0.8 mi); Naturaland Trust Trail (#14) (1.5 mi of 5.8 mi); Pinnacle Pass Trail (#20) (9.6 mi); Rim of the Gap Trail (#6) (4.3 mi)

Length: 17.8 mi round-trip, combined, (28.5 km); **moderate** to **strenuous;** USGS map: Table Rock, Brevard, Cleveland, Sandingstone Mtn.; trailhead: parking area A at Caesars Head Station.

Jeff Brewer and I hiked part of this loop in preparation for a longer combination of hikes with Steven Hughes and Dennis Parrish a week later. The time was a warm late March, after all the leafless hardwoods had been bleached by winter weather. We followed the **Frank Coggins Trail** across US 276, first on a section of gravel road, then on a footpath through hardwoods and rhododendron to a jct with **Rim of the Gap Trail** (#6) near Cliff Falls and **Naturaland Trust Trail** (#14) at 0.8 mi. We turned R and ascended on the **Naturaland Trust Trail,** parallel to a stream. At 1.1 mi we passed L of Firewater Falls, and at 1.2 mi a jct R with a white-blazed connector trail to **Frank Coggins Trail** and **Coldspring Connector Trail** (#7).

After crossing US 276 again at 1.7 mi, we descended to cross a private road. For the next 0.6 mi the trail clings to the cliffs of Caesars Head; rocky, rooty, mossy, wet, and steep in places. Along the way is Rockcliff Falls (flume) in a damp sanctuary of hemlock and rhododendron. At 2.3 mi we turned off **Naturaland Trust Trail** to follow the preserve's longest trail: **Pinnacle Pass Trail** (#20). From a wide ridge in an open hardwood forest, we partly followed an old woods road to again cross US 276 after 0.6 mi.

For the next 0.1 mi, there were two short switchbacks among poplar and maple, and beds of trout lilies. At 3.0 mi (0.7 on the **Pinnacle Pass Trail)** we arrived at an old logging road, where we began a descent on 17 curves and switchbacks to the banks and bridges of Oil Camp Creek. In the descent were oak, hemlock, locust, ash, wild hydrangea, mountain laurel, and fern. At 4.2 mi were campsites used by hunters.

The easy descent was over at 5.4 mi, when we crossed a cement bridge to begin the winding climb of about 1,460 ft in elevation. (Downstream on the road for 0.5 mi is a gate and parking area accessible from River Falls Road, SR 97.) The climb has rocky multiple switchbacks among trickling streams. Scattered Virginia yellow pine grows among large granite boulders, and patches of fern, trailing arbutus, yucca, and yellow-root are near the trail. A guy wire assists in the crossing of slick Eastern Stream at 6.1 mi. At 7.2 mi (4.9 mi on **Pinnacle Pass Trail),** we had outstanding views S toward Green Mountain. Nearby was the crossing of Eastern Stream again, where it formed an unusual garden of bog plants, ferns, mosses, and pitcher plants on a dangerous rock slope.

The treadway became easier when we reached an old forest road at 7.3 mi. We turned R. At 8 mi we intersected with **John Sloan Trail** (#21), L. (On the mountaintop it serves as an easy 0.9-mi connector to **Rim of the Gap Trail.** Its use could make a return loop for a total of 11.4 mi.) Continuing on the old road, there was a jct at 8.8 mi with **6 & 20 Connector Trail** (#22), L. Steven suggested that we call it **Hickory Nut Trail,** because the 0.1-mi connector to **Rim of the Gap Trail** had at least four species of hickories in concentration. (The connector could make a return loop, for a total of 12.1 mi.)

We reached the top of the ridgeline of Little Pinnacle Mountain at 9.3 mi and began a descent to Middle Saluda River. Through the trees and at scenic rock outcroppings were spectacular views of Cleveland Cliff, Standingstone Mountain, and Hospital Rock Falls, N, and toward the foothills E and SE. At 10.6 mi the descent began on more than 18 switchbacks before reaching a jct with **Rim of the Gap Trail** at 11.8 mi (9.6 mi on the **Pinnacle Pass Trail**). (It is 0.4 mi R on a descent of the **Rim of the Gap Trail** to **Jones Gap Trail,** and another 0.2 mi to Jones Gap Station parking area C. Primitive camping is allowed here with reservations at designated campsites.)

To complete the loop, we ascended from the valley on the yellow-blazed **Rim of the Gap Trail** (#6). We passed the jct with **6 & 20 Connector Trail,** L, at 14.2 mi (2 mi on **Rim of the Gap Trail),** and **John Sloan Trail** (#22) L, at 14.9 mi. To the R are superb views of Rainbow Falls, near Camp Greenville. After a descent among rock ledges and dense evergreens, we stayed close to granite walls, where constant seepage had created a garden of mosses and ferns. Views of Jones Gap area are outstanding; even the roar of the river below can be heard.

At 16.3 mi we held onto metal cables at a treacherous cascading stream crossing. To complete the loop, we returned on the **Frank Coggins Trail** at the jct with the **Naturaland Trust Trail** at 16.5 mi. From here it was 0.8 mi back to the Caesars Head Station and parking area.

Fourth Loop
Tom Miller Trail (0.7 mi) (#2); Jones Gap Trail (5.3 mi) (#1)

Length: 10.6 mi, combined backtrack (16.9 km); **moderate** to **strenuous;** USGS Maps: Table Rock, Brevard, Cleveland, Sandingstone Mountain; trailheads: see below.

Access: The W trailheads are at Raven Cliff Falls parking area and Middle Saluda River bridge on US 276, 1.1 mi and 2.4 mi N from Caesars Head Station Visitor Center. Access to the E trailhead is at the Jones Gap Station parking area at the end of Jones Gap Rd., and SR 97, River Falls Rd., 5.8 mi from US 276/SC 11. To locate River Falls Rd., look for the station sign at the road jct on US 276/SC 11, near the K-mart, 1 mi W of Cleveland and 4.9 mi E of the W jct of US 276 and SC 11.

At the Raven CLiff Falls parking area B, there is one linear option to parking area C at Jones Gap Station (5.3 mi) and the same distance if leaving from the Middle Saluda River bridge on US 276. Both entrances are part of the alternate routes of the **Foothills Trail.** If planning a loop rather than backtracking, the longest is 11.5 mi by using **Rim of the Gap Trail** (#6), part of **Frank Coggins Trail** (#15), **Coldspring Connector Trail** (#7), and part of **Coldspring Branch Trail** (#3). Other loop options with partial backtracking on **Jones Gap Trail** are Trail #8 (under construction in 1998), **Coldspring Branch Trail** (#3), or **Bill Kimball Trail** (#5) (2.1 mi).

We began our hike on the N side of the parking area B at US 276 on the **Tom Miller Trail** (former **Jones Gap Access Trail,** and also serving as an alternate route of the **Foothills Trail,** which ends at the parking area C of Jones Gap Station). Through hardwoods, we made a steep descent to a grove of hemlock and rhododendron by the Middle Saluda River (a small stream at this point). At 0.7 mi we made a jct, R, with the **Jones Gap Trail,** the old Jones Toll Road. (To the L it is 0.7 mi to US 276, the route formerly used for the W entrance of the Jones Gap Trail. You may notice that the Park Service has built rock water bars to prevent erosion.)

167

The famous Jones Toll Road operated from 1848 to 1910 and was engineered by Solomon Jones (1802–1899), "roadmaker of the mountains." Born in Flat Rock, North Carolina, this tall, mild, blue-eyed mountaineer married Mary Hamilton at the age of 20 and later served on the Hendersonville Public Health Commission. He is best remembered by the road that bears his name. Lacking engineering instruments, he used his natural talent and sense of contour grades to begin the road in 1840. Eight years later, without slave labor, it was completed. Mrs. Hattie Finlay Jones, a descendant who lives in Greenville, told this story about Solomon's road: "He turned loose a pig and followed it five and a half miles up the slope." The State of South Carolina permitted Solomon to install a tollgate at the foot of the mountain, near River Falls and Drakes Inn. (In addition to Solomon receiving a toll, his daughter and heir, Mrs. June Jones Cox, received $50 a month from the state for the project for a number of years.) Over the years the toll fee varied, but in 1858 a one-horse wagon paid 25 cents, a two-horse carriage was 85 cents, a goat or pig was 1 cent, and a pedestrian paid 5 cents.

In 1851 Solomon built a home on 4,000 acres in the nearby Oil Camp region; and for about 20 years, beginning in 1870, he sold real estate. Later he moved to the summit of Mt. Hebron. On his gravestone is this epitaph:

> HERE LIES SOLOMON JONES
>
> THE ROADMAKER, A TRUE PATRIOT
>
> HE LABORED FIFTY YEARS TO LEAVE
>
> THE WORLD BETTER THAN HE FOUND IT.

We followed the blue-blazed **Jones Gap Trail** and at 1 mi crossed the stream on a footlog. Near here is the state's largest reported yellow birch, with a circumference of more than 8 ft, and the largest witch hazel, more than 9 in around. Also nearby is Dargan's Cascade, flumes, and pools of clear water, evidence of a splashing river that drops 1,680 ft through 4 mi of the gorge. On our L were the slopes toward the Tennessee Valley Divide on the South Carolina/North Carolina border and the Little Rich Mountains. To the R was the steep ridge E to the Little Pinnacle Mountains. For the next 0.4 mi on the trail is one of the best examples of Solomon's engineering. He constructed a switchback that would pass, except for the short curves, for a railway grade. Wildflowers are prominent in this area—trillium, crested dwarf iris, Solomon's seal, bloodroot, and fringe tree. At 1.8 mi we entered a deep cove, and for the next mi we crossed numerous streams plunging down from the slope. At 2.2 mi is the state's largest reported mocker-nut hickory (more than 10 ft in circumference) and the state's co-champion Fraser magnolia (more than 5 feet). A yellow poplar stand afforded some sunlight on the road at 2.6 mi. At 3.2 mi we reached a jct, R, with 2.6-mi **Coldspring Branch Trail.**

(The orange-blazed **Coldspring Branch Trail** crosses the middle Saluda River on a footbridge, crosses an old wagon-road intersection, and begins a gradual ascent. Maple, poplar, hemlock, fetterbush, and wildflowers are prominent. At 0.2 mi it makes a jct with **Bill Kimball Trail,** R. [The 2.5-mi **Bill Kimball Trail** ascends steeply to encounter two major switchbacks. After reaching the top of a ridge called "The Thumb," it is over a 300-ft granite cliff. The trail rejoins the **Coldspring Branch Trail** at 2 mi, 0.5 mi before the US 276 parking area] Continuing on the **Coldspring Branch Trail,** it is necessary to rock-hop the branch six times to turn away at 1.3 mi. We then ascended on a wagon road to a ridge crest at 1.9 mi, turned L, and arrived at US 276 at 2.6 mi. A R turn onto the highway was 150 yd from the parking area.)

Continuing downstream on the **Jones Gap Trail,** we followed the path to the L, paralleling the river and noticing deer, turkey, and raccoon tracks. We also passed a number of the selected campsites that require a permit from the visitor centers. At 3.8 mi we passed L of scenic Ben's Sluice, and at 4.4 mi we followed a section of trail, rerouted R to cross the John Reid Clonts bridge. (To the L is an old trail now called **Rainbow Falls Trail** [#4], that ascends steeply 0.6 mi to Rainbow Falls.) The trail rejoins the old trail at 4.7 mi. We passed campsites along the river and at 5.1 mi noticed an enormous landslide, R, that exposed a spectacular rock face on Little Pinnacle Mountain. At 5.3 mi we arrived at the Jones Gap Station parking area.

Hospital Rock Trail (4.7 mi) (#30); Cleveland Connector Trail (0.5 mi) (#32); Falls Creek Trail (1.6 mi (#31)

Length: 6.8 mi combined (10.9 km); **strenuous** (elevation change: 1,840 ft); USGS Maps: Cleveland and Standingstone Mountain; trailheads: parking area at Jones Gap Station for SW entrance of **Hospital Rock Trail,** and roadside parking on Falls Creek Road for SE trailhead of **Falls Creek Trail.**

This linear combination of trails (with the exception of **Cleveland Connector Trail)** is exceptionally rugged and steep, has many switchbacks, but provides scenic views of cliffs, waterfalls, and the Middle Saluda River valley. Jeff Brewer and I chose an early spring to hike these trails to have best views without tree foliage. Large patches of violets and saxifrage were blooming. The scope of evergreens, gray granite, and lichens, and splashing whitewater from the winter season gave us a surreal and unforgettable journey.

From the parking area at Jones Gap Station, we followed the trail entrance signs to cross an arched footbridge over Middle Saluda River. After a R turn we registered at the trailhead at 0.2 mi, where we entered a forest of hemlock, hardwoods, and rhododendron. Ascending, we passed under a power line at 0.5 mi. At 1.1 mi, L, is Hospital Rock, a large overhang named from a legend that the site was a hide-out for Civil War deserters. A 1.2 mi is a sheer rock face, R. to the L at 2.3 mi is **Cleveland Connector Trail.** (It is an old CCC road to the North Carolina state line and a 1.4-mi road to a paved road a Camp Greenville. On the way is Symmes Chapel, an area with sweeping views S of Jones Gap Gorge and Little Pinnacle Mountain.)

Continuing on **Hospital Rock Trail,** we temporarily followed an old road through hardwoods and mountain laurel in a short section of a Wildlife Management Area (used by wild-game hunters in

170

the last three months of the year and in April). After a descent to cross tributaries of Headforemost Creek, we switched from footpaths to old forest roads to parallel Falls Creek and the end of **Hospital Rock Trail** at 4.7 mi. Merging into **Falls Creek Trail,** we passed through a tunnel of rhododendron, more switchbacks and rocky outcrops, then to the base of spectacular Falls Creek Waterfall, L, at 5.2 mi. After a series of switchbacks, old roads, and steps, we descended on an old road to a gate at Falls Creek Road, the trail's E end. It is 2.9 mi on paved roads back to Jones Gap Station. (Access to E end trailhead is 4 mi on River Falls Road from US 276/SC 11, described for **Jones Gap Trail** above, then a turn R on Duckworth Road to cross a bridge over Middle Saluda River and into a residential area. After 0.7 mi turn R on Falls Creek Road, pass Palmetto Bible Camp R at 0.9 mi, a lake waterfall L at 1.1 mi, and immediately to the trailhead and roadside parking, L.)

Oconee State Park (Oconee County)

Oconee State Park is scenic, peaceful, and characteristic of everything inviting about the Appalachians. Centered among mountain ranges, lakes, rivers, waterfalls, and historic places, the 1,165-acre park was donated to the state by Oconee County in 1935. Surrounded by wilderness regions of the Andrew Pickens District of the Sumter National Forest, the park is only 10 mi from the Chattooga River, a National Wild and Scenic River. To the N is the Ellicott Rock Wilderness Area; the Upper and Lower Whitewater Falls, among the highest in eastern America; Walhalla Fish Hatchery, one of the largest trout hatcheries in the world; and Jocassee Lake, probably the state's most beautiful. South of the park is the Stumphouse Mountain Tunnel and the legendary Isaqueena Falls, and Tugaloo Lake. To the E is Oconee Station, an old Indian fort and the oldest building (1760) in the county.

In the park is the SW terminus of the **Foothills Trail,** the state's longest until the state's **Palmetto Trail** is completed (see

Chapter VI). Also, the trailhead for **Tamassee Knob Trail** begins near the park boundary at the corner of **Foothills Trail** and Station Mountain Road (see Chapter I, Section 1). In the heart of the park is 1.5-mi **Lake Trail,** an easy loop that begins at the rock building near the boat rentals. Among hardwoods and rhododendron it passes near cabins, picnic shelters, a playground, and volleyball courts.

The park offers 140 campsites and 10 walk-in tent sites, 19 cabins, a primitive group camp for organized groups, a park store, a camper's recreation building and a community recreation building, picnic areas, a 20-acre lake for fishing, swimming, and pedal boating, a playground, carpet golf, and hiking trails. There is also a museum and visitor center that displays CCC tools and equipment, early farm life artifacts, and trout-fishing equipment, including a bamboo fly rod once owned by President Theodore Roosevelt.

Information: Oconee State Park, 624 State Park Rd., Mountain Rest, SC 29664; (864) 638–5353.

Access: From Walhalla on SC 28 go 11 mi N to jct of SC 28 and SC 107. Follow SC 107 for 2 mi to the park entrance. From Cashiers in North Carolina, follow SC 107 S.

Oconee Trail (5.6 mi); Old Waterwheel Trail (0.4 mi)

Length: 6.0 mi round-trip, combined (9.6 km); **moderate;** USGS Maps: Tamassee, Walhalla; trailhead: Trading Post.

From the parking lot behind the Trading Post, follow the signs and green blazes. Descend from a knoll and cross a small stream that feeds a lake. Pass through a forest of rhododendron, oak, poplar, white pine, and mountain laurel. Cross a ravine at 0.4 mi, and cross the dam at the lake (stocked with bream and bass) for a turn R at 1.0 mi. Pass a campground sign at 1.7 mi and turn L to cross a dry streambed at 1.8 mi. At 2.2 mi cross a creek on a footbridge to ascend a ridge. Follow the green blazes and descend off the ridge on switchbacks. In a ravine at 3.2 mi, cross to reach an intersection with the **Old Waterwheel Trail** at 3.9 mi, R and L, on an old dirt road.

Go R and follow orange blazes for 0.2 mi to the site of an old overshot waterwheel. It was used when the area was a CCC Camp during the 1930s. The turn of the wheel powered a piston pump to elevate and store water. Backtrack and, at the intersection with the **Oconee Trail,** continue R. After 0.5 mi there is a jct with the cabin road that serves cabins #7–13. Continue R to intersect with the **Foothills Trail** after another 0.6 mi. Keep L and follow the paved road for a return to the Trading Post and parking area.

Foothills Trail (Park Section)

Length: 1.2 mi (1.9 km); **easy;** USGS Maps: Tamassee, Walhalla; trailhead: Foothills Trail sign.

To reach this trailhead go 0.5 mi E on the paved road from the trading post and campground to the **Foothills Trail** sign on the SE cabin-area road. Parking space is limited. From this point you can go 0.4 mi within the park boundary to a jct on the R with the **Tamassee Knob Trail** or to the L on the **Foothills Trail.** If you take the latter, you can hike to the Long Mountain Lookout Tower for a round trip of 4.4 mi. If you hike the **Tamassee Knob Trail** for a round trip, it is 5 mi. (See section on the Andrew Pickens Ranger District, Sumter National Forest, in Chapter I for descriptions of these trails.)

Paris Mountain State Park (Greenville County)

In 1935 the state acquired 1,275 acres of forest from the city of Greenville to create the Paris Mountain State Park. The acreage included mountaintop ridges of Virginia pine, rugged slopes with dense stands of rosebay rhododendron, and clear cascading streams. One of these streams was impounded in 1898 as a reservoir for the Greenville Water Works. It served the city until the early 1930s, when the Table Rock and North Saluda reservoirs took its place. The CCC developed the area in 1935–1940, and the park opened in June 1937. Some of the CCC stone and wooden buildings, such as the bathhouse, remain in use.

Paris Mountain got its name from Captain Richard Pearis (Paris), the first white settler in the Greenville area, c. 1766. He held a trust of 10 sq m (present-day Greenville), which had been given to him by George II of England.

Facilities in the park are a 50-site campground, a primitive campground, an amphitheater, picnic areas, a bathhouse, a lake for swimming and fishing, a campground for organized youth camping, playground equipment, hiking trails, and nature-study areas. The park has more than 75 species of trees and shrubs, more than 80 species of wildflowers, and more than 30 species of birds. Finches and wrens are frequently seen.

Information: Paris Mountain State Park, 2401 State Park Rd., Greenville, SC 29609; (864) 244–5565.

Access: From I-385 in Greenville take US 276 N toward Travelers Rest, but soon turn R on SC 253 (Paris Mountain Rd.). Follow signs and turn L.

Sulphur Springs Loop Trail (4.0 mi); Brissy Ridge Trail (2.3 mi)

Length: 6.3 mi round-trip (10.1 km); **strenuous;** USGS Map: Greenville NW. NE; trailhead: Sulphur Springs Picnic Area.

Dick Hunt and I began this white-blazed **Sulphur Springs Loop Trail** at the Sulphur Springs Picnic Area parking lot. After 100 yd we crossed a footbridge over a creek. Continuing upstream, we passed under large oaks, pines, and poplars. Hugging the creek banks and on the steep slopes were alder, yellow root, mountain laurel, and rosebay rhododendron. Ferns, partridge berry, and mosses covered the level spots. We crossed the creek again at 0.3 mi near a large gazebo and continued upstream. New Jersey tea, sensitive briar, goat's pea, and Indian plantain grew on the red-clay banks among rocks and exposed tree roots. At 0.6 mi we rock-hopped the creek in a grove of fetterbush and low-hanging rhododendron. We took the trail to the R across the creek, climbed the stone steps, and rock-hopped the stream again. At 1 mi were wild hydrangea, sweet pepperbush, and rosebay rhododendron. We ascended on a steep grade where the stream cascaded on our R, and rock-hopped again at 1.3 mi where the creek splashed over a tier of rocks.

We began a steep climb through a stand of chestnut oak and rocky terrain. After a small dip over the ridge came the final ascent along a slope to the mountaintop. At 1.7 mi we reached an old roadbed (now 1.6-mi blue-blazed **Fire Tower Bike Trail),** once used to reach a former firetower. Across the road were the foundations of the firetower, rock and brick chimneys of a former forester's home, and artifacts of other outbuildings. We continued on a gradual grade hiking E to pass a jct with the yellow-blazed **Brissy Ridge Trail.** We turned R, then made a jct on the L with the other loop jct of **Brissy Ridge Trail,** and R to the trailhead of **Fire Tower Bike Trail** at 3.3 mi. After crossing the paved Camp Buckhorn Road near a gate, we descended to cross the road again for a return to the picnic area at 4 mi. (The **Brissy Ridge Trail** loops around Camp Buckhorn, crosses the camp entrance road, crosses Buckhorn Creek, and completes the loop near the gate described above.)

Lake Placid Nature Trail

Length: 0.7 mi (1.1 km); **easy;** USGS Map: Greenville NE; trailhead: bathhouse.

I started this trail at the bathhouse, aware that bathers close to the trail would wonder what I was doing pushing a measuring wheel. I had gone about 50 yd when Jamie Rodgers, a nine-year-old boy with freckles, rode up beside me on his Mongoose bike. "Can I go with you?" he asked. His bike bumped over the little footbridge at the lake headwaters. He had ridden the trail so many times that he knew each tree at each interpretive post—beech, sycamore, black locust, poplar, hickory, and dogwood. "I live just down the road from the park, I come up here every day," he said. At 0.4 mi I walked down to the base of the dam, but Jamie chose the nearby road to avoid the rocks and the creek. We continued on the trail by a picnic shelter and crossed a wood viaduct with five stone pillars built by the CCC. At 0.7 mi we returned by the swimming area. "Would you like to go around again?" Jamie asked, poised on his Mongoose as if to race with "Clicker," the measuring wheel.

Rose Hill Plantation State Park (Union County)

Between 1828 and 1832 a federal-style, three-story house of red brick and split-shingle roof was constructed on a rolling hill S of Union in Union County. This lovely home had a frontdoor fanlight, a graceful spiral stairway in the center of the main hall, a ballroom, and, on the third floor, a classroom for the owner's 14 children (just five of whom lived) from two marriages. In the 1850s the house was remodeled with stucco over the bricks and two-story porches.

It was "Rose Hill," the home of William H. Gist (1807–1874), who was elected to the South Carolina House of Representatives in 1840 and to the Senate in 1844. Four years later he was elected lieutenant governor and ten years later, governor. He is often referred to as the state's "Secession Governor." But he was more than a political figure; he was also manager of his cotton plantation at Rose Hill. In 1960 the mansion and 44 acres were purchased for a state park.

Visitors today will see a completely remodeled structure with a rebuilt outhouse kitchen and a number of other outbuildings. One exhibit building has a display of plantation life and cotton culture; another has four carriages. "I hope we can get the carriages restored," Chris Hightower, park superintendent, said as he showed me the plantation grounds.

Information: Rose Hill Plantation State Park, 2677 Sardis Rd., Union, SC 29379; (864) 427–5966.

Access: From jct of US 176 and SC 215 in Union, go 8 mi S on SR 16 to park entrance.

Rose Hill Nature Trail

Length: 0.6 mi (1 km); **easy;** USGS Map: Whitmire N; trailhead: behind the group picnic shelter.

I entered the forest from the open field behind the group picnic shelter and followed the trail signs. The forest was mainly oaks and pines. Honeysuckle formed a forest ground cover and a number of wildflowers, such as rattlesnake orchids, were noticeable. At 0.4 mi I turned sharply L and ascended to the rose gardens. Adjoining them is the formal garden in the shape of the Confederate flag. (The trail has a 0.5-mi spur that descends to the Tyger River and a floodplain. It was built by a local Boy Scout troop.)

Sadlers Creek State Park (Anderson County)

Sadlers Creek State Park comprises 395 acres of hardwood and pine forest on the N side of Hartwell Lake. The land was leased from the U.S. Army Corps of Engineers in 1966. The park offers fishing, boating, water skiing, and camping. In addition to the 100 campsites on the peninsula, it has a primitive campground, recreation building, picnic area, playground, and community activities building.

Although the Cherokee Indians once lived in the area, only a few artifacts have been found. A few English settlers' house foundations have also been found; an old brick foundation was located near the park superintendent's residence. "My uncle, Gordon Smith, once lived there," former park ranger Herbert Jones said.

How red was the clay on the shoreline with a red sunset up the lake! Silhouetted ducks came up the clay banks for food. By dark the screech owls were giving their eerie sounds over the din of the cicadas.

Information: Sadlers Creek State Park, 940 Sadlers Creek State Park Rd., Anderson, SC 29624; (864) 226–8950.

Access: From the jct of SC 24 and 187, take SC 187 for 7 mi to the park road on the R and go 1.2 mi to the park entrance.

Pine Grove Trail

Length: 0.6 mi (1 km); **easy;** USGS Map: Hartwell NE; trailhead: pavilion parking area.

From the parking area at the pavilion, I went R, near the restroom, and followed the trail sign. On a well-graded and well-maintained trail I passed through a mixed forest by the lake. I saw oaks, hickory, pines, maple, honey locust, dogwood, wild cherry, sumac, deerberry, redbud, and honeysuckle. Chunks of quartz added beauty to the winding path. At 0.2 mi I crossed a paved road with a cul-de-sac to the L, made a curve around a bench (designed as a love seat), crossed the road again, and returned to the point of origin at 0.6 mi.

Table Rock State Park (Pickens County)

No one seems to know his name, but many know the legend of a prodigious Cherokee chieftain god who used the "Sah-ka-na-ga," Great Blue Hills of God, as he wished. To dine he sat on a 2,600-ft mountain, and for his table he used a granite mountain, now called Table Rock. It is 3,124 ft high and composed of feldspar, biotite, quartz, and amphibole. It has patches of vegetation on the summit already mixed like a garden salad for the chieftain. This colossal table of volcanic origin is part of the 3,083-acre Table Rock State Park.

Development of the base area by settlers began in the early nineteenth century, and by 1845 a hotel was constructed for a vacation resort. In 1935 the state acquired the park area as a gift from the city of Greenville and Pickens County. Three years later the park opened to the public after development by the CCC.

Park facilities include Pinnacle Lake, a 36-acre swimming, boating, and fishing area; a picnic area; a carpet golf course; a nature center; two campgrounds with a total of 100 units; a country store; a community recreation center; a meeting house; 14 cabins; a bathhouse; a lodge and restaurant (closed on Mondays, except Labor Day); and three exciting trails for hiking.

Information: Table Rock State Park, 246 Table Rock State Park Rd., Pickens, SC 29671; (864) 878–9813/6641.

Access: Turn off SC 11 at the park signs, 4 mi E of the jct with US 178 and 4.7 mi W of the jct with SC 8.

Table Rock Trail

Length: 6.8 mi round-trip (10.9 km); **strenuous;** USGS Map: Table Rock; trailhead: Nature Center.

I started on the **Table Rock Trail,** (a National Recreation trail) early one morning with a group of friends. After 0.1 mi we left the asphalt trail near a waterfall on Carrick Creek, crossed the creek on a wooden bridge, and at 0.2 mi turned R on the red-blazed trail. (The green-blazed **Carrick Creek Trail** also follows this route for the first 0.5 mi.) A warning sign reminded us not to underestimate our time and be caught on the trails after dark. We walked through a ground cover of partridge berry in a basic oak and hickory forest with scattered pines and hemlock. After crossing Green Creek for the last time, the **Carrick Creek Trail** veered L at 0.5 mi and the **Table Rock Trail** ascended steeply in an open forest. Gigantic boulders appeared poised to roll down the steep mountainside, smashing the Cherokee chieftain's toes. At 1.6 mi we reached a rain shelter built by the CCC in 1937. At 1.8 mi we climbed to the jct with Pinnacle Ridge at Panther Gap. At 2.5 mi we reached Governor's Rock; the rock steps here were carved out of the granite by a battery-powered air hammer. At 2.7 mi there was a spring (but it is recommended that you not drink from it).

We reached the forest-covered summit at 3 mi, then descended for another 0.4 mi to a sweeping view of Table Rock Lake, Caesar's Head, and the smaller foothills.

Sitting at this scenic place were Taylor Watts, Kevin Clarey, and Less Parks, three first-class Boy Scouts of Troop 26 in Easley. "We tried to run up the mountain," said Les, the youngest, still short of breath. They were camping at the park's primitive campsite.

As I left the chieftain's dining table, I thought about what Mike Hendrix, park superintendent, had said to me the day before:

"Everything about this park I like: the lake, the streams, Table Rock. It's like a magnet—once you are on it, it's hard to get off."

Pinnacle Mountain Trail

Length: 7.0 mi round-trip, combined (11.3 km); **exceptionally strenuous;** USGS Maps: Table Rock, Eastatoe Gap; trailhead: Nature Center.

To reach the top of Pinnacle Mountain, I made a loop by ascending the **Table Rock Trail** for 1.8 mi to Panther Gap. Here I turned L on Pinnacle Ridge at a yellow-blazed trail, which climbed to the first peak but skirted the S slope of the second peak to Hemlock Gap at 2.8 mi. (At this point is an 0.7-mi connector trail, Mill Creek Pass, L, which descends to intersect the **Pinnacle Trail/** alternate **Foothills Trail.)** Continuing ahead on a steep ascent, I reached the summit (3,425 ft) at 3.7 mi, the highest point in the park.

I was disappointed that there was no view. Instead, a sign warned me that I would "be prosecuted to the full limit of the law" if I trespassed on the watershed of the City of Greenville a few yards N. A former climber, Chet, had written on the sign, "I did it for Jan." There was solace in seeing a garden of wildflowers—horsemint, meadow rue, yellow flowering bear's foot, New York fern, and more Carolina pink (a scarlet gentian-shaped flower with five yellow corolla lobes) than I have seen anywhere. Although *Lilium canadense,* Canada lily, grows nowhere else in the state but in this area, I found what I think is a rare red *Lilium grayi,* the orange bell lily.

I descended 0.2 mi on the **Pinnacle Trail** to where it joins the **Foothills Trail** for a descent and return to the Nature Center. At 4.3 mi was a magnificent view of the farms and forest S of the Pinnacle. Wild quinine and blackberries grew on damp spots of the rock face. The Mill Creek Pass connector jct was at 4.7 mi. From here the narrow trail descended steeply on slippery rocks and roots along Carrick Creek. At 6.2 mi I rejoined the green-blazed Carrick Creek Trail and exited at the Nature Center for a round trip of 7.0 mi.

Carrick Creek Trail

Length: 1.9 mi (3.0 km); **easy** to **moderate;** USGS Map: Table Rock; trailhead: Nature Center.

From the Nature Center I followed the same route as for the **Table Rock Trail,** but after 0.5 mi turned L on the green-blazed **Carrick Creek Trail.** In a mixed hardwood forest were dogwoods, sourwood, and mountain laurel. I crossed a small stream at 1 mi and reached a jct with the **Pinnacle Trail** and **Foothills Trail** at 1.1 mi. I turned L, descended, and crossed Carrick Creek a number of times. Sheets of water seemed to slide through the flumes, lightly from rocky lips, and cascade over one another at rugged strips of rocks. (Please obey the signs and do not swim or slide down the rock slopes.)

SECTION 2
Upper Midlands

Major reservoirs (Russell, Thurmond, Wateree, Murray, Wylie, Monticello, and Greenwood), other lakes, and rivers in this region provide superb facilities for boating and fishing. More national forest acreage is here than anywhere else in the state, and some of the longest hiking and equestrian trails are here also. History is emphasized at such state parks as Andrew Jackson, Dreher Island, and Landsford. Hickory Knob is the only state park with a resort system.

Andrew Jackson State Park (Lancaster County)

Andrew Jackson State Park is the state's only historic park honoring a U.S. president. Donated to the state by Lancaster County in 1953, the 360-acre park has a museum that features the farm and household life of the nineteenth-century piedmont settlers in an area formerly belonging to the Waxhaw Indians. The park has a

25-site campground near an 18-acre lake with bass, crappie, bream, and catfish; a children's playground; a boat dock; a "meeting house" for groups and organizations; a primitive campground; a fishing pier; an outdoor amphitheater; a 1-mi **Lake Trail;** a picnic area; a replica of an old schoolhouse, and a nature trail.

In a manicured meadow is the park's impressive focal point: an equestrian statue of the young Andrew Jackson, a gift from sculptress Anna Hyatt Huntington (Huntington Beach State Park is named in honor of her and her husband). Children from around the state gave nickels and dimes for the purchase of the base. An inscription explains:

> We, the children of Lancaster County, South Carolina, are interested in a youthful statue of Andrew Jackson because he was born among the red clay hills of our county and here he spent the formative years of his life. . . .
>
> Sixth grade, H.R. Rice Elementary School
> Nancy Crockett, Teacher and Principal
> May 15, 1967

Although it is not certain in which of the Carolinas Andrew Jackson was born, historians agree that, after young Andrew's father died, he spent his boyhood in South Carolina living with his mother's Scot-Irish relatives, the Crawfords. By the time he was 14, he showed an interest in the development of the nation. He rode with Major William Richardson Davie's troops in the American Revolution and was captured by the British but returned to his family because of his age.

Information: Andrew Jackson State Park, 196 Andrew Jackson Park Rd., Lancaster, SC 29720; (803) 285–3344.

Access: From Lancaster go N on US 521 for 8 mi; or from Rock Hill at I-77, go E on SC 5 for 11.9 mi and L on US 521 for 0.6 mi to park entrance.

Andrew Jackson Nature Trail
Length: 1.1 mi (1.8 km); **easy;** USGS Map: Van Wyck; trailhead: parking area.

From the parking area Steve Harris and I passed the "meeting house," a chapel-like structure in the pines, dedicated to Viola C. Floyd (1901–1978) for her service as historian, teacher, and community leader. The trail meandered over a ground cover of reindeer moss under pines and cedars. After passing a picnic area at 0.3 mi, we entered an open space at 0.6 mi where blackberry and honeysuckle competed with young sweet gum. A doe and fawn, partially in a patch of lespedeza, were ahead of us. At 0.9 mi we crossed the park road again into bunches of lyre-leaf sage, ragwort, and Queen Anne's lace before we returned to the "meeting house" and parking area.

Baker Creek State Park (McCormick County)

In 1967 the state leased 1,305 acres for 25 years from the U.S. Army Corps of Engineers to establish Baker Creek State Park. With rolling hills of clay and quartz, and pines bordering Thurmond Lake (formerly Clark Hill reservoir), the topography is so ideal for camping, fishing, and relaxing, it is a model for a natural park. It has 100 campsites with electricity, water, comfort stations, and hot showers. There are picnic areas, a boat dock, a playground, carpet golf, a pavilion bathhouse, a swimming area, a primitive campground, and trails for hikers and equestrians.

Information: Baker Creek State Park, Route 3, Box 50, McCormick, SC 29835; (864) 443–2457.

Access: From downtown McCormick take US 378 SW for 3.7 mi to jct with SR 329 on R. Follow SR 329 for 2 mi into the park.

Wild Mint Trail

Length: 0.8 mi (1.3 km); **easy;** USGS Maps: McCormick, Willington; trailhead: between campsites 56 and 57.

From camping area #2 between campsites 56 and 57, I descended to the edge of the lake and followed the trail sign. I read the trail brochure, but campers had removed some of the posts at the 14 stations, and at other locations the plant specimen had vanished. But there was more to see than the listed species. Along the trail were buttonbush, holly, redbud, wild plum, wild cherry, sweet gum, persimmon (from whose heartwood golf-club heads are made), loblolly and shortleaf pines, mulberry, dogwood, and indigo. At 0.3 mi I crossed a paved road and immediately smelled that familiar odor of cloves; it was wild mint, thus the name of the trail. After a loop curve on the hilltop, I returned to cross the road again and complete the loop.

Baker Creek Walking Trail
Length: 0.7 mi (1.1 km); **easy;** USGS Maps: McCormick, Willington; trailhead: picnic area #1.

I began this loop around a picnic area at the sign near an electric meter, uphill from the boat ramp. The forest was mostly pines and oaks with scattered ash, cedar, and dogwood. Jessamine and *vaccinium* were prominent; indigo, sticky fox glove, and wild onion provided spots of color. After crossing the road at 0.4 mi, I returned to the point of origin.

Calhoun Falls State Park (Abbeville County)

Fishing (bass, bluegill, crappie, and catfish) is a major offering of this new park, opened in 1992. Developed on the SE shore of 26,650-acre Lake Russell, it is a joint project of PRT and the U.S. Corps of Engineers near the town of Calhoun Falls. The park received its name from the town, which was in turn named for John C. Calhoun's property in the area. The "falls" are thought to refer to a section of rapids in the Savannah River now covered by Lake Russell. Facilities in the park include a full service campground, tennis courts, picnic area with shelters, playground, boat ramp, fishing pier, park store, bathhouse, and lake swimming beach.

Information: Calhoun Falls State Park, 46 Maintenance Shop Rd., Calhoun Falls, SC 29628; (864) 447–8267.

Access: On SC 81 2 mi N of Calhoun Falls and 7 mi S of Lowndesville.

Cedar Bluff Nature Trail

Length: 1.7 mi round-trip (2.7 km); **easy;** USGS Map: Calhoun Falls; trailhead: tennis courts and campground #1.

After entering the park from SC 81, drive to the parking area near the tennis courts. The trail entrance is on the N side of the road. The central loop runs through a forest of hardwoods and cedar. Deer and turkey are natural inhabitants. The loop trail is wide and well designed.

Chester State Park (Chester County)

Chester State Park has 523 acres of mixed forest and includes a 160-acre lake. Deer, raccoon, squirrel, and dove have a sanctuary in the forest, but it is a different story for the bass, crappie, bream, and catfish that abound for the anglers in the lake. Fishing boats may be rented at the boat dock (private boats are not allowed in the park). The park was purchased by the state in 1934 from the Lake View Corporation and other landowners. Facilities include a community recreation building, picnic area, 25-site campground, equestrian arena, field-archery range, primitive campground, and hiking trail.

Information: Chester State Park, 759 State Park Dr., Chester, SC 29706; (803) 385–2680.

Access: From the jct of SC 9 and US 321 Bypass and SC 72 in Chester, go S on SC 72 for 2 mi to park entrance.

Caney Fork Falls Trail

Length: 1.3 mi (2.1 km); **easy;** USGS Map: Chester; trailhead: parking area.

From the parking area I followed trail signs at the boathouse and entered a young mixed forest on a well-maintained and well-graded trail. Coreopsis, wild pink, five finger, wild larkspur, deerberry, and silverberry were in bloom. At 0.3 mi I passed a picnic area where the majority of trees were hickory, elm, oak, sycamore, and hackberry. After passing the campground at 0.7 mi, the trees were much larger and the trail became wider. Leaving the forest, I crossed the dam and returned to the parking zone by the picnic area and falls at 1.3 mi.

Dreher Island State Park (Newberry County)

The 348-acre Dreher Island State Park has multiple peninsulas in 50,000-acre Lake Murray, NW of Columbia. When it was leased from the South Carolina Electric and Gas Company in 1970, there was some controversy about the park's safety. It had been a WWII bombing range, and in 1958 the Air Force uncovered and destroyed approximately 2,200 duds on the premises. In 1972 Mike Stevens, historic research coordinator of PRT in Columbia, recommended that the park honor the B-25 bomber of WWII, its pilots (one of whom was General Jimmy Doolittle), and its missions over Japan, by naming the park a "World War II Interpretive Park."

Most of the early settlers in this area were Scot-Irish and German. One German community was called "Dutch Fork," the site of George Drehr's Mill (note the old spelling). William (Billy) H. Dreher, for whom the park is named, was a descendant of the "Dutch Fork" Germans.

Facilities in the park include 112 campsites, a camp recreation building, a primitive campground, a trading post, a tackle shop, a community recreation building, a number of picnic areas, two playgrounds, fishing, three boat ramps, a swimming area, a youth camp, and five lakeside villas.

Information: Dreher Island State Park, 3677 State Park Rd., Prosperity, SC 29127; (803) 364–4152.

Access: From US 76 in Little Mountain, take SR 271 for 2.8 mi to SR 20. Follow SR 20 for 3.5 mi to jct with SR 26. Turn L on SR 26, and follow SR 26 to SR 571 and then to the park for 4 mi. If from US 76 in Prosperity, follow SR 26 all the way to SR 571. If from I–26, Exit 91 at Chapin, then follow park signs and SR 48, SR 29, and SR 231 W to the park for 12 mi.

Billy Dreher Nature Trail

Length: 0.2 mi (0.3 km); **easy;** USGS Map: Lake Murray W; trailhead: behind the community rec bldg at parking area.

I noticed a sign that read, BILLY DREHER NATURE TRAIL, AN EAGLE PROJECT BY DAVID HASKELL, TROOP 95, 1981. I walked under tall oaks, pines, walnuts, mulberry, and gums, many of which were dressed in English ivy. After 0.1 mi I saw the foundation and fallen chimney of Billy's ancestral homeplace. The trail circled back to the parking area.

Who was Billy Dreher? Research in the PRT office and in the Lexington and Newberry Counties register of deeds offices led me to Harriette Chapman Epting (Mrs. James H. Epting). She told me that Billy was born June 13, 1857; died April 8, 1938; and was buried in the Prosperity cemetery. He was a farmer, and he "loved his spirits in earthenware jugs," she said. "He also loved the women, but he never married."

She said she was not related to Billy, but Billy's niece, Lillian, was the half-sister of her grandfather, John Jacob Chapman. Billy had three sisters: Almenia (mother of Lillian), Martha (who married a Dennis), and Louisa (who married a Price). Lillian, who never married, moved in with her uncle Billy at the homeplace to take care of him, but in 1929 they moved off the island because Lake Murray was impounded between 1927 and 1930. They moved to Prosperity to live with Billy's sisters. Lillian survived them all, but needed someone to take care of her in her old age. That person was Harriette, who at the death of Lillian was willed the Dreher property.

"I have Billy's metal driver's license in my purse," Harriette said. "I've carried them since Aunt Lillian gave them to me. Do you think I could use Billy's license to have a permanent pass to the park?" she said, smiling. "Why don't we ask?" I replied.

Hickory Knob State Resort Park
(McCormick County)

They cleared all the hickories off this knob when they created the state's first deluxe country club-style resort park in 1973. But there are plenty of hickories for those who love them around the lake's edge and golf courses and in the rich forest. There are 1,090 acres here, leased from the U.S. Army Corps of Engineers in 1969. It has everything for vacationers who "are looking for the right place . . . one that is removed from the hectic pace of everyday living . . . accessible and economical," says a park advertisement.

On top of the knob is the lodge complex with a motel, restaurant, swimming pool, and tennis courts. Another motel and a conference building are near the lake, close to the marina. All this can easily accommodate 300 guests. In a crescent from the knob are 18 cabins complete with color TVs and telephones. The park also includes a playground, a large boat dock, a tackle shop, a fishing pier, a boat ramp, a skeet and trap range, a putting green, and an archery course. And the 6,560-yard championship golf course, with full service, designed by golf architect Tom Jackson, gives this beautiful park its country-club atmosphere. There is a 75-site campground with all the usual conveniences for tent campers and RVs.

Information: Hickory Knob State Resort Park, Route 1, Box 199-B, McCormick, SC 29835; (800) 491–1764.

Access: From McCormick take US 378 SW for 5.8 mi to SC 7. Turn R on SC 7 and go 1.5 mi to the park entrance.

Turkey Ridge Trail and Beaver Run Nature Trail
Length: (together) **1.3 mi** round-trip, combined (2.1 km); **easy;** USGS Map: Willington; trailhead: near parking area at the Lodge Complex.

After parking at the Lodge Complex, I walked to the edge of the forest, where there is a trail sign. I followed the **Turkey Ridge Trail,** and at 0.2 mi the trail curved by the lake where almost silent ripples were transformed into sequins by the sun. On the 1-mi **Beaver Run Nature Trail,** I passed under tall, silent loblolly pines. "When the pines tranced as by a wizard's will, doth some lone Dryad haunt the breezeless air," wrote Charleston poet Paul H. Hayne in "The Voice of the Pines." Silent as the pines was the understory of sweet gum, oak, sassafras, black tupelo, black willow, dogwood, and wild cherry, some heavy with trumpet creeper (*Campsis radicans*) and twining honeysuckle. Only the sourwood had a sound from swarms of honeybees seeking clear nectar from the fragrant, urn-shaped flowers. This was a place of peace.

Lake Greenwood State Park (Greenwood County)

In 1938 Greenwood County donated 914 acres to the state for a Civilian Conservation Corps campground. From this transfer came the development of Lake Greenwood State Park. Although a few graveyards have been located within the boundary, the greater historical significance is its location near Ninety Six, once a trading village on the Keowee Path, and Star Fort, a British outpost in the Revolutionary War. The old Island Ford Road, begun in 1776, went through this area, which was part of "The Treat Survey" mentioned in early documents.

Situated on the south side of Lake Greenwood, the park has 125 campsites in two campgrounds, a primitive camp, a trading post and tackle shop, a campground recreational building, a picnic area, a lake swimming area, a playground, carpet golf, and a boat ramp. There is also a 3-mi **Lake View Trail.**

Information: Lake Greenwood State Park, 302 State Park Rd., Ninety Six, SC 29666; (864) 543–3535.

Access: From Ninety Six go 3.4 mi E on SC 34 to SR 41. Turn L on SR 41 and go 1.5 mi to park entrance across SC 702.

Greenwood Lake Nature Trail

Length: 0.8 mi (1.3 km); **easy;** USGS Map: Dyson; trailhead: behind the Recreation Building.

I entered the unmarked but well-maintained loop trail behind the Recreation Building in a pine forest with an understory of gum, dogwood, mulberry, and wild cherry. The first L fork led into a more mixed forest that included oak and elm as part of the top canopy. Honeysuckle covered the ground. At 0.4 mi I passed the lake on the L and returned to the point of origin.

Lake Wateree State Park (Fairfield County)

Lake Wateree State Park takes its name from the Wateree River, which was dammed to make the lake. It is a beautiful 238-acre park between I-77 and Lake Wateree, near Great Falls. It is open all year and has outdoor recreation areas for family camping with full service, picnicking, sailing, boating, and fishing for white and largemouth bass, stripers, catfish, bream, and crappie. It has a commissary-tackle shop, boat ramps, and in-boat fueling station.

Information: Lake Wateree State Park, Route 4, Box 282-E-5, Winnsboro, SC 29180; (803) 482–6126.

Access: From I-77 E of Winnsboro, take SC 41 E to US 21. Turn L and go N 2.1 mi to jct with SC 101, River Rd., and turn R. Follow SC 101 4 mi to the park entrance, L, for a total of 8.8 mi from I-77.

Desportes Island Nature Trail

Length: 0.7 mi (1.1 km); **easy;** USGS Map: Flint Hill; trailhead: entrance road.

The trail is a partial loop at the E end, and it begins on the entrance road across the jct with the campground entrance. Another entrance is at the edge of the parking lot at the tackle shop. The trail can be used by the physically handicapped. Along the way we saw wildflowers, ferns, loblolly pines, oaks, and sparkleberry. In all seasons there are wild turkey, deer, duck, and other waterfowl.

Landsford Canal State Park (Chester County)

Landsford Canal began in 1820 when the Board of Public Works contracted with Robert Leckie to build a dam, canal bed, guard lock, four lifting locks, the necessary bridges and culverts, and a lock keeper's house. It was to be constructed on land given by William Richardson Davie, a patriot who would benefit from the connection of the canal with his mill at the construction site. The basic units of measurement for determining the individual features were the perch, which has 24 cubic ft, and the chain, which was 66 ft. Apparently the initial calculations were incorrect, because Leckie petitioned the state legislature for additional funds in 1823. Abram Blanding was authorized to make a second measurement.

The canal was the northernmost of one of four built to circumnavigate the shoals and falls of the Catawba and Wateree Rivers. Constructed on the W bank of the Catawba, the Landsford Canal dropped 32 ft in 9,600 ft (a 33 percent slope). Hornblende and siente found on the site were used, but the granite in the locks may have come from the York District or from a quarry near Great Falls.

Of the many canals built in the state before the 1840s, only the Landsford remains without substantial alterations. It is uncertain how long it operated because of the continuous problems with flooding and dry seasons. When Duke Power Company donated 200 acres of this area to the state in 1970, both archaeological and environmental studies began. At present the recreational facilities include a picnic area, a community meeting house, a museum, and a hiking trail traveling past the remnants of the 1820 canal works for a blend of natural and cultural history. A short walk behind the museum to a sand bar on the Catawba River has been constructed by an Eagle Scout and called **Eagle Point Trail.**

Information: Landsford Canal State Park, 2051 Park Dr., Catawba, SC 29704; (803) 789–5800.

Access: From Rowell at jct of US 21 and SR 327 (Landsford Rd.), go 1.6 mi on Landsford Rd. to park entrance (SR 690) and 0.5 mi to the river and parking area. (Another access point is 2.2 mi past the park entrance, L off Landsford Rd., to another parking area.)

Support Facilities: For the nearest campground see Andrew Jackson State Park.

Landsford Canal and Nature Trail

Length: 3 mi round-trip (4.8 km); **easy;** USGS Maps: Catawba, Van Wyck; trailhead: parking area.

When Steve Harris and I arrived at the parking area, Walt Schrader, a veteran hiker, was there waiting for us. "This is one of my favorite parks and trails," he said, elaborating on the historic value of the park before going off to a Sierra Club engagement.

From the parking area Steve and I went 0.1 mi in a cleared picnic area to the trailhead. We chose to walk the W bank of the old canal. We were in a climax forest, where for 140 years nature had been unhindered. Tall oaks, elm, beech, poplar, sweetgum, hickory, sycamore, river birch, and walnut competed for the sunlight. Underneath were columbine, wild geranium, mandrake, atamasco lily, and Japanese honeysuckle. Redbud, holly, dogwood, cedar, ironwood, and buckeye were scattered to form pockets of subcanopy. At 0.7 mi we passed the **Nature Trail** sign on the L, and at 1.1 mi we reached a canal lock. At 1.4 mi we passed another lock; a few yards ahead was the southern parking area.

On our return we took the **Nature Trail,** which meandered along the bank of the river rapids. Here we saw spiderwort, elderberry, ferns, wild onion, switchcane, muscadine, and horsetail. We saw only one deer, but other mammals in the park are raccoon, squirrel, fox, skunk, bobcat, opossum, rabbit, and mink. The avian population consists of more than 45 species with large populations of robin, junco, sparrow, nuthatch, and warbler. The southern bald eagle has been sighted in the park. Among the reptiles are two poisonous snakes, the copperhead and timber rattler. (The only snakes we saw were garter and ringneck.) We heard plenty of amphibians, of which the tree frog and the cricket frog were the most vociferous. At 3 mi we returned to the parking area.

Sesquicentennial State Park (Richland County)

The 1,445-acre Sesquicentennial State Park was opened to the public in 1940; it had been donated to the state by the Columbia Sesqui-Centennial Commission in 1937, the city's 150th anniversary. Generally referred to as "Sesqui," it is a park of outstanding facilities, natural beauty with nature-study potential, and historic value. Among the facilities are group camping areas, an 87-site family camping area, a nature center, picnic and swimming areas, trails, and sport fields. **Sesqui Bike Trail** is 6.1 mi. Lake fishing and pedal boating are also provided. A 1756 log house has been relocated from the county for display in the park near the main road soccer and tennis field. A full-time naturalist provides high-quality interpretive programs through the year.

Information: Sesquicentennial State Park, 9564 Two Notch Rd., Columbia, SC 29223; (803) 788–2706.

Access: From I-20, exit 74, at US 1 NE of Columbia, proceed 3 mi NE on US 1 to park entrance on R.

Sandhill Nature Trail

Length: 2 mi (3.2 km); **easy;** USGS Map: Fort Jackson N; trailhead: parking area near the bathhouse.

From the parking area I went L of the bathhouse, following the trail clockwise through loblolly pines around the 30-acre lake. I crossed a small stream at 0.5 mi among oak, dogwood, bay, poplar, bracken, and sassafras and crossed a boardwalk and a footbridge over an active brook at 0.6 mi. After another 0.1 mi a spur trail R led to an angler's tranquil pier. I continued R at the trail jct at 0.9 mi and R at the park road at 1.5 mi. The lake border had a number of wildflowers, including the *Drosera capillaris* sundew, a low plant with a pink corolla and sticky insect-catching leaves. (In contrast, the *Drosera intermedia*, which grows in the adjoining county of Lexington, has leaves that sparkle away from the rosette, and its corolla is usually white.) Other plants were ditch stonecrop, alumroot, honewort, pitcher plants, and prickly pear cactus. I passed through the picnic area to a footbridge and reached the jct with the **Wild Plum Nature Trail** at 1.9 mi. (A loop on the 0.2-mi **Wild Plum Nature Trail** led across the branch below the dam.) I continued along the rim of the lake to complete the loop at the bathhouse and parking area.

Sesqui Physical Fitness Trail

Length: 3.5 mi (5.6 km); **easy;** USGS Map: Fort Jackson N; trailhead: road jct near the Log House.

This exercise and jogging trail (and hiking trail) began on the sand and gravel road and continued clockwise to form a loop from the Log House and soccer and tennis area. I passed a white cedar (*Chamaecyparis thyoides*) bog on the R. At 0.4 mi on the road, a FOOT TRAIL ONLY sign is on the R for fitness stations.

At 1 mi there was a jct with a road on the L, but I continued R and passed a jct with the **Sandhill Nature Trail** at 1.4 mi. I passed the picnic area and kept R at the next jct at 1.8 mi. At 2 mi there was a jogging-trail sign. Keeping R at other jct, I returned to the Log House at 3.5 mi. Forests along the road were mainly pine and scrub oak, and there was one of 200 acres of planted pine. Another 100 acres in the bottomlands had primarily hardwoods.

SECTION 3
Lower Midlands

From the capital city of Columbia to the heart of Santee/Cooper Country, this region is generally flat with quiet blackwater rivers. Named the sandhills because it was once the beach of an ancient ocean, the region has forests of tall pines, historic sites, and unique geological depressions at Woods Bay.

Aiken State Park (Aiken County)

Purchased in 1934, the Aiken State Park opened two years later with 1,067 acres. Its location on the Aiken Plateau includes four spring-fed lakes and the winding South Edisto River. Millions of years ago the area was a beach for an ancient ocean. Facilities in the park include 25 campsites (under an exceptionally beautiful canopy of longleaf pines), a youth camp for Boy Scouts, picnic areas, a lake for swimming, fishing (for bream, bass, and crappie), pedal boating, and hiking trails.

Information: Aiken State Park, 1145 State Park Rd., Windsor, SC 29856; (803) 649–2857.

Access: From the jct of SC 4 and SR 78 in Windsor, take SR 78 5 mi N to park entrance.

Jungle Trail

Length: 2.4 mi (3.8 km); **easy;** USGS Map: Seivern; trailhead: parking area at swimming lake.

I started at dawn from the parking area of the picnic and swimming lake and soon noticed that the trail was being relocated to raise it from a boggy level. Water in this area comes from the clear spring water that feeds the lakes. At 0.1 mi I took the L fork. Bays, wax myrtles, ostrich ferns, sweet pepperbushes, and switchcane were thick on the trail borders. At 0.3 mi I went L again where bracken, sensitive ferns, and blueberries were frequent. At 0.8 mi I took the L at an intersection to the Fishlake picnic area. I turned R on the paved road to the Riverside picnic area, where a strong artesian well provided cold drinking water. Reentering the woods, I faced the intersection again and took the L toward Cypress Stump picnic area. Along the way I stopped to feast on the ripe blueberries; a deer saw me, watched a few seconds, then bolted into deeper woods. At 1.5 mi I saw where turpentine had been extracted from the longleaf pine. After 0.2 mi I crossed the paved road and a stream to the Cypress Swamp picnic area. Immediately I curved R to cross the road again and enter the forest. At 1.9 mi I crossed a boardwalk and heard considerable noise from the forest. I saw cardinals, warblers, and towhees busy with their morning chores. The loop was now complete at 2.3 mi, where I turned L to return to the parking area, for a total of 2.4 mi.

Barnwell State Park (Barnwell County)

Barnwell State Park, with 307 acres, was donated to the state by Barnwell County in 1937; the park opened in 1939. Historians say that the first American-made steam locomotive, built for the South Carolina Railroad Company, made its maiden run out of Charleston to this area in 1833. The nearby town of Blackville was named after Alexander Black, who secured funding for the railroad. Park facilities include 25 campsites, five vacation cabins, picnic areas, a community recreational building, lake swimming and fishing, a playground, and hiking trails.

Information: Barnwell State Park, 223 State Park Rd., Blackville, SC 29817; (803) 284–2212.

Access: From Blackville at jct of US 78, go S on SC 3 for 3 mi, R.

Barnwell Lake Trail

Length: 1.5 mi combined (2.4 km); **easy;** USGS Map: Blackville; trailhead: family campground.

Every time I have been to this trail, it has rained. On the rainy morning that I measured the trail, I left from campsite 11, followed the trail to the dam at 0.1 mi, crossed a boardwalk, and skirted R of the camp cottages. I continued ahead through the forest of poplar, holly, and bay near a marsh. I followed the edge of the second lake by a swimming area and the community center at 0.6 mi. Large oaks and pines were here. I descended to the spillway on a service road where other large trees make the understory sparse. When I reached the paved road bridge at 0.7 mi, I turned R over the bridge and made a sharp R to streamside. (A trailhead about 0.2 mi above this point is at an overlook of the lower lake.)

Following upstream over boardwalks, I reached the dam at 0.8 mi, turned L, and entered the woods to reach a picnic shelter area at 1.1 mi. To the R was an unusually attractive fishing pier and observation deck. I completed the loop at 1.4 mi and turned L to my point of origin at 1.5 mi. (An 0.2-mile fisherman's trail continues along the upper lake to an old spring in a bog.)

Lee State Park (Lee County)

Lee State Park, opened to the public in 1941, contains 2,839 acres of natural pristine forest, snowy white sandhills, sequestered swamps, and outstanding recreational facilities for swimming, camping, fishing, picnicking, and community-center activities. The area is a delight for birders, hikers, and equestrians. **Lee Horse Trail** is 12 mi. For those interested in nature study, there is the usually languid Lynches River, the Sandhill Natural Area, and hidden oxbow lakes. A 4.5-mi loop road and self-guiding auto trail, which can also be hiked, provides a dozen stops at historic, scenic, and other unique points of interest. One unique point is on Mulberry Island, where two artesian wells bubble in cairns, and another is an elevated privy near a picnic area. A horse show ring is used by local horse clubs. Campground facilities include 50 sites, and there is a special campground on the loop road for Boy Scouts.

Information: Lee State Park, Route 2, Box 1212, Lee State Park Rd., Bishopville, SC 29010; (803) 428–3833.

Access: From I-20 at jct of SR 22, go NW 1 mi on SR 22 to park entrance. (From US 15 and SC 34, 3.4 mi N of Bishopville, take SR 22 R and go 3.6 mi on SR 22 to park entrance on R.)

Artesian Nature Trail

Length: 1 mi (1.6 km); **easy;** USGS Map: Bishopville E; trailhead: picnic and parking area.

From the park entrance I drove 1 mi and turned L to the picnic area and community building at the parking area. After parking I

hiked across the dam, the site of an old gristmill. Spanish moss hung from oaks. At 0.1 mi I turned R, followed the banks of three small former fish-hatchery lakes, and entered a forest with a swamp on the L. Vegetation was loblolly, oak, hickory, holly, and dogwood. Exceptionally large sweet gums and tulip poplar towered on the L. I crossed on the entrance road in a sand barren at 0.5 mi and a small stream at 0.7 mi. I continued around the edge of the forest by beds of partridge berry and spots of pipsissewa to two gurgling artesian wells feeding the lake at 0.8 mi. The trail returns to the dam and the parking area at 1 mi.

Sandhill Nature Trail

Length: 0.6 mi (0.9 km); **easy;** USGS Map: Bishopville E; trailhead: park campground.

I entered by the sign from across the road at the campground. After 0.1 mi was the loop-trail fork: either direction led through loblolly, longleaf pine, scrub oak, holly, and a variety of *vaccinium* specimens. An example of nature's art was the lime-green reindeer moss intertwined with yellow jessamine over patterns of xeric white sand. After the loop, I returned to the campground.

Lynches River State Park (Florence County)

The 668-acre Lynches River State Park was purchased in 1971. Since then it has progressed through two development stages and entered its third for recreational facilities. It has a community recreation center, a picnic area, playground equipment, a ball field, nature trails, and a swimming pool, which opened in 1982. Office hours are Monday through Sunday, 11:00 A.M. to noon.

Information: Lynches River State Park, 1110 Ben Gauge Rd., Coward, SC 29530; (843) 389–2785.

Access: From Florence go S on US 52 for 10 mi to SR 147 on the R, then go 1.8 mi on SR 147 to the park entrance on the R.

Stagecoach Trail

Length: 1.1 mi round-trip, combined (1.7 km); **easy;** USGS Map: Florence W; trailhead: parking area by the river.

From the parking area we followed the trail sign through a large grove of wild azaleas, where oaks and hickory were draped with Spanish moss. There were thick stands of sparkleberry, mosses, and wild orchids. At 0.3 mi we veered L at a fork, and at 0.4 mi we crossed a stream and noticed holly, dogwood, river birch, and fetterbush before entering a pine forest at 0.5 mi. We turned R on an old stagecoach roadbed, and at 0.9 mi we left the road R and followed a narrow trail back to the parking area at 1.1 mi.

Poinsett State Park (Sumter County)

Poinsett State Park is a 1,000-acre hilly and unique park in an other-wise-flat area near the Wateree Swamp on the W side of Manchester State Forest. Donated to the state in 1934 by Sumter County, the park facilities consist of 50 campsites, four vacation cabins, primitive and group campgrounds, a recreation building, a picnic area, a lake for swimming and fishing, playground equipment, pedal boats, and some unusual natural features. One of the features is Fuller's Earth, a sedimentary formation that is high in silica. Its name comes from an early use by cloth processors—fullers—to absorb or remove greases from wool. Coquina is another unusual feature here. You will notice this rock, made of naturally cemented shell fragments, probably 50 million years old, used in construction of the bathhouse and other structures. The presence of coquina indicates that at one time this area was covered by the ocean.

More than 50 species of birds have been seen in the park, and more than 65 species of trees and shrubs have been classified. The park has a 6-mi **Equestrian Trail,** accessible from the Equestrian Camping Area, off River Road, that may become used also for the **Palmetto Trail.** There is a 2-mi. **Scout Trail,** accessible from picnic shelter #2, which ascends to the Youth Camping Area.

The park is named in honor of Charlestonian Joel Roberts Poinsett (1779–1851), a distinguished Latin American diplomat and naturalist whom one historian has called the "most versatile and cosmopolitan American of his time." In 1828, when Poinsett was U.S. minister to Mexico, he brought home a wild plant (*Euphorbia pulcherrima*) that his fellow scientists named "poinsettia" in his honor.

Information: Poinsett State Park, 6660 Poinsett Park Rd., Wedgefield, SC 29168; (803) 494–8177.

Access: From the jct of US 76, US 378, and SC 601 (1.7 mi W of Shaw Air Force Base), go S on SC 601 for 9.9 mi to SR 63 and turn R. Go 1.7 mi farther to park entrance. From downtown Sumter go 10.5 mi W on SC 763 to SC 261 and turn L on SC 261 to the park entrance.

Coquina Nature Trail (1.4 mi); Hilltop Trail (0.5 mi); Laurel Group Trail (0.5 mi)

Length: 2.4 mi combined (3.8 km); **easy;** USGS Map: Poinsett State Park; trailhead: parking area.

From the parking area near the bathhouse, I followed the trail signs across the lower area of the lake to the spillway and ascended in a surprisingly sylvan environment. Here were galax, mountain laurel, and trailing arbutus, in contrast with coastal plain Spanish moss farther up the hillside. After passing a rain shelter, I reached a jct with **Hilltop Trail** at 0.8 mi. **Coquina Nature Trail** veered L, while **Hilltop Trail** continued R. I chose the **Hilltop Trail,** hiking on a ridge. Because it was wintertime, all the oaks were gray and bleak, and the Spanish moss blended in with them. A strong wind swayed the moss mournfully, and the afternoon sun made eerie shadows. It was a choreographic *montrer* of Black Mingo dancing skeletons. At 1.2 mi I descended to the jct with the **Laurel Group Trail** on the R. (From here the spur trail was 0.2 mi.) I followed the trail L and rejoined the **Coquina Nature Trail** along Shank's Creek. At 1.9 mi I crossed a boardwalk in a swamp area of bays, fetterbush, and birch. More swaying banners of Spanish moss welcomed me back to the parking area.

Redcliffe State Historic Site (Aiken County)

Donated to the state in 1973 by John Shaw Billings, a descendant of the Hammond family, the 369-acre estate of Redcliffe is a showpiece of Greek Revival architecture, Southern antiques, art collections, and landscaping. It was first the home of former governor James Henry Hammond (1807–1864), who had it constructed between 1857 and 1859 on an airy slope of red-clay cliffs near the Savannah River. Hundreds of fruit trees for the orchards and grapevines for the vineyards were planted, including the impressive avenue of magnolias, which decorates the entrance to the mansion. The park has a picnic area, but no campground. The site features regular programs and small festivals throughout the year, and educational experiences at the park are popular with school groups.

Information: Redcliffe Plantation State Park, 181 Redcliffe Rd., Beech Island, SC 29841; (803) 827–1473.

Access: From US 278, 1.5 mi E of Beech Island, take SR 580 (Hammond Rd.), go 0.2 mi to Redcliffe Rd., and make a R into the park.

Redcliffe Trail

Length: 1.7 mi (2.7 km); **easy;** USGS Map: Hollow Creek; trailhead: parking area.

I left the mansion, crossed a portion of the spacious lawn, and entered the woods near a park residence. The trail was on an eroded road, which descended deeply into a forest. It began to rain, first a trickle in the gully of red clay, then a deluge. The road became a red river as I wobbled, balancing myself awkwardly with a camera, notebook, and measuring wheel under my raingear. At 0.6 mi was the lake, green as malachite. Surrounding me was the allure of a tropical rain forest, with tall oaks, poplars, pines, and the largest crepe myrtles I have ever seen. Cedar and dogwood were enveloped by an intertwining of wet wisteria, ivy, honeysuckle, and Spanish moss. A lone pinkroot bloomed by the trail. I crossed the head of the lake at 0.7 mi and turned R into a tunnel of cane. From here I ascended on an improving roadbed to a more even contour at 1 mi, where I turned L at a road jct. I left a forest of hickory, oaks, pines, and sassafras at 1.3 mi for a beautiful view of farm fields and the mansion. After another 0.4 mi on the edge of the field and entrance road, I was back at the parking area.

Rivers' Bridge State Park (Bamberg County)

This historic area is the state's only state park commemorating the Confederacy. After you enter the park from SC 641 on SR 8 (7.5 mi E of Sycamore, or 7 mi W of Ehrhardt off SC 64), go 0.6 mi to the site of the Battle of Rivers' Bridge on the left. Plaques on the breastworks explain how General William T. Sherman's army advanced north toward the Salkehatchie Swamp in early February 1865. Protecting the 16 bridges through the swamp were Confederate infantry, artillery, and cavalry forces of 1,200 men. Musket fire protected the bridges, but the Federal forces felled trees to make a crossing 6 mi upstream, safe from the breastworks. The result was that the Confederate general Lafayette McLaws withdrew his troops. Although the delay did not prevent Sherman's forces from marching to burn McPhersonville and Columbia, the delay may well have saved other cities north of Columbia as the war was drawing to a close.

Of the 390 park acres, the first 90 (which encompassed the battle sites) were given to the Confederate Memorial Association in 1938 by John D. Jenny. Adjoining land was subsequently purchased, and in 1945 the state acquired the area for recreation and historic emphasis. Park facilities provide a swimming pool, a recreation building, a picnic area, a 25-site campground, a playground, fishing in the Salkehatchie River, primitive camping, and a nature trail.

Information: Rivers' Bridge State Park, Route 1, Box 190, Ehrhardt, SC 29081; (803) 267–3675.

Lupine Nature Trail

Length: 0.4 mi (0.6 km); **easy;** USGS Map: Olar; trailhead: campsite #8.

I entered the park recreational area and followed a sign to the family campground. From campsite #8 I began the hike through a young forest of holly, pines, oaks, and other hardwoods. There was a wide display of yellow jessamine and reindeer moss in the open areas. Scattered Spanish moss hung from some of the oaks. Although this was a short, quiet trail, it was excellent for nature study. The roseate lupine here was probably *Lupinus villosus,* similar to another species generally found in the sandhills range.

Santee State Park (Orangeburg County)

The 2,496-acre Santee State Park has nearly 1.5 million visitors annually, ranking second among the state parks. The explanation for this heavy traffic to an inland park is that Santee is the gateway to nationally famous Santee-Cooper Country, a sportsman's paradise covering three counties. In this paradise are 171,000 acres in Lakes Marion and Moultrie with 450 mi of shoreline, a national wildlife refuge, a golf course, beach resorts, historic sites, and the crossroads of arteries I-95 and I-26. The Santee Cooper Commission reports that the area is rated in the nation's top five fishing spots and "one of America's top 10 vacation spots." The area is the home of the freshwater king of fighting fish, the striped bass, but white and black bass, crappie, and bream are more general near the park area. The park occupies the S shore of Lake Marion, between the village of Santee E and Poplar Creek W.

I met Wilber and Margie Redd from Williston, who were fishing on the park pier. "We've been coming here for 15 years," Wilber said. "Who catches the most fish?" I asked. They agreed it was an even score. "But I kinda think Margie holds a record," he said, explaining how one windy morning he had lost a rod and reel in the lake. That afternoon Margie thought she had a big one, but much to her surprise and his pleasure she had hooked the eye of the lost rod and reel.

Park facilities include 30 of the popular cabins and 174 campsites, a restaurant (open Thursdays–Sundays only), picnic areas, a tennis court, a conference room, a swimming area, a primitive campground (for organized groups only), a recreation building, an interpretive center, a playground, a fishing pier, and hiking and bicycle trails. (One of the hiking trails, **Lakeshore Nature Trail,** was destroyed by Hurricane Hugo in 1989.) There is a 3.4-mi. **Bike Trail.**

Information: For the general area contact Santee Cooper Country, P.O. Box 40, Santee, SC 29142; (803) 854–2131. For the park contact Santee State Park, 251 State Park Rd., Santee, SC 29142; (803) 854–2408.

Access: From I-95 or US 301 jct in Santee go W on SC 6 for 1 mi to the park sign, and follow park directional signs.

Support Facilities: The park cabins are completely furnished, including even silverware, and accommodate a maximum of six persons. Each cabin has two bedrooms. Reservations must be made well in advance. If you are not staying in the cabins or campground and prefer an outside facility, a nearby KOA is off Exit 102 on I-95, 0.4 mi on SR 400. Open all year, the campground has 200 sites, full svc, and excellent rec fac. Address: KOA Santee-Lake Marion, Route 2, Box 84, Summerton, SC 29148; (803) 478–2262.

Other things to see and do nearby are the Santee Wildlife Refuge and Fort Watson Battle Site, 4 mi N on US 15-301, and Eutaw Springs Battlefield Site, 12 mi SE off SC 6.

Limestone Nature Trail

Length: 1 mi (1.6 km); **easy;** USGS Maps: Summerton, Vance; trailhead: parking area near pavilion and swimming area.

I followed the signs along the bank of a cove where wax myrtle leaned as if to embrace me with its fragrance. Interpretive signs were along the path. I crossed a boardwalk to a trail fork. (L led 0.2 mi to East Park Road.) I turned R and crossed a moist ground area with buckeye and papaw, then continued back through a mixed forest to signpost #6 and backtracked to the swimming area. This trail is excellent for a trip with the park naturalist, who is usually on duty from June through August.

Oakpinolly Nature Trail

Length: 0.9 mi (1.5 km); **easy;** USGS Maps: Summerton, Vance; trailhead: Interpretive Center on West Park Road.

Access to this loop trail is from the Interpretive Center, the tennis court, or the "Village Round" in the cabin area. You will be on a generally open forest trail padded with pine needles and adventuresome grapevines. One spot halfway through the forest has switchcanes, ostrich ferns, and wild azaleas.

Woods Bay State Park
(Clarendon, Florence, and Sumter Counties)

There are hundreds of shallow, elliptical depressions known as bays in the state's coastal plains. The bays are also found in SE North Carolina and NE Georgia. Some of the depressions are dry, others are swampy, and a few others are beautiful lakes. They range in diameter from a few hundred feet to 5 miles. Attempted explanations of this natural phenomenon include the meteorite theory, the ancient-ocean-springs theory, and the ancient-ocean-lagoons theory.

Woods Bay State Park has 1,541 acres, most of which are an open savannah near the pointed E end of the egg-shaped bay, with dense cypress swamp elsewhere. At the edge of the bay are sandy flats with loblolly pines and turkey oaks, and on the N side adjacent to the bay is the mill point pond. The park was named after Andrew Woods, who once owned a gristmill at the pond. Wildlife is prominent and includes numerous species of wading, perching, and preying birds. The land was purchased in 1973, and the facilities are limited to nature study and hiking, picnicking, and fishing. There is also a Nature Center, from which nature programs are provided. The park is closed Tuesdays and Wednesdays.

Information: Woods Bay State Park, 11020 Woods Bay Rd., Olanta, SC 29114; (843) 659–4445.

Access: From I-95 (Exit 141) and SC 53, take SC 53 NE for 1.3 mi. Turn R on SR 597, and go 1.6 mi. Turn L on SR 48, and go 2 mi to park entrance on R.

Mill Pond Nature Trail

Length: 0.9 mi (1.4 km); **easy;** USGS Map: Lake City; trailhead: picnic area.

The trail began at the picnic area near the parking lot and circled the mill pond. As the park superintendent and I followed the dikes, we saw Spanish moss hanging from the cypress, gums, and pines. Growing near the edge of the pond were Virginia willow, sweet pepperbush, sweetbay, fern, and lizard's tail. In parts of the pond area were water lilies. At 0.5 mi we reached a boardwalk that reached out into the bay and a nearby canoe trail. We walked out on the boardwalk for 0.1 mi. The superintendent said that the park had alligators and that at night there were the sounds of frogs— tree chirper, bull, and leopard. Leaving the boardwalk, we saw white bells, yellow sundew, and bladderwort. On the way back to the parking lot, a Carolina anole ran up a sapling. The park also has bobcat, osprey, barred owl, anhinga, duck, egret, and heron.

SECTION 4
Lowcountry and Coast

A diversity of wetlands, swamps, salt marshes, islands, beaches, bays, and floodplain forests make this region appealing for explorers, canoeists, fishermen, and biologists. Some of the state's primary rivers—Savannah, Edisto, Cooper, Santee, Great Pee Dee—empty into the Atlantic Ocean. Wildlife refuges and the Francis Marion National Forest provide wildlife habitats. State parks are in or near the historic seacoast cities of Myrtle Beach, Georgetown, Charleston, and Beaufort.

Charles Towne Landing (Charleston County)

Charles Towne Landing, site of the state's first permanent English settlement in 1670, has such a wide range of attractions that hikers can "accumulate 3 miles before they realize it," a park public information specialist said. Other visitors may prefer a bicycle trail or to take an easy route on a tram tour. But everyone halts to look and listen on the **Animal Forest Trail,** an unforgettable delight for the entire family.

This natural preserve and historic site, which bills itself as "America's most unique state park," has 664 acres of untouched forests, landscaped pavilions, marshland, fragrant gardens, and special educational features. First visit the Visitor Service Complex for information. From there you may hike, rent a bike, or take a tram out to the dock from the Transportation Center. More than 200 picnic tables are in the park, but camping is not allowed. Park facilities may be reserved for group picnics and banquets. *Carolina* is a 30-minute film introduction to Charleston and the low country shown daily in the theater. Park hours are daily from 9:00 A.M. to 5:00 P.M. (9:00 A.M. to 6:00 P.M. in the summer), and admission is nominal.

Information: Charles Towne Landing State Park, 1500 Old Town Rd., Charleston, SC 29407-6099; (843) 852–4200.

Access: Entrance is off SC 171 in Charleston on the W side of the Ashley River, 0.6 mi SW from the jct of SC 7 and SC 171.

Support Facilities: One of the nearest commercial campgrounds is Oak Plantation Camps on US 17, 9 mi S from jct of US 17 and I-26. Full svc, rec fac. Open all year. Address is Route 2, Box 559, John's Island, SC 29455; (843) 766–5936.

Charles Towne Garden Trails (2.4 mi) and Animal Forest Trail (0.8 mi)

Length: 3.2 mi combined (5.1 km); **easy;** USGS Map: Charleston; trailhead: Transportation Center.

From the Transportation Center, I entered a network of trails through 80 acres of many varieties of azaleas and camellias among 75 other species of flowers, trees, and shrubs. Unmarked avenues pass in between or circle the three lakes in the gardens and reach the original settlement area at 0.5 mi. I turned R, to the wharf, where a full-scale replica of the 53-ft seventeenth-century trading vessel *Adventure* is docked. On the way back I veered R at the Fortified Area and entered the 1670 Experimental Crops Garden, where rice, indigo, cotton, and sugarcane are grown in season. I continued to the Settlers' Life Area on the R, a reconstructed period village at 1 mi. I continued for 0.1 mi into the Animal Forest, a 20-acre natural-habitat zoo. Watching me as I watched them were red foxes, raccoons, skunks, deer wolves, elk, otters, pumas, bison, bobcats, bears, owls, alligators, and other native animals along an 0.8-mi section of the forest. "My favorite animal is the timber wolf," a park aide said. "They are so beautiful . . . so full of mystery." At the exit from the forest, the 10,000-sq-ft Geodesic Dome was on the R; the building is available for dinners, dances, trade shows, and educational programs. Returning to the Transportation Center, I completed a hike of 2.5 mi; for another 0.7 mi I could have taken the paths within the azalea and camellia gardens.

After Hurricane Hugo in 1989, a new nature trail, in the shape of a figure eight, was designed to originate a trailhead at the end of the parking lot to the L. This trail meanders through a marsh, wetlands, a forest, and a meadow of wildflowers. There are interpretive signs.

Colleton State Park (Colleton County)

Colleton State Park, the state's smallest with only 35 acres, is nestled between the Edisto River and Canadys Steam Electric Generating Plant. Used by the U.S. government as a CCC camp in the 1930s, the area was donated to the state in 1944. Facilities include a 25-site campground and picnicking grounds. Other features are an old canal, once used to float logs downstream to a sawmill; boating; and fishing.

Information: Colleton State Park, US 15, Canadys, SC 29433; (843) 538–8206.

Access: At the jct of SC 61 and US 15, 10 mi N of Walterboro, go 0.5 mi N on US 15 to the park entrance on L. From I-95 take Exit 68.

Cypress Swamp Nature Trail
Length: 0.4 mi (0.6 km); **easy;** USGS Map: St. George; trailhead: campsite #19.

I entered a mixed mature forest with scattered sections of Spanish moss and an understory of sweet pepperbush, buckeye, and sassafras. After reading the park road, I turned L to return to the campground. The area was clean and well maintained. About 50 yd from the trailhead, there is a boardwalk that leads 100 ft through a cypress swamp to the river for an ideal canoe launch.

Edisto Beach State Park (Colleton County)

Edisto Island, named for the peaceful Edisto Indians, is between the North Edisto and South Edisto Rivers and faces the Atlantic

Ocean. A 1,255-acre section of this enchanting island has been set apart from commercial development to form the semitropical Edisto Beach State Park. It is a jewel of diverse natural areas for botanists, archaeologists, and ornithologists. Beachcombers find plenty of shells—cockle, calico, scallop, whelk, olive—particularly after storms; sometimes they find petrified and fossilized fragments of ancient animal and plant life. Dense live oaks draped with Spanish moss, tall pines, and palmettos provide a canopy for haunting trails leading to vast open salt marshes. Facilities in the park include 106 family campsites, five vacation cabins, a picnic area, primitive camping, a camp store, an amphitheater, carpet golf, and oceanfront swimming and fishing.

Information: Edisto Beach State Park, 8377 State Cabin Rd., Edisto Island, SC 29438; (843) 869–2756/2156.

Access: From the jct of US 17 and SC 174 at Osborn (7 mi E of Jacksonboro), go 22 mi on SC 174 to park entrance on L.

Indian Mound Trail

Length: 3.6 mi round-trip (5.7 km); **easy;** USGS Maps: Edisto Beach, Edisto Island; trailhead: On R of road to cabins.

During my first visit to this peaceful island, I met an unofficial sentry, Johnny Metfield, relaxing at the park gate where I was waiting to see a ranger. I told Johnny I was going to hike the **Indian Mound Trail.** "The Indian Mounds?" he said, no longer appearing relaxed. "I don't think you wanta go there; them mounds are full of spirits . . . it's spooky back in them swamps . . . and there are moccasins, too." My interest was only enhanced. (Some call this Spanish Mound.)

From the first state park sign on SR 174, turn R on the road toward the cabins, and continue 0.2 mi to a sign on the R. Prepare yourself: There are biting insects, poison ivy, and poisonous snakes in the area. In hot weather an insect repellent is essential.

I began on the old road, which has a heavy canopy of live oaks, but turned L on an unmarked trail at 0.1 mi. Red cedar, palmetto, loblolly pine, sassafras, yaupon, and wax myrtle formed thick boundaries among sections of the oaks. I saw many woodpeckers and squirrels and heard numerous animal sounds of unknown origin. At 0.4 mi the trail forked. (To the R was a short hike back to the park, handy for those who change their minds.) I continued L to a salt marsh and crossed on a boardwalk at 0.9 mi. Here the marsh provided food and shelter for waterfowl, marine life, and shellfish. Nearly halfway across the marsh, I heard the call of a marsh hen. Below me were thousands of busy periwinkles.

When I reentered the depths of the forest, a slight breeze moved the vegetation. I expected a Fizzgig of the *Dark Crystal* to leap at me with a shriek from a vine-covered stump. After 1 mi I turned L at a fork in the old road and reached the Indian Shell Mound near Scott Creek at 1.8 mi. This mound, like others in the park, may have been formed from Indian ceremonies, or it may have been simply a large pile of shell refuse. Some of the mounds may be 4,000 years old. (Please do not disturb the mounds.) I backtracked on the old road, careful not to get lost as I explored the mysteries of the spur roads into the world of the Gelflings.

Givhans Ferry State Park
(Colleton and Dorchester Counties)

The outstanding feature of the 988-acre Givhans Ferry State Park is the Edisto River, on whose scenic high bluffs visitors can picnic, rent cottages, camp, hike, or use carpet-soft lawns for ballgames. Away from commercial noise, the park provides a tranquil 25-site campground and a community center. In the river are red-breast bream, bass, jackfish, catfish, crappie, and (much to my surprise on one fishing trip) flounder. Some of the regular visitors say they have seen alligators in the river.

Captain Philip Givhan, a Revolutionary War officer and road commissioner, and his descendants maintained a ferry at this site. It was the primary crossing of the Edisto between Charleston and the upper W part of the state before the coming of railroads and highways. Mrs. W. F. Kinard of the Givhans community said that a popular local story is that the name Givhan came from the ferryman shouting for assistance with the cables: "Give me a hand." The Givhan home, over a bluff by the river, was burned by General Sherman's army in November 1864, after the destruction of the Colleton courthouse in Walterboro. (The gravestone on the bluff, near the park's community center, for an infant named Mary E. Ford, is thought to be from a family passing through the area in 1818.)

In the twentieth century the City of Charleston bought the property for its 24-mi Edisto-Goose Creek Tunnel water supply from the Edisto River. In 1934 the property was donated to the state with the provision that the water intake and tunnel area be protected.

I came off the nature trail on a sultry summer afternoon and met Roy Limehouse, a tall, dedicated ranger, who was picking up garbage cans in the campground. He said that as a teenager he'd spent more time in the park than anywhere else. "Campers are like my family," he said. At that moment some children riding bicycles waved and called him by name. "This job is the best thing that ever happened to me," he said with a broad smile. "Well . . . almost, my baby girl has to be the best." (Limehouse is now a ranger at Hunting Island State Park.)

Information: Givhans Ferry State Park, 746 Givhans Ferry Rd., Ridgeville, SC 29472; (843) 873–0692/875–1457.

Access: Enter the park on SR 30 near the jct with SC 61, 3 mi E of the community of Givhans.

River Bluff Nature Trail

Length: 1.5 mi round-trip (2 km); **easy;** USGS Maps: Maple Cone Swamp, Ridgeville; trailhead: picnic parking area.

From the most W picnic area, I began by the trail sign and descended slightly by the Charleston water intake on the L. Trees included magnolia, beech, pine, holly, and oak. After 0.1 mi I came to a deep ravine, L, and a number of spur trails made by exploring hikers. At 0.5 mi a footbridge crossed what is locally called the canal. I followed an old road bordered with sweet pepperbushes, yellow jessamines, sensitive and ostrich ferns, and downy false fox-gloves. Partridge berry patches were frequent. I reached a ballfield at 0.9 mi and turned R again in a few yards into the forest.

Although not listed as a trail, there is a 5-mi service road across the road from the park entrance, which, like a crescent, goes into the forest and returns 0.7 mi from the park entrance on SR 30. When hiking this road, use caution, as there are rattlesnakes in the area.

Hunting Island State Park (Beaufort County)

With 5,000 acres of forest, marsh, lagoon, and beach, the semi-tropical Hunting Island State Park should be on your must list of parks to visit. It is one of the state's most-visited parks; more than 1¼ million visitors register annually. A wide range of recreational facilities includes 200 sites for camping and 15 vacation cabins under the palmettos and pines. There are 4 mi of beach for tanning, swimming, surfing, and shell collecting. Robert Browning must have had such a beach in mind when he wrote of a large yellow half-moon and a "sea scented beach" in his poem "Meeting at Night."

This barrier island acquired its name from the popularity of hunting its abundant wildlife. When the state acquired the property from Beaufort County in 1938, it redeveloped the island with protective measures for the wildlife, the marshes, and the thick forests of palmetto and slash pine. This park is a place to observe South Carolina state trees in all their splendor. And if you wish to imagine islands made famous by Robert Louis Stevenson (or Spanish navigator Juan Fernandez), then search no longer; I think Stevenson had a park like this in mind when he wrote in his *Walking Tours,* where "thoughts take colors from what you see."

A climb of 181 steps in the Hunting Island Lighthouse (which is on the National Register of Historic Places) provides a magnificent view of the island and its estuaries. The first lighthouse was built in 1859, but beach erosion required the construction of another in 1875. By 1889 the sea had again threatened the light, and it was relocated to its current site. Using incandescent oil vapor, its candlepower was 100,000 and the light could be seen 18 mi away. In 1933 operation of the lighthouse was discontinued.

Other facilities on the island are a park store, a nature center, a recreation building, a children's playground, and picnic areas. There is also a 5-mi **Island Nature Trail,** a mountain-biking trail that can also be used for hiking. Its access is behind the Visitor's Center or across the road from the Marsh Boardwalk parking area. Fishing is best for whiting, spot, trout, bass, and drum in the summer and autumn. For hiking, birding, and nature study, the opportunities are constant and challenging. And on your way to or from the island, you can walk some of the historic streets in Beaufort, the state's oldest town.

Information: Hunting Island State Park, 2555 Sea Island Pkwy, Hunting Island, SC 29920; (843) 838–2011.

Access: From the town of Beaufort at the bridge over the Beaufort River, go 16 mi on US 21 to Hunting Island across Johnston Creek. The campground entrance is on the L, SR 348. After another 0.7 mi on US 21, the main park entrance is on the L.

Lighthouse Nature Trail

Length: 0.9 mi (1.4 km); **easy;** USGS Map: St. Helena Sound; trailhead: parking area by the lighthouse.

From the lighthouse I crossed the paved area to the carpet-golf locality. Following the sign through a parking area, I took a wide trail road into a forest of palmettos and oaks with a dense understory of yaupon for 0.4 mi to the beach. Instead of backtracking, I made a loop by taking the beach route to the parking area at the lighthouse.

Marsh Boardwalk Trail

Length: 0.5 mi (0.8 km); **easy;** USGS Map: Fripps Inlet; trailhead: Fripps Inland Road on SR 406.

From the park entrance on US 21, we went 1.8 mi farther on US 21, which became SR 406, to the parking area on the R. It was a day when the marsh grass was green, the tide was up, and the herons, gulls, and egrets fought the wind. A walk on this **National Recreation Trail,** a boardwalk with creosoted pilings, took us across the salt marsh to several small islands with white sand, pines, live oaks, and palmetto. Interpretive displays at two kiosks adjacent to the boardwalk provided information on the plant and animal species living in the marsh. In the summer a park naturalist provides guided walks for visitors, and sometimes crabbers and fishermen use the trail for access to a salt-marsh creek at the end of the trail. As we returned we heard the water lapping the pilings and saw the marsh grass wave in the wind—acres and acres of it, as far as we could see. They were lustrous and stately, but what Dickey wrote in "The Salt Marsh" was right: They were "fields without promise of harvest." On our next visit we would see the marsh grass dead and gray, stalks scattered on the board-walk by another wind and another tide.

Huntington Beach State Park (Georgetown County)

Named in honor of Archer M. and Anna Hyatt Huntington of New York City, who owned the property from 1930 to 1960, this 2,500-acre scenic beach area is on the S end of South Carolina's "Grand Strand." The park has retained the Huntingtons' former winter home and sculpture studio, the 63-room "Atalaya" (meaning watchtower), modeled on a royal court from the Spanish province of Granada. After Mr. Huntington's death in 1955, the furnishings of Atalaya were moved to New York City, and the studio sculpture equipment was transferred to the couple's Brookgreen Gardens (across US 17 from the park entrance).

Facilities in the park include a campground with 127 campsites (usually filled early in the day during the summer), ocean swimming, surf fishing, organized summer nature programs (one of which is to study the 255 species of birds that inhabit the park), picnicking, and hiking. Several viewing stands are scattered throughout the park.

Information: Huntington Beach State Park, Murrells Inlet, SC 29576; (843) 237-4440/9255.

Access: Across the highway, US 17, from Brookgreen Gardens (18 mi S of Myrtle Beach and 18 mi N of Georgetown), turn onto the park road, and drive 1 mi to the park entrance gate.

Boardwalk Trail (0.1 mi); Kerrigan Nature Trail (0.3 mi); Sandpiper Pond Nature Trail (2 mi)

Length: 2.4 mi combined (3.8 km); **easy;** USGS Map: Brookgreen; trailhead: left on North Beach Road.

From the Boardwalk parking area we walked on a bridge over a salt marsh to observation decks. We saw birds of prey, such as marsh hawk, and waterfowl, such as common egret, great blue heron, marsh hen, and coot. During one visit at low tide we saw fiddlecrabs, blue crabs, mussels, oysters, and periwinkles.

Across the road from the **Boardwalk Trail** is the entrance to the **Sandpiper Pond Nature Trail.** It parallels the North Beach Road and showcases shore vegetation until it ends at North Beach. There is an observation deck for viewing Sandpiper Pond. The **Kerrigan Nature Trail** is behind the Trading Post.

Little Pee Dee State Park (Dillon County)

In this park I have identified more than 80 trees and flowering plants—from orange milkwort to elephant's foot—and at least seven species of oaks. A wide range of songbirds kept my attention through the afternoon, and I went to sleep that night listening to a cacophony—but sometimes a harmonious choir—of frogs: tree chirpers, clackers, leopards, and young bulls.

Across the lake, over the spillway, and left on an old road is a

1.2-mi, round-trip hike. The park also has a number of fire lanes you can hike, but check with the ranger first. Park facilities include 50 campsites, picnic areas, fishing, hiking, swimming, and nature study.

Named after the Peedee Indians who once owned the area, the location has also been called "The Devil's Woodyard." Composer Stephen Foster originally used "Peedee" in his ballad "Old Folks at Home," but in the second version changed it to Swanee.

Information: Little Pee Dee State Park, 1298 State Park Rd., Dillon, SC 29530; (843) 774–8872.

Access: Take SC 57 SE out of Dillon for 11 mi to SR 22, turn L, and go 2 mi to the park entrance. It is 1.1 mi to the campground.

Beaver Pond Nature Trail

Length: 1.3 mi round-trip (2.1 km); **easy;** USGS Map: Fork; trailhead: near campground parking lot.

The trail begins, L, on the entrance road just before the campground. I followed it through an area of planted pines, near the edge of the bay. After 0.6 mi I reached a beaver pond. Here were beavers, a beaver hut, and ducks. The trail continued in a loop through a forest of mixed pine and hardwoods.

Myrtle Beach State Park (Horry County)

As I entered the park after dark, the headlights of my van revealed an adult raccoon exploring a small stream by the roadside. I slowed to a stop. Two young raccoons peered at me curiously from a sapling. Those nocturnal mammals, and more like them, live on the 312-acre Myrtle Beach State Park, a preserve only 3 mi S of downtown Myrtle Beach. A state park since 1934, it has more than 1 million visitors annually, more than any other state park. Its name comes from the fragrant coastal shrub, the wax myrtle, known for its use in bayberry candles, dyes, medicines, and spices.

The noise from US 17 and the adjacent commercial district appears to have little effect on the tranquillity of the animal life or camping in a park that is part of the "campground capital of the world." Its 347 campsites are usually filled from Memorial Day through Labor Day, serving nearly 190,000 campers annually. Reservations can be made one year ahead of time, but forty campsites are allowed on a first come, first-served basis. There are cabins and apartments available for rent, by reservation. Other facilities and activities are surf and pier fishing, swimming in the ocean, picnicking, and hiking. A store with groceries and fishing and camping supplies are also in the park. In addition, there are a nature center and year-round natural history programs.

Information: Myrtle Beach State Park, 4401 South Kings Hwy., Myrtle Beach, SC 29575; (843) 238–5325.

Access: From the intersection of US 17, Ocean Blvd., and the entrance to Myrtle Beach AFB, go S on US 17 0.1 mi to park entrance on L.

Support Facilities: If the campground is filled, you have more than 12,000 campsites to choose from at commercial campgrounds in the Myrtle Beach area. But they also fill up quickly; it is wise to make reservations during the summer. Two campgrounds near the park are Pirateland Family Campground, Hwy. Bus. US 17, (843) 238–5151; Ocean Lakes Family Campground, Hwy. Bus. US 17, S, (843) 238–5636. Reduced rates apply in fall and winter months.

Sculptured Oak Nature Trail

Length: 1.3 mi (2.0 km); **easy;** USGS Map: Myrtle Beach; trailhead: near visitor center. Park in the nature center parking lot.

After entering the park from the park fee station, I passed a picnic area on the L (where you can park) and entered the trail opposite the road. (I parked at the pier parking area and walked back 0.2 mi to the entrance.) The trail went under tall loblolly pine, poplar, elm, hickory, holly, and live oak. The magnolia trees were exceptionally tall. Wild ginger and partridge berry grew in the duff. I crossed a stream at 0.1 mi and a boardwalk at 0.7 mi. This came out on the sand dunes, and I crossed a small estuary at the beach at 0.8 mi to the parking area at the pier. (If it is high tide, you may prefer to backtrack.) The trail offers great bird-watching during the spring and fall migration of songbirds. Other hiking in the park is primarily on the beach.

Old Santee Canal State Park (Berkeley County)

The 250-acre Old Santee Canal State Park is the site of America's first summit canal. It began operation in 1800. A day-use park, its key feature is the historic Santee Canal, which connected the Santee River with the Cooper River. Facilities include a picnic shelter, canoe rentals, boardwalks, trails, an Interpretive Center, two theaters, and a gift shop. The Stony Landing Plantation House and the Berkeley County Museum are also here. In addition to a land trail through the park, there is a 1-mi canoe trail.

Information: Old Santee Canal State Park, 900 Stoney Landing Rd., Moncks Corner, SC 29461; (843) 899–5200.

Access: At Moncks Corner take the US 52 Bypass 1 mi E and turn off on a street going SE to the park entrance.

Old Santee Canal Trail

Length: 3.0 mi round-trip (4.8 km); **easy;** USGS Map: Cordesville; trailhead: parking area.

The main trail is a loop of some earthen pathways and nearly 1.5 mi of boardwalks. The 3-ft- and 6-ft-wide boardwalks meander through scenic swamp sections of bottomland hardwoods of live oak, sycamore, black gum, and hickory. Spanish moss and reeds are among the large cypress areas. Wildlife includes osprey, wading birds, and other waterfowl. (The boardwalk is designed to accommodate the physically handicapped.)

SECTION 5
Other State Properties

Hanging Rock Battle Monument
(Lancaster County)

This scenic Revolutionary War battle area is maintained as a state historic site. It has an 0.5-mi hiking/auto trail encircling a hillside of enormous weather-rounded and split-granite boulders. One huge rock balances precariously over another in a stand of white oaks. From the summit of the rocks is a view of Hanging Rock Creek flowing through a hardwood forest. Among these boulders on August 6, 1780, Colonel Thomas Sumter defeated British major John Carden of the Prince of Wales American Regiment. The area is on the Heath Springs USGS Map.

Information: Parks, Recreation, and Tourism, Suite 110, Edgar A. Brown Bldg., 1205 Pendleton St., Columbia, SC 29201; (803) 758–3622.

Access: From the jct of US 521 and SR 15 in Heath Springs, go 1.7 mi on SR 15 to the sign for the James Ingram Home (where George Washington spent a night in 1771), and turn L on SR 467. After 0.8 mi turn R on a dirt road, the **Hanging Rock Battle Trail.**

Sand Hills State Forest
(Chesterfield and Darlington Counties)

In 1939 the South Carolina State Commission of Forestry received 46,000 acres as part of the U.S. Department of Agriculture's Resettlement Administration program. Under this program, infertile land was restored for timber harvesting, wildlife and fish management research, and recreation. Since the late 1930s nearly 30 million pine seedlings of slash, longleaf, and loblolly have been planted. Timber management avoids soil damage and uncontrolled fires. Revenue from timber sales has made the forest self-sustaining, and one-fourth of its income is paid to the local counties in lieu of taxes.

Increasing the wildlife population is another intensive operation. Thirteen ponds have been stocked with bream, catfish, and bass. Numerous patches of lespedeza, rye, peas, and millet have been planted for deer, dove, squirrel, and quail. Both fishing and hunting are open to the public, but a state license is required.

There are short nature trails at the Sugar Loaf Mountain area, and many of the 200-plus mi of truck trails are suitable for hiking. I have hiked some of the roads in the wintertime to study wildlife and in June to pick blueberries. Camping is allowed in the forest in specific areas with a permit.

Information: Forest Director, Sand Hills State Forest, Box 128, Patrick, SC 29584; (843) 498–6478.

Sugar Loaf Recreation Area

This area has facilities for fishing, picnicking, birding, nature study, and hiking.

Access: At the jct of US 1 and SR 29 (12.9 mi S of Cheraw State Park and 1.1 mi S of Sand Hills State Forest Headquarters), take SR 29, Ruby Rd., NW for 3 mi, and turn R at SR 63, Scotch Rd. After 0.3 mi turn R at the gate, and follow the road 0.7 mi to the lake and another 0.8 mi to Sugar Loaf Mountain.

Sugar Loaf Mountain Trail

Length: 0.6 mi (1 km); **easy;** USGS Maps: Middendorf, Patrick; trailhead: parking area.

Thoreau contended that some areas where one walks are sacred. I felt that way about this area when Scott Smith and I walked the prescribed trail at Sugar Loaf Mountain and Horseshoe Mountain. We first climbed the steps on Sugar Loaf, a 160-ft, dome-shaped mound of ferrous sandstone. A monadnock (a rocky mass that has resisted erosion), Sugar Loaf has lost much of its protective cap over millions of years. Thoreau observed in his many hikes that the finest stonecutters were not of copper or steel, but "air and water working at their leisure with a liberal allowance of time." So it is at Sugar Loaf.

What surprised us most was that plants of both exeric and mesic environments were growing near each other. Dr. Doug Raynor of the South Carolina Wildlife and Marine Resources Department explained that impervious rock layers hold the rainfall in some areas, while in other places seepage dominates. We saw tree huckleberry, staggerbush, mountain laurel, trailing arbutus, fern, titi, leucothoe, leopard's bane, jessamine, aster, and something I had not seen anywhere else—the tiny Wells pyxie-moss (*Pyxidanthera barbulata var. brevefolia*), a nationally endangered species. (I later learned that the tiny Bradley fern, *Asplenium bradleyi,* is so rare that it may be endemic only to Sugar Loaf.) After Sugar Loaf we hiked Horseshoe, a nearly 55-ft-tall mound shaped like its name. Here, as at Sugar Loaf, the sandstone had a variety of colors, and the chief trees were longleaf pine and turkey oak.

Santee Coastal Reserve (Charleston County)

Before the arrival of the French Huguenots in the late 1600s (Arnaud Bruno de Charbusiers may have been the first settler in 1691), the land that is now this coastal sanctuary was inhabited by the Santee Indians. Afterwards, in the eighteenth and first half of the nineteenth centuries, the area prospered on rice and sea island cotton. Joseph Blake, at the zenith of his plantation power and before the Civil War, had 900 slaves on a preserve of 1,252 acres known as "Washo." But what slave labor had created, the Civil War, powerful hurricanes, and the ricebirds had destroyed by the end of the 1800s.

In 1898 the Santee Club was founded and organized by Captain Hugh R. Garden for sport hunting. In addition to purchasing

Blake's Plantation, Ormond Hall, and Little Murphy Island, the club leased a number of other islands and "reserves" of old rice fields. The club adhered to a strict system of conservation and never exceeded more than 30 members. One of the early members was President Grover Cleveland. Game wardens assisted in protecting what was considered to be the "largest wading bird rookery in the east." Poaching has always been a problem. In its efforts to protect the waterfowl, the club maintained and repaired more than 100 dikes.

The Santee Club was dissolved in 1974, and the property, with 23,024 acres, was given to the Nature Conservancy, a national nonprofit organization committed to preserving natural diversity. It has been said that it was the "most valuable gift in private conservation's history." The property included 3,600 acres of mainland longleaf pine, excluding Blake's Plantation. Except for the Blake Reserve, the Conservancy deeded most of the sanctuary to the state through the Heritage Trust Program; the state's Department of Natural Resources took over the management. With the dissolution of the Santee Club, a new club, the Collins Creek Club, was organized. It pays annual fees to receive hunting rights for 25 years.

The reserve adjoins the Francis Marion National Forest on the SW, the Cape Romain National Wildlife Refuge on the S, and the North Santee River on the N. On the E and SE are maritime forest, sand dunes, and the Atlantic beach. Most of the refuge is marsh, but sections in the SW are upland and some bald cypress ponds, swamps, and Carolina bays. The Intracoastal Waterway splits through the center, and the South Santee River forms part of the delta on the N side. Approximately 8,000 acres are on Murphy Island, and 5,000 acres are on Cedar Island.

These areas are part of the Santee River Focus Area (SRFA), a state component of the Atlantic Coast Joint Venture (ACJV), which makes up the North American Waterfowl Management Plan. The objective of the SRFA is to protect, preserve, and enhance wetland wildlife habitat in the Santee River floodplain. Its managed marsh acreage represents 32 percent of the state total.

There are 14 Carolina bays—oval or elliptical depressions—in the reserve. The easternmost bays have cypress, poplar, maple, and red and sweet bays, but the other bays are more savannalike, and herbaceous species are favored. Twelve species of orchids are here and at least five species of lilies. Two rare plants, yellow fringeless orchid (*Habenarla integra*) and blue Burmannia (*Burmannia biflora*) are found in the area.

Probably every Atlantic species of shorebirds is found on the 11 mi of beaches. A former property manager, Billy Cody, said the reserve had "sheltered as many as 120,000 to 170,000 ducks at one time." He remembers when the sky would be darkened with flocks of pintail, teal, widgeon, and mallard. Other birds are quails, crows, owls, hawks, swallowtail kites, and numerous species of songbirds. The mammal population includes deer, fox, raccoon, bobcat, opossum, and "wild" boar. Among the reptilian species are the rat snake and garter snake. Alligators and loggerhead sea turtles are also on the refuge. Marine and estuarine fish include flounder, sheepshead, largemouth bass, spot, whiting, striped bass, mullet, and lady fish.

The Santee Coastal Reserve and the Washo Reserve are open to the public from 8:00 A.M. to 5:00 P.M., Monday through Saturday and 1:00 to 5:00 P.M. on Sunday. They are closed from November 1 to February 1, except by permission from the South Carolina Department of Natural Resources. Vehicular traffic is limited to designated routes. Hunting and fishing are restricted by state, federal, and reserve laws. Dogs, cats, and other pets are not permitted. Although camping is allowed in some restricted areas, a free permit is required from the reserve headquarters.

Information: Santee Coastal Reserve, South Carolina Wildlife and Marine Resources Department, Box 37, McClellanville, SC 29458; (843) 546–8665.

Access: From US 17/701 N (1.6 mi N of Moores Corner), take SR 857 R at the Santee Coastal sign. Go 2.7 mi, and turn R at a community center onto a sandy road to the reserve. (Heading S on

US 17/701, take SR 857 L 1 mi after the South Santee River bridge, and continue 1.5 mi to the community center.)

Support Facilities: Buck Hall Campground, Francis Marion National Forest. From jct of US 17/701 and SC 45 at McClellanville, go S on US 17/701 for 7.4 mi to FR 242 on L. From Awendaw on US 17/701, it is 2.3 mi N to entrance sign R on FR 242. Facilities are for camping, fishing, and picnicking near the Intracoastal Waterway.

Santee Coastal Reserve Nature Trails

Length: 11.4 mi round-trip, combined (18.2 km); **easy;** USGS Maps: Cape Roman, Minim Island; trailhead: parking area.

After we turned onto the sandy road from the community center at SR 857, Scott Smith and I drove 1.8 mi to the **Woodland Trail,** a nature trail on the L. We hiked this old roadbed in an area of pines for 0.6 mi and returned to the main road after a 1.2-mi round trip. Ahead on the main road we drove another 0.9 mi to a nature trail sign on the R in an open grassy field. (This led to the Washo Reserve boardwalk and 2.9-mi **Marshland Trail.)** From here we hiked another 0.7 mi, 1.4-mi round trip, through an avenue of live oaks, swaying Spanish moss, and pines. Large anthills were en route. Ahead was the reserve parking area and the office to the L, where a huge live oak spread 150 ft and had a circumference of 24 ft.

From the parking area we walked across a dike on an old vehicle road and followed the trail signs. (The trail intersects the **Marshland Trail** and serves as an access route to the 7.2-mi biking and hiking trail to the Intracoastal Waterway and the Santee River. From the biking and hiking trail is a connection for a 4.2-mi canoe trail in the impoundment.) At 0.9 mi we passed an observation deck on the R. We watched the backwater lap against the lacustrine trees and shrubs before continuing through the forest. Along the route we saw places where wild hogs had been rooting in the soft mud, particularly under oaks. At 1.8 mi we reached a wildlife observation blind and boardwalk to the L. We were leaving the titi, wax myrtle, and sea oxeye for borders of sedge, rush, and cordgrass. As far as we could see, there were acres of water lilies, fragrant as laurustine, and beyond them were more marshes and hummocks to Murphy Island. Waterfowl were abundant. We observed this magnificent area for a long time and wondered what it's like at night. "Probably full of sounds and mystery," I said. "Drayton Mayrant has said that 'sea islands have jungle gods, regnant here while all the mainland sleeps.' "

Whitten Center (Laurens County)

Whitten Center, named in honor of its founder, Dr. Benjamin O. Whitten, opened in September 1920. It is a 1,808-acre community in Clinton with more than 1,000 clients and is one of four similar state facilities for the handicapped. On the wall in a hallway is an embroidered sign, the Beatitudes for the Retarded Child, by C. Parsley. In part it states ". . . Blessed are they who can softly say 'try harder, you'll do better on another day.' Blessed are they who understand my limited mind. . . ."

In addition to the center's programs in health, development, and service support, it has a camping and nature program. Jeff Stackhouse, director of the program, told me that the network of trails at the center was designated for the clients, but that visitors with permission were welcome. "Our experimental outdoor program for the clients," he said, "provides day camping, overnight camping, horseback riding, fishing, hiking, pedal boat riding, archery, picnicking, birdwatching, and other educational outings."

Information: Whitten Center Camping and Nature Programs, Box 239, Clinton, SC 29325; (803) 833–2733.

Access: From Clinton go SE 2 mi on US 76 to entrance on the L.

Creek Trail and Explorer Trail
Length: 4.3 mi round-trip, combined (6.9 km); **easy** to **moderate;** USGS Map: Joanna; trailhead: parking area at Unit 24.

Dick Hunt and I went to the Camping and Nature Center past Unit 31 and followed the service road to the **Creek Trail** for 0.5 mi. At the labeled C jct, we followed the signs across the Sands Creek footbridge to the **Explorer Trail.** Here we turned R and hiked 0.8 mi in an open grassy area with elderberry, milkwort, peppergrass, ironweed, and rose pink. We rock-hopped across Sands Creek and curved R to a jct with the **Creek Trail.** It was another 0.5 mi back to the C jct. This time we followed the other section of the **Explorer Trail** for 1.7 mi around pond #2 to make another loop L at G jct, K jct, and E jct. At D jct we made a R and hiked 0.5 mi back to C jct on the **Creek Trail.** (Although we explored some of the side trails, we did not count their distance in our combined mileage.) From C jct we ascended the service road to the Camping and Nature Center for a total of 4.3 mi.

Wildcat Wayside (Greenville County)

Wildcat Wayside is a 63-acre state park limited to picnicking and nature study. It was transferred to the state-park system in 1971 from the state highway department.

Information: Program Coordinator, State Park, Dept. of PRT, 1205 Pendleton St., Columbia, SC 29201; (803) 734–0156, toll-free (888) 887–2757.

Access: From the jct of US 276 and SC 11, at Cleveland go W for 5 mi to the Wayside on the R. From the US 276 and SC 11 jct W, go E 0.7 mi to park on L.

Wildcat Nature Trail
Length: 0.8 mi round-trip (1.3 km); **easy;** USGS Map: Cleveland; trailhead: parking area.

From the parking area we climbed the steps of the bank, crossed a bridge over a cascade and entered an old picnic ground. We crossed another bridge at 0.1 mi and followed a pleasant trail under large hemlocks by Wildcat Branch. At 0.4 mi we reached the base of a high slab of a granite slide, over which the branch flows. Mountain laurel, rhododendron, and wildflowers grew along the trail.

Wildlife Management Areas

Administered by the South Carolina Department of Natural Resources (SCDNR), the Wildlife Management Area (WMA) Program initiated in the early 1950s offers 1,253,314 acres (609,788 owned by NFS and 643,526 owned by state corporations and private individuals) to the public, both hunters and nonhunters. The many campgrounds and scenic areas offer year-round recreation and enjoyment, but hiking and camping are allowed on the corporate and private properties only with permission. Although hiking is allowed anywhere in the national forests, camping may be restricted and permits necessary. Nonhunting hikers are cautioned by the WMA Program to know the hunting seasons where they hike and to wear the internationally recognized orange caps and jackets.

To clarify the boundaries of these areas, the WMA Program cautions all users to remember that only properties displaying signs with the diamond-shaped, yellow and black SCDNR logo are open to the public. In 1980 the department launched the RESPECT Campaign, a project to encourage all outdoorsmen to protect the state's natural resources and its outdoor sports by adhering to ethical rules of conduct in the field: respect for nature, respect for the game pursued, respect for the landowner, respect for fellow sportsmen, and respect for the law.

The SCDNR has listed the corporate and private individuals who have generously contributed their holdings for the public's enjoyment and have provided their land through cooperative agreements with the department. Without these lands, public use as now provided in the state would be impossible. One of the agreements between the state and landowners is that, if a landowner feels that visitors are being destructive, inconsiderate, or disrespectful of their privilege to the land, the area will be made unavailable for public use. The following landowners have contributed the acreage listed to the department's WMA Program:

U.S. Forest Service 609,788
Champion International Corporation 169,491
Bowater, Inc. 93,465
Crescent Land & Timber Corporation 81,293
S.C. DNR Commission 100,152
S.C. Forestry Commission 61,945
S.C. Public Service Authority 17,883
International Paper Company (Augusta) 8,966
Clemson University 11,265
John Hancock Life Insurance Company (Greenwood) 8,747
Marsh Furniture Company 8,044
U.S. Army Corps of Engineers (Clarks Hill) 7,974
Union Camp Corporation 5,038
Willamette Industries, Inc. 11,415
S.C. Electric & Gas Company 5,753
Canal Industries 5,159
John Hancock Life Insurance Company (Midlands) 1,979
Timberlands, Inc. 5,000
Westvaco 1,538
Georgia Power Company 3,336
Wachovia-Brown Trust 3,252
S.C. Public Service Authority (Pee-Dee–Witherbee) 2,659
U.S. Army Corps of Engineers (Santee) 2,491
Estelle W. Dunbar Estate 745
Union Camp (West) 816
Belk-Simpson Company 546
Springland, In. 1,695
Lavinia B. George 569
Alderman-Shaw Company 408
Kennecott Mine 290
H. J. Smith 286
City of Clinton 276
Gary Wood 240

James Spruill 847
Department of Energy 10,012
Department of Parks, Recreation and Tourism 7,571
Dorothy Beaty 209
Lanny R. Gregory 150
James M. and Jack L. Brown 135
William and Joab Lesesne 92

There are four major WMAs—Mountain, Western Piedmont, Central Piedmont, and Francis Marion—and 18 secondary WMA lands. All of these are shown in detail on free maps published by the SCDNR. Contact the department for these maps and for the *South Carolina Rules and Regulations* brochure that covers hunting and fishing. Designated trails in WMAs that lie outside of national forests are rare, but the potential for seeing the state's wildlife and natural environment is there.

Organized in 1952 at the regular session of the legislature, the department is charged by law to provide the public with the management, protection, research, conservation, and preservation of the state's vital wildlife, marine, and natural resources.

Information: The SCDNR is located downtown at the capital complex in the Rembert C. Dennis Building. The address is South Carolina Department of Natural Resources, P.O. Box 167, Columbia, SC 29202; (803) 734–3888.

Webb Wildlife Center (Hampton County)

Near Garnett and adjoining the Savannah River is the Webb Wildlife Center and Management Area, a research and demonstration facility. The center offers year-round outdoor recreation—fishing, hunting, hiking, canoeing, birding, and nature study. Fishing is not allowed on Sundays and days scheduled for public deer hunting. Although hunting is restricted to specific seasons, public hunting is the primary objective for this area. In addition, the center offers educational programs in wildlife and forest management for organized groups and school groups.

In 1941 the state Game and Fish Department purchased 5,741 acres, which include the historic property that was owned by John Tison, Sr., in 1771. Approximately 75 percent is upland stands of longleaf, slash, loblolly, shortleaf, and pond pine. A hardwood forest of oaks—live, willow, laurel, water, and overcup—elm, ash, and maple is on the upper floodplains; and on the river swamp, floodplains are stands of old-growth bald cypress and water tupelo. Animal life includes wild turkey, deer, quail, raccoon, bobcat, rabbit, gray and fox squirrels, dove, osprey, hawk, wading and migratory birds, alligator, and the rare bird-voiced tree frog. A scientific and educational-use permit is required to visit the property. To avoid conflict with other groups, requests for permission must be made in advance by telephone or letter. No camping is allowed, except by prior arrangements and for educational purposes.

The center is named after James W. Webb, the state's first wildlife biologist and a former executive director of the Wildlife and Marine Resources Department. He is remembered for administering some of the best conservation programs in the nation.

(Another wildlife management area is Tillman Sand Ridge in Jasper County, 5 mi W of Tillman on SC 17-119. Visitors are encouraged to hike, bird-watch, and observe wildlife when hunting is not in season. Contact the Webb Wildlife Center for a map.)

Information: Webb Wildlife Center, Garnett, SC 29922; (803) 625–3569.

Access: In Garnett at jct of US 321 and SR 20, go W on SR 20 for 2.8 mi to the Webb Wildlife Center entrance on L. Drive on a straight road lined with live oaks and Spanish moss. After 1.4 mi on entrance road, reach the center's hq.

Support Facilities: Access to Americamps-Point South campground is from I-95 jct (exit 33) with US 17. Go 0.1 mi N on US 17, then 0.5 mi N on road behind Best Western Motel. Full svc, rec fac. Open all year. Address: Americamps, Point South, Yemassee, SC 29945; (843) 726–5728.

Savannah River Swamp Trail

Length: 3.6 mi round-trip (5.7 km); **easy;** USGS Map: Brighton; trailhead: Bluff Lake parking area.

From the center's office we drove for 2 mi on a dirt road to the trailhead at Bluff Lake. It had rained, and some of the sloughs had water, but it was not deep enough to keep us from hiking all the way to the Savannah River and back. Parts of the trail were grassy and almost dry, though it was wet elsewhere. Among the types of oaks were overcup, laurel, willow, and water. The wildlife biologist at the center mentioned that we should watch where we walked, because a cottonmouth moccasin could be on the trail. Bald cypress, water tupelo, and elm were more prominent in the lower sections of the river swamp. The cypress is best described by William Gilmore Simms (1806–1870) in "The Edge of the Swamp":

> Cypresses,
> Each a great ghastly giant, eld and gray,
> Stride o'er the dusk, dank tract—with buttresses
> Spread round, apart, not seeming to sustain,
> Yet link'd by secret twines, that underneath,
> Blend with each arching trunk. . . .

Chapter IV
County and Municipal Trails

In city Gardens of pines and palms,
We walked with wings of wind.
                    Walt Rayherd, "Surcease"

SECTION 1
Counties

Palmetto Islands County Park
(Charleston County)

Palmetto Islands County Park is a 943-acre, family-oriented natural park, whose attributes include semitropical forests, marshes, lakes, tidal wetlands, meadows, and a series of 16 islands. The park is designed to bring its visitors close to the low country's largest natural land asset, the marsh. Natural trails wind throughout the park, and boardwalks cross marsh areas, allowing visitors to view plant and animal life found in a typical marsh environment.

In addition to foot trails, the park also offers a 1.5-mi bicycle trail, a water playground designed especially for families, picnic areas and shelters, a 50-ft observation tower, fishing in Boone Hall Creek, pedal-boat rentals, nature study, and a Big Toy Playground for children of all ages. The park is for day use only, usually opening at 9:00 A.M. and closing between 5:00 and 7:00 P.M., depending on the season. This park (and other park facilities at Folly Beach County Park and Beachwalker Park) is owned and operated by the Charleston County Park and Recreation Commission.

Information: Palmetto Islands County Park, 444 Needlerush Pkwy., Mt. Pleasant, SC 29464; (843) 884–0832.

Access: NE of Charleston on US 17, 7 mi from the Cooper River bridge, take the Long Point Rd., L, SR 97. (For southbound traffic it is 1.2 mi S on US 17 from the jct of US 17 and SC 41.) Go 1.1 mi to the park entrance on Needlerush Parkway, R, which dead-ends at the park gate.

Osprey Trail, Nature Island Trail, and Marsh Trail

Length: 1.6 mi, combined (2.6 km); **easy;** USGS Maps: Fort Moultrie, Charleston; trailhead: park center.

We followed the 0.2-mi **Osprey Trail** from the park center to a marsh, where a boardwalk offered an excellent view of large osprey nests high on top of power lines. From here we followed the bicycle trail W to the trailhead of the longest and most unique trail in the park, the 0.8-mi **Nature Island Trail.** After crossing a boardwalk to an island, we found an extensive self-guided nature trail. (An accompanying brochure assisted us in learning about its unique characteristics through identifying various plants and land features.) The plants we saw along this trail included live oak, water oak, fresh-water gum, yaupon, palmetto, yellow jessamine, red cedar, and pine. Because the 0.6-mi **Marsh Trail** is at the E end of the park, we could have driven to the most eastern parking area, or walked the bicycle trail for about 0.5 mi to the connection. Vegetation includes spartina grass, black needlerush, sea oxeye, groundsel tree, wax myrtle, and Cherokee bean. This trail also has boardwalks.

Pocotaligo Swamp Park (Clarendon County)

The Pocotaligo River has headwaters in Sumter County: streams such as Green Swamp, Pocalla Creek, Nasty Branch, Brunson Swamp, Long Branch, and Hatchet Camp Branch. It flows across Clarendon County to join the Black River, flowing into Williamsburg County. Pocotaligo moves through miles of concealed silent swamps, wild and shrouded in secrets since the days of the Indians, its wildlife sequestered. A glimpse into its murky magnificence is from a boardwalk trail at a small park on the north edge of Manning.

Information: Manning Dept. of Parks and Rec., 411 N. Brooks St., Manning, SC 29102; (803) 435–8424/8477.

Access: From downtown Manning go N on US 301 for 1.6 mi to entrance on L, S of the river's bridge.

Pocotaligo Swamp Trail

Length: 0.5 mi round-trip (0.8 km); **easy;** USGS Map: Manning; trailhead: parking area.

From the parking and picnic area, we followed the signs to the boardwalk. Ghostly Spanish moss hung from the black gum, bald cypress, bay, willow oak, water tupelo, and red maple along an interpretive trail. From an observation deck we watched a group of turtles crowd each other off a log. All too soon we were at the end of the boardwalk, where the faster-moving river seemed to say that it was taking its secrets to the sea.

Pleasant Ridge County Park (Greenville County)

Pleasant Ridge, formerly known as Pleasantburg, is a 300-acre county park that was first donated by Greenville County to the state system in 1950, but transferred back to the county in 1988. During the 1930s a CCC campground was here. Facilities include a 25-site campground with hook-ups, hot showers, and two cabins (completely furnished), a picnic area, a lake for swimming and fishing, and a playground.

Information: Pleasant Ridge County Park, Route 2, Cleveland, SC 29635; (864) 836–6589.

Access: On SC 11, 2.5 mi E from jct of US 276 at Cleveland and 2 mi W from jct of SC 11 and US 25.

Pleasant Ridge Nature Trail

Length: 0.7 mi (1.1 km); **easy;** USGS Map: Tigerville; trailhead: picnic area.

From the trailhead at the picnic area I followed the trail sign and crossed a footbridge to an old wagon road, which was bordered by yellow root, hemlock, rhododendron, and mountain laurel. On a ridge were the remnants of a log cabin, probably from a CCC campground. At 0.2 mi I left the old road and went L into an oak and hickory forest. The understory is of holly, mountain laurel, and dogwood.

Across a stream at 0.4 mi was the site of an old whiskey still; at this point I turned L. At 0.5 mi a spur trail led off to the R to the lake area. I crossed another stream and descended on an old, wet, rocky road. Cascading on the L was a stream with a heavy bank of fetterbush. Completing the loop, I returned to the trail origin.

Laurens County Park (Laurens County)

The park has a sheltered picnic area, a children's playground, tennis and basketball courts, a baseball field, and a fishing lake.

Information: County Park, P.O. Box 445, Laurens, SC 29360; (864) 984-5484.

Access: The park is 3.1 mi E of Laurens on US 76. Take a L on SR 274 and go 1.3 mi to park entrance on the R.

Laurens County Park Nature Trail

Length: 0.8 mi (1.3 km); **easy;** USGS Map: Laurens S; trailhead: picnic area.

The nature trail begins in the picnic area under hardwoods at a sign. After crossing the dam at 0.1 mi, we entered the hardwood forest to make a loop around the lake. Vegetation was mainly young oaks, pines, beech, ironwood, hickory, and dogwood. Wildflowers we saw included downy false and sticky foxglove, false flax, and asters. Ferns grew near the two streams. At 0.5 mi we crossed the lake's headwaters and returned through a mixed forest to the point of origin.

Chau Ram Park (Oconee County)

Chau Ram Park is one of three recreational facilities provided by the Oconee County Parks and Recreation Commission. The other two are High Falls Park and South Cove Park on Lake Keowee, but only Chau Ram has a trail. Facilities at Chau Ram include campsites with water and electric hook-up, a picnic area, a playground, a recreational building for special events and group activities, fishing and swimming at the Chauga River, and carpet golf.

Information: Oconee County Parks and Recreation Commission, P.O. Box 188, Walhalla, SC 29691; (864) 638–4212.

Access: From Westminster take US 76 W for 2.5 mi to entrance on the L.

Chauga Nature Trail

Length: 0.5 mi (0.8 km); **easy;** USGS Map: Holly Springs; trailhead: campground.

In the campground I entered the trail at campsite #22 and followed on a slope where goat's pea, huckleberry, bracken, galax, and trailing arbutus grew. Trees and shrubs included hawthorn, pink rhododendron, mountain laurel, dogwood, pine, and oak. The trail descended on switchbacks in a rocky and steep area to scenic views of the roaring Chauga cascades at 0.2 mi. Huge boulders and flat rocks made this an unusually picturesque locale. Moss and ferns graced the hillside. I crossed a small stream at the picnic area and ascended the hillside to the point of origin at 0.5 mi.

Campobello-Gramling School Outdoor Laboratory (Spartanburg County)

This unique outdoor laboratory was the result of cooperative efforts of the school, the Spartanburg Conservation District, and the South Carolina Land Resources Commission. In the summer of 1997, a local Boy Scout group renovated the laboratory area as an

Eagle Scout project. Funding was from local businesses and a national sports company.

Information: Contact Principal, Campobello-Gramling Elementary School, Campobello, SC 29322; (864) 472–6495.

Access: From the jct of US 176 and SC 11 in Campobello, go S on US 176 for 1.6 mi to Campobello-Gramling Elementary School on the R.

Campobello-Gramling Trail

Length: 0.8 mi, round-trip (1.3 km); **easy;** USGS Map: Inman; trailhead: SW corner of the school.

From the parking area I went to the SW corner of the school and followed the trail laboratory sign. A number of the botanical specimens were labeled; some of the additional ones were strawberry bush, mock strawberry, pipsissewa, partridge berry, penstemon, Christmas fern, and endangered orchids. Trees were mostly young pines, oaks, sourwood, poplar, maple, hickory, and sweet gum. I crossed two footbridges and backtracked after reaching Motlow Creek.

Museum of York County (York County)

In October 1982 the Rock Hill *Evening Herald* ran a 12-page supplement on the Museum of York County. It was about a dream come true; a dream in the 1950s of the Junior Welfare League of Rock Hill and of leaders such as Maurice Stans and J. Lee Settlemyre. There are myriad attractions in this museum: a planetarium, an environmental theater, and four galleries: the Grant Gallery (named in honor of Vernon Grant, Rock Hill's nationally known artist), the Springs Gallery, an Alternative Gallery, and Local Accents (which features work by area artists). The museum also boasts the Hall of the Western Hemisphere, but the most spectacular attraction is the Maurice Stans African Hall's dioramas, with the world's largest collection of mounted African hooved mammals.

A curator of natural history told me that the museum "docent program," which uses volunteer teachers, was of great assistance. "I enjoy the students who come to learn. . . . When they appreciate what you are doing, it makes it all worthwhile," she said. It was closing time; she locked up, and as we were leaving I realized that one of my students, Steve Harris, was so engrossed in the exhibit that he was locked inside the museum. "Somebody would have found him," she assured me, as she reopened the door.

Another special feature at the museum is the nature trail, which has a wood carving of the state bird, the Carolina wren, and flower, yellow jessamine, at the trailhead. Picnicking is allowed. The museum is open Monday through Saturday 10 A.M. TO 5:00 P.M. and Sunday 1:00 to 5:00 P.M.

Information: Museum of York County, 4621 Mount Gallant Rd., Rock Hill, SC 29732; (803) 329–2121.

Access: From I–77 take Exit 82A to SC-161; at second light turn right on Mount Gallant Rd.

York County Nature Trail

Length: 0.5 mi (0.8 km); **easy;** USGS Map: Rock Hill; trailhead: behind the museum.

Steve and I took with us a map of the carefully planned trail within a 10-acre garden of plant selections from the coastal, piedmont, and mountain areas. We counted more than 50 species. At 0.3 mi we could see Big Dutchman's Creek from an observation deck. After completing the loop we returned to the amphitheater, picnic area, and trail entrance.

SECTION 2
Municipalities

Aiken (Aiken County)

Founded in 1834, Aiken is a fashionable year-round resort and a popular sports center for thoroughbred training, fox hunts, drag hunts, and golf in the winter months. Some of the nation's top horses are trained here, and the Racing Hall of Fame, established by the local Jaycees, is at Hopeland Gardens. The annual Triple Crown—harness racing, trials, and steeplejack—is held each March. The city's chief industry is textiles, and among its more significant buildings is the Aiken County Museum on Chesterfield Street; it houses an exhibition of the area's early history. Here also is the famous Hitchcock Woods, a 1,200-acre forest preserve. Maintaining the area park system is the Aiken Recreation Department, which has two parks with trails: Hopeland Gardens and Virginia Acres Park. The park system is currently in an expanded period of growth and development.

Information: Aiken Recreation Dept., P.O. Box 1177, Aiken, SC 29801; (803) 642–7630.

Support Facilities: The closest camping is Pine Acres Campground. From jct of I-20 and US 1 (Exit 22), go S on US 1 for 4 mi. Open all year, full svc, no rec fac; (803) 648–5715.

Hopeland Gardens

The 14-acre Hopeland Gardens is a tranquil area with a network of paved walkways, a lake, floral gardens, and outdoor stage for plays and concerts, and a special trail for the handicapped.

Access: From jct of US 78, SC 302, and SC 19, downtown, go S on SC 19 for 1 mi to the corner of Whiskey Road and Dupree Place. Turn on Dupree Place to the parking entrance on L.

Hopeland Gardens Trail

Length: 0.3 mi (0.5 km); **easy;** USGS Map: Aiken; trailhead: in front of the Thoroughbred Hall of Fame.

From the parking area I took an avenue of ivy and tall oaks to the Thoroughbred Hall of Fame building. I followed the signs on a paved trail where 28 permanent labels in print and Braille described the plants, including some that are fragrant. (The trail is also constructed to accommodate wheelchairs.) Other trails in the park interconnected or looped back to the point of origin.

Virginia Acres Park

With a diversity of sports facilities, the Virginia Acres Park also houses the Odell Weeks Recreation Center and city park headquarters. There are eight lighted tennis courts; two shuffleboard courts; four outdoor and two indoor basketball courts; four racquetball courts, both outside and inside; one soccer field; two picnic shelters; and a trail for jogging, walking, in-line skating, and track.

Access: The park is on SC 19, Whiskey Road, E of the city, between SC 302, Pine Log Rd., and Price Ave.

Camden (Kershaw County)

The historic town of Camden celebrated its 250th anniversary in the spring of 1983 as the state's oldest inland city. Originally situated by the Wateree River, it was first named Fredericksburg. The name was changed 10 years later to Pine Tree Hill when the settlers moved to higher ground. In 1768 it was appropriately named in honor of the British champion of colonial rights Charles Pratt, Lord Camden.

Camden is a city of traditions, of charm and style, of restored homes and public buildings, and of culture and a high quality of life. And it is a shrine for horse racing. Some observers credit its

health and beauty to Haiglar, King of the Catawbas and friend of the early settlers, whose image is on the tower of the former City Hall as a weather vane. He, if no one else can, informs the city which way the wind blows.

The Camden area has nearly 275 mi of equestrian trails. Famous as one of America's finest thoroughbred racehorse centers for 150 years, Camden is the host each fall to the Colonial Cup International Steeplechase and to the Carolina Cup in the spring.

Historic Camden Revolutionary War Site

Some of Camden's and Kershaw County's late eighteenth- and early nineteenth-century structures have been restored by the Camden District Heritage Foundation, which began the work in 1970. Archaeological research identified the sites of buildings in the original settlement near the 1200 block of Broad Street. Three of the restored buildings—the Craven frame cottage and the Bradley and Drakeford log cabins—are now filled with museum exhibits and dioramas. The Craven House serves as the tour office, museum shop, and administrative office. The Joseph Kershaw House, headquarters for Lord Charles Cornwallis, has been rebuilt. The museum is open 10:00 A.M. to 5:00 P.M. Tuesday through Saturday, and 1:00 to 5:00 P.M. Sunday. Guided tours are Tuesday from 10:30 A.M. to 3:00 P.M., Saturday from 10:00 A.M. to 4:00 P.M., and Sunday 1:00 to 4:00 P.M.

Information: Contact any of the following in Camden, SC 29020: Historic Camden, P.O. Box 710, (803) 432–9841; Kershaw County Historical Society, P.O. Box 501, (803) 425–1123; Greater Kershaw County Chamber of Commerce, 724 S. Broad St., (803) 432–2525; or Camden Archives and Museum, 1314 Broad St., (803) 425–6050.

Access: From I-20 at the US 521 jct, it is 1.4 mi N and on the R. From downtown turn S on US 251 at jct with US 521/1/601 and continue for 0.9 mi.

Historic Camden Trail

Length: 0.7 mi round-trip, combined (1.1 km); **easy;** USGS Map: Camden S; trailhead: Visitor Center parking area.

From the Exchange in the center, we walked on a dirt road to the magazine area of earthworks, turning R to the forest of tall oaks and a wide path. Yellow jessamine was fragrant. At 0.2 mi we passed under a power line near Big Pine Tree Creek. The trail turned R, and we passed a pond, then returned to the parking area E of the maintenance building at 0.4 mi. After reentering the dirt road, we followed it to the Joseph Kershaw mansion and returned at 0.3 mi.

Pine Tree Hill Trail

Length: 9.8 mi round-trip (15.7 km); **easy;** USGS Maps: Camden S, Camden; trailhead: Historic Camden Revolutionary War Site parking area.

Access to the Pine Tree Hill Trail is at the parking area. This trail winds through the historic section of Camden.

I chose a Sunday morning to hike to avoid traffic. From the parking area I crossed Broad Street and walked on Meeting Street to the Presbyterian meetinghouse and cemetery, then to the Quaker Burying Ground, site 3. On September 3, 1759, Samuel Wyly leased this area to the Quakers for a cemetery and meetinghouse under "the terms of 999 years at a yearly rental of one peppercorn, if lawfully demanded." The Quakers later leased the property to the town of Camden for 99 years at a rate of $1.00 a year. The cemetery has the graves of three Kershaw County heroes: Richard H. Hilton and John C. Villepique, recipients of the WWI Congressional Medal of Honor, and Richard Kirkland, the compassionate Confederate soldier who risked his life for dying Union soldiers at the Battle of Fredericksburg.

At 0.2 mi I returned to Broad Street and turned L to site 4, where Baron Johann de Kalb, hero of the Battle of Camden, was buried by the British with full military honors in August 1780. In 1825 his remains were moved to site 63 on De Kalb Street. At 0.5

mi I arrived at the jct of Bull and Broad Streets, once the center of town. President George Washington addressed a gathering of local citizens on May 27, 1791, during his first Southern tour. On the 600 block of Bull Street is site 6, the burial enclosure of Colonel Joseph Kershaw, founding father of Camden, for whom the county is named.

Back on Broad Street I turned L and reached the 600 block and site 8 at 0.7 mi. Erected in 1826, the original Mills Court House was designed by Robert Mills, a native South Carolinian who designed the Washington Monument in the nation's capital. The courthouse was rebuilt three times and used until 1906. It is now the Masonic Lodge. At site 9, across the street from the lodge, is the site of the Revolutionary gaol (jail) built in 1771. This is the jail where 14-year-old Andrew Jackson was imprisoned briefly (see Andrew Jackson State Park in Chapter III). Legend has it that young Andrew watched the Battle of Hobkirk Hill from a hole he had cut in the second-story wall.

At the jct of Broad and York Streets, I turned R and went to the Fine Arts Center on Lyttleton Street and on to Fair Street, where the Bonds Conway house, site 11, has been moved from 411 York Street. The story of Bonds is significant because, in 1793, at the age of 30, he was the first black citizen in Camden to buy his own freedom.

I returned on York Street to Market Street and turned R at 1.4 mi. I was puzzled about site 13 on Market Street until I read my guidebook. Instead of a mausoleum, it was a Civil War storage place for arms and ammunition. I continued on Meeting Street to Arthur Lane, turned L, and went back to Broad Street to site 15, at the corner of Broad Street and Rutledge. Here, at the top of a tower, is a replica of a 5-ft iron effigy (c. 1820) of Catawba Indian King Haiglar, "the Patron Saint of Camden."

Site 17, on the 1100 block of Broad Street, is the site of Lafayette Hall, once the home of John Carter. It burned in 1903, but a cedar tree planted in 1825 still stands. The new courthouse is here now. At 2.1 mi I passed site 18, followed by sites 19 to 22, which were private architectural landmarks.

At site 23 I reached Broad and Laurens Streets at Monument Square. The area has large oaks and pines and mounds of azaleas in a parklike area honoring the Confederate dead. One monument honors Lt. Colonel James Polk Dickinson (1816–1847), who died in the Mexican War. An inscription reads:

> How beautiful in death,
> The warrior's cause appears,
> Embalmed by fond affection's breath
> And bathed in woman's tears.

On the SE section of the square is the Camden Archives and Museum, a repository for historic documents and objects such as the original tower clockworks and the King Haiglar weathervane. After passing historic private homes at sites 24 to 30 along Broad Street from the 1400 block to the 2000 block, I arrived at Hobkirk Hill at 3.8 mi. Site 31 marks the area on the ridge overlooking Camden where General Nathanael Greene's troops were defeated after a brief battle with Lord Francis Rawdon's British forces just before dawn on April 25, 1781, at the Battle of Hobkirk Hill.

The next 18 sites (33 to 50) are elegant private homes. I admired them as I passed by using the following route: Kirkwood Lane from Broad Street to Ancrum Road; Ancrum Road to Union Street and turn R; turn R at Lakeview Avenue; turn L at Brevard Place; turn R on Mill Street; turn L on Greene Street; turn L on Fair Street to sites 39 and 40; and return to Greene Street. At the jct of Greene and Lyttleton Streets, I turned L on Lyttleton (missing sites 43 and 44) and continued on to site 51, Rectory Square, at Lyttleton and Chestnut Streets. I had walked 7 mi; I sat down at the square's pantheon to rest and eat a snack from my day pack. Around me were six columns, each memorializing one of Camden's Confederate war generals—James Cantey, James Chesnut, Zach Deas, John D. Kennedy, Joseph B. Kershaw, and John B. Villepique. The pantheon was erected in 1911 from funds raised by the schoolchildren of Camden. A marker read:

The silent pillar, gold and gray,
Claimed kindred with their sacred clay;
Their spirits wrap the dusty mountain;
Their memory sparkles o'er the fountain.

I left the square under the shade of large oaks and by gardens of azaleas and crepe myrtle. I continued S on Lyttleton Street to Laurens Street, turned L and walked for 2 blocks to see site 54, and returned to go W on Laurens Street to see sites 56 and 57. Backtracking to Lyttleton, I turned R and followed Lyttleton Street to Haile Street. Here I turned L on Haile Street and walked 2 blocks to see site 60, to my R on Mill Street. I backtracked to Lyttleton Street, turned L, and reached Hampton Park at 8.3 mi.

Hampton Park was named for General Wade Hampton, Confederate officer and later governor of the state. A monument here honors Sergeant Richard Kirkland, who at the Battle of Fredericksburg, December 13, 1862, carried water again and again in the line of fire to the suffering and dying Union soldiers. Named the "Angel of Mayre's Heights" by the troops, he died nine months later in the Battle of Chickamauga, at age 20. Of the 71,000 South Carolinians who served in the Civil War, he was one of the 12,922 who died. The monument was erected as a tribute from the schoolchildren of Camden in 1910.

From Hampton Park I turned R on De Kalb Street to the monument where Maj. General Baron de Kalb, Revolutionary War hero, was reinterred in 1825. Behind the monument, the Bethesda Presbyterian Church worship service was over, and most of the parishioners had gone home to Sunday dinner. I left my day pack and measuring wheel near the entrance and went in to sit quietly, admire this 1822 architectural masterpiece by Robert Mills, and think about the five porches of Bethesda in John 5:2.

I walked back to my car for a total of 9.8 mi. (I could have taken a shorter route had I not backtracked to view the sites in numerical order.) Hikers may wish to purchase the 48-page *Historic Site Directory* from any of the agencies listed above. Boy Scouts may earn the Pine Tree Hill medal and patch by hiking this trail and taking a written test; contact the Boy Scouts of America, P.O. Box 144, Columbia, SC 29202; (803) 765–9070.

Charleston (Charleston County)

Charleston is often referred to as "America's most historic city." In 1670 "Charles Towne" was established in the Carolinas by Anthony Ashley Cooper, Earl of Shaftesbury. His establishment of American nobility titles for the owners of large plantations laid the foundations and opened a gateway for much of the city's elegance and refinement.

The state's second largest city, it was once the state capital. Today its charm, its beauty, and its heritage are carefully preserved. "We are proud of our heritage," said Mayor Joseph P. Riley, Jr. "It is a city for everyone . . . any time of year." Others have described it as a "city of romance," "a city of cultivated manners," "the best example of civility," "a living history book," "the Carolina city of old-world charm," and "a proud survivor of every calamity." James Dickey described the city as "full of walled gardens, which I love more than any other construction of man."

Charleston has nine major museums, including Patriots Point, which is the world's largest naval and maritime museum, and the Charleston Museum (1713), which is the oldest in America. Architectural rehabilitation and stabilization of dozens of historic buildings have been the principal concern of the Historic Charleston Foundation, founded in 1947. Visitors can tour the 789-acre historic district on foot, by horse-drawn carriage, or by a variety of motorized vehicles.

There are more than 12 historic churches. The city parks and gardens and recreational facilities are numerous, and the Spoleto Festival U.S.A. attracts an international audience each spring. Tour boats leave daily from the Municipal Marina and the Patriots Point Marina, heading to Fort Sumter. (See discussion of the Fort Sumter National Historical Monument in Chapter II.)

In West Ashley there is a developing 9-mi West Ashley Greenway on an old railroad grade. Some parts are paved, and it is used by joggers, walkers, and bikers. Access is at the jct of SC 171 and Windenere Drive. (For city park information see the address ahead.)

The Charleston Visitors Center provides a great variety of information and visit-planning assistance; a visitor's guide/map of the city is available with a numbered list of 46 points of historic interest. Another guide is an 18-page booklet with a map, titled *The Complete Walking Tour of Historic Charleston.* It is written by Nita Swann and illustrated with the artwork of Nicki Williams, Betty Schwark, and Jim Gensmer. The guide lists 65 historic sites (and 23 alternate sites) and is available from the Visitors Center. The "Old Walled City" dates from 1703, and the lines of former fortifications can be traced in the area. It is recommended that you first go to the Visitors Center, 81 Mary Street, for directional maps. From there you should park your car at the adjacent parking lots and use the D.A.S.H. for transportation throughout the historic district.

Old Walled City Trail

Length: 2.3 mi (3.7 km); **easy;** USGS Map: Charleston; trailhead: 23 Cumberland St.

From the Old Powder Magazine (1703) at 23 Cumberland Street, we began a walk of the "Old Walled City." At the corner of Cumberland and Meeting was the Carteret Bastion, the NW corner of the old wall. We turned L on Meeting Street; on the R was Gibbes Art Gallery. On the L was the Circular Congregational Church, organized in 1681, although the current building was constructed in 1891. On Meeting Street across from Chalmers Street is Hibernian Hall (1799). At 100 Meeting Street is America's first fireproof building, erected in 1822.

Near the corner of Meeting and Broad are a number of historic firsts: City Hall (1801), County Court House (1792), United States Post Office and Federal Court (1896), and St. Michael's Protestant Episcopal Church, the oldest church edifice in the city (1751). Its bells were imported from England in 1764. Near here, on Broad

Street, are the Confederate Home and the Citizens and Southern National Bank Building (1797); and at the corner of Broad and Church Streets is "Cabbage Row." This spot inspired the setting of "Catfish Row" in the *Porgy and Bess* operetta.

From here we continued R on Church Street to the Heyward Washington House (1770), home of Thomas Heyward, a signer of the Declaration of Independence. At Tradd Street we turned R to Meeting Street and turned L to the First (Scots) Presbyterian Church, organized in 1731 but built in 1841. At 51 Meeting Street we visited the Nathaniel Russell House (1809), and at 16 Meeting Street, the Calhoun Mansion (1876).

After 0.8 mi we reached South Battery Street and turned R to make a curve of 0.4 mi around the White Point Gardens to Murray Boulevard and "The Battery" area. The gardens are landscaped with shrubs and flowers, and monuments are placed in the area to represent the cycle of American wars in which Charleston has been involved.

At the corner of Murray Boulevard, we turned L and followed East Battery Street to the Edmonston-Alston House, then to Missroon House at 44 East Battery. The Vanderhorst Row (1800) was at 76–80 East Bay Street. At 83–107 East Bay we passed the Rainbow Row houses, named for the pastel colors of the historic buildings. To our R was the Old Exchange and Custom House (1767–71) at 122 Bay Street. From here we turned L on Broad Street to the South Carolina National Bank (1817). At the corner of Broad and Church, we turned R to Chalmers Street and saw the Pink House (1745), a three-story house with one room on each floor. Continuing on Church Street, we visited Dock Street (1809) and the French Huguenot Church (1844–45) at the corner of Church and Queen Streets. At 146 Church Street was St. Philip's Episcopal Church (1838), the church that had the oldest original congregation (1670). The Old City Market Area (1788–1804) is between Meeting and East Bay Streets on North Market and South Market Streets. After a visit there we walked back to the Cumberland Street parking area at 2.3 mi.

Information: For a visitor's guide contact Charleston Trident Convention and Visitors Bureau, 81 Mary St. (P.O. Box 975), Charleston, SC 29402; (843) 853–8000; toll-free (800) 868–8118. City of Charleston Rec Dept., 30 Murray Dr., Hampton Park, Charleston, SC 29403; (843) 724–7327.

Chester (Chester County)

Named by settlers from Pennsylvania in 1755, the town is the county seat and has a population of about 7,000. Located in the center of the county, it is also the hub of six rail routes of the Seaboard Coast Line, Carolina and Northwestern, Lancaster and Chester, and Southern railways. Eleven highways spread out like a fan from the center of town. Its recreation program is owned by the city but administered by Chester County Parks and Recreation Department. One of the parks is Wylie Park, which has seven tennis courts, a large swimming pool, a picnic area, a basketball court, and a nature area.

Information: Chester County Parks and Rec Dept., P.O. Box 580, Chester, SC 29706; (803) 581–6200.

Access: From the jct of SC 72, US Bypass 321 and SC 9, and West End St., go 0.6 mi on West End to the park and the park hq.

Wylie Park Trail

Length: 0.3 mi (0.5 km); **easy;** USGS Map: Chester; trailhead: park road.

From West End Street I entered the gate at the picnic area and went to the trail entrance on the L. Although the trail was unmarked, it could be taken in a loop by returning to the paved road and the point of origin. In a mixed forest of pines, cedar, oaks, gum, and wild cherry, the honeysuckle and wisteria were cozy to them all. Ebony spleenwort leaned over the trail to force fragrance in my face, and atamasco lilies were growing near the wet spots. A sign at the gate read: PRESENTED BY JOSEPH WYLIE TO THE CITY OF CHESTER FOR THEIR COMFORT, PLEASURE AND INNOCENT AMUSEMENT, 1899.

Columbia (Lexington and Richland Counties)

Columbia, the capital city in the center of the state, the focal point of state government since 1790, has been described by historians, politicians, and writers from many perspectives. Probably only one writer, James Dickey, has assessed its value meridionally. "But the best thing," he wrote in *The Starry Place Between the Antlers*, "is the way it balances Appalachia and the Atlantic."

Its wide boulevards—Assembly, Gervais, Senate, and Sumter—frame the capitol building, a masterpiece of Southern elegance and design. The imposing statehouse is built of native granite in Roman Corinthian style. It is more than the heart of state government; it is also a center for wholesale and retail trade, industry, finance, and education. Within a few blocks of the capitol building are the University of South Carolina (1801) and the Richland County Courthouse. In addition to USC, other institutes of higher education are Allen University (1870), Lutheran Theological Southern Seminary (1830), Columbia College (1854), Benedict College (1870), and Columbia Bible College (1923).

In 1790 the General Assembly met in the statehouse, and the following year George Washington visited the city during his Southern tour. South Carolina was the first state to secede from the union, and it was here that the Ordinance of Secession was drawn on December 17, 1860, at Columbia's First Baptist Church on 1306 Hampton Street. More than four years later, February 17, 1865, General William T. Sherman's army marched N from Savannah and occupied Columbia. At least 1,386 buildings were burned within 84 blocks, as revenge, claim some historians.

Attractions in the city include the Town Theatre (since 1919), one of the nation's oldest little theaters, on Sumter Street; McKissick Museum and Columbia Museum of Art and Science; Robert Mills Historic House and Park (Mills was the designer of the Washington Monument in Washington, DC); the South Carolina Archives Building; Woodrow Wilson's boyhood home; and the 50-acre Riverbanks Zoological Park and Botanical Garden, one of the nation's finest. Fort Jackson, on the E boundary of the city, is one of the nation's largest U.S. Army training centers.

The Department of Parks and Recreation maintains 37 parks. Those with walking trails are described below. The parks range from open green areas and playgrounds to large community parks with gymnasiums to small neighborhood parks.

Information: Parks and Rec Dept., 1932 Calhoun St., Columbia, SC 29201; (803) 733-8331.

Support Facilities: (See Sesquicentennial State Park.)

Earlwood Park

Earlwood Park Trail
Length: 0.5 mi (0.8 km); **easy;** USGS Map: Columbia N; trailhead: parking area.

Access: 2 blocks S from the jct of SC 16 and Main St.

Although the walking area is not a designated trail system, I walked through oaks and pines and willows. A paved jogging trail near the entrance is at 0.2 mi. Other facilities are provided for picnicking and tennis.

Maxcy Gregg Park

Maxcy Gregg Park Trail
Length: 0.3 mi (0.5 km); **easy;** USGS Map: Southwest Columbia; trailhead: parking area.

Access: This park is on 500 Pickens St. and at the Blossom St. and Pickens St. jct. Serving as a natural area with gardens, it is also the setting for an Olympic-style pool. I walked for 0.3 mi one way along the banks of the stream among live oaks, magnolias, poplars, and cultivated gardens of azaleas, camellias, and seasonal floral displays.

Historic Columbia Canal and Riverfront Park

The Historic Columbia Canal and Riverfront Park is located near the confluence of the Broad and Saluda Rivers, where they become the Congaree River. Interpretive markers explain the history and services of the Columbia Canal, the Pump House, and the old waterwork system markers also discuss other historic structures as well as the local plant and animal life.

Constructed by the state more than 150 years ago, the purpose of the canal was to bypass the dangerous shoals at the jct of the rivers. Although the canal's usefulness decreased after the railroads, it was rebuilt in the 1890s for the purpose of generating electricity. It has been in use ever since.

The waterworks at the canal continues to serve the city also. The waterworks' filtering capacity currently exceeds 70 million gallons of water daily.

Columbia Canal Trail

Length: 5 mi round-trip (8.0 km); **easy;** USGS Map: Columbia N; trailhead: parking lot.

Access: Turn S from Elmwood St. Huger St. to Laurel St., R; or N from Hampton St. on William St. (or Huger St.) to Laurel, L.

From the parking area we descended to a footbridge that crosses the Columbia Canal to the levee and the Congaree River. At 0.2 mi was the historic waterworks. From here we turned upstream on the levee on a paved, scenic trail used for jogging, bicycling, and walking. The area is landscaped with white and pink crepe myrtle. Natural shrubs, wildflowers, sycamore, and sweet gum are prominent. A sign at 0.4 mi, near the picnic area, describes the river cooters. We walked under the I-26 bridge and railroad at 0.7 mi. The paved area ended at 0.9 mi and gravel began. When the trail ended at 2.5 mi, at a diversion dam, we backtracked.

Sidney Park

Sidney Park Trail
Length: 0.5 mi (0.8 km); **easy;** USGS Map: Southwest Columbia; trailhead: parking area.

Access: From Riverfront/Canal Park (Elmwood to Huger Sts.), take a L to Laurel St. to the inner-city park.

The park is a natural 17.5-acre green area with a lake and manmade waterfall in the middle of downtown Columbia. There is a sidewalk trail, picnic area, amphitheater, playgrounds (one of which is designed for visitors who are physically impaired), and views of the lake and city from the Watermark Cafe.

Darlington (Darlington County)

Darlington, the county seat, is best known for its leadership in tobacco marketing and the Darlington International Raceway. In addition it has the Joe Weatherly Stock Car Hall of Fame Museum with the largest collection of race cars in the world. It is also the largest automobile auction market in the nation. As for parks, the largest is beautiful Williams Park (approximately 400 acres). A small, unique park is the Frank and Mark Sue Wells Park, at the corner of Avenue A and South Main Street by the railroad track. This miniature park has a picnic table; a 100-yd designed trail **(Wells Park Trail);** shrubbery; and a few trees, including cedar, pecan, and catalpa.

Information: Director, Rec Dept., P.O. Box 94, Darlington, SC 29532; (843) 393–3626.

Williams Park Trail
Length: 1.8 mi combined (2.9 km); **easy;** USGS Map: Darlington; trailhead: parking area.

From downtown at the courthouse square, take SC 34, Cashua Street NE, go 2 blocks to SR 446, Spring Street, and turn L. Go 0.2

mi to parking area on R between Park Drive and Swift Creek bridge.

From the parking area we followed the trail R through large elm, ash, poplar, gum, and mulberry. In some places wisteria was encroaching on the dogwood, mulberry, redbud, and azalea, and at other locations it had intertwined itself in competition with the Spanish moss to high-hanging displays of green and purple and gray. Jewelweeds, Scotch brooms, ferns, and daylilies were not far from the tentacles of the wisteria. There was an abundance of songbirds. At 0.3 mi we reached a jct, the path on the R leading to North Spain Street. We passed an old well pump. To our L the trail looped back to the parking area, and to our R was Park Street at 0.4 mi. We first hiked a less-used trail ahead for 0.5 mi to an exit at Cashua Street near Bellyache Creek bridge. Backtracking, we completed the loop mentioned above. The trail passed two sheds, crossed three boardwalks in a swampy area over Swift Creek, and wove through tall birch, cypress, oak, and gum. Arrow arum and lizard's tail were prevalent, and benches in beds of ground ivy were along the trail. Returning to the parking area, we crossed three more boardwalks at Swift Creek. Across the street was the smallest chapel I have ever been in. It could accommodate only two or three people. A sign told us it was for meditation. (I have since learned from the Chamber of Commerce that it is maintained by Bill Brasington of 105 Evans Circle.)

Florence (Florence County)

In 1846 General William W. Harllee of Marion received a state charter to construct a railroad from Manchester to Wilmington. Construction began in 1853, and a station for the North Eastern Railroad was based at present-day Florence. The early settlers and developers needed a name for the station; the railroad construction superintendent suggested Florence, the name of General Harllee's oldest daughter. In 1871 the town was chartered, and in 1888 a county by the same name was established by the state legislature. Today Florence remains the hub of extensive railroad lines and is a major retail and wholesale distribution center. It is also a beautiful city, with city parks, museums, and the **Florence Beauty Trail,** with brilliant floral displays.

The 12-mi motor trail is in the central and SW area of the city around the parks and by a country club. The trail starts at Timrod Park on Coit Street, at the corner of Cherokee Road. It is sponsored by the Rotary Club in association with the Greater Florence Chamber of Commerce. There are trail signs along the way. The brilliant floral display of trees, shrubs, and flowers is at its peak from late March to early April.

Information: City of Florence Rec Dept., P.O. Box 1476, Florence, SC 29503; (843) 665–3253.

Jeffries Creek Park

Jeffries Creek Trail
Length: 0.8 mi combined (1.6 km); **easy;** USGS Map: Florence W; trailhead: parking area.

From the jct of US 52/301, South Irby Street, and Second Loop Road in downtown Florence, drive 1.5 mi to Edisto Drive Extension and turn R. After 0.7 mi turn L on Wisteria Drive and proceed 0.2 mi to park entrance. You can also proceed 0.5 mi farther ahead, to the South Deberry Boulevard entrance, under tall ash, poplar, maple, oak, elm, and sweet gum, where Spanish moss hangs in clusters.

We turned L over a bridge. Bordering the well-graded trail were ferns, mandrake, elderberry, switchcane, and willow. At 0.3 mi we crossed a bridge to the picnic area and to the end of the island. We backtracked to follow the trail over more bridges and to another picnic area and children's playground. Exit L here goes to the street. We returned to West Wisteria Street after 0.8 mi in the 55-acre park.

Lucas Park

Lucas Park Trail

Length: 0.6 mi round-trip (.09 km); **easy;** USGS Map: Florence W; trailhead: Azalea Lane.

Downtown at the jct of US 52/301 and Cherokee Road, turn W on Cherokee Road and go 2 blocks to Camellia Drive or 3 blocks to Park Avenue on the L. Go 2 blocks on Park Avenue to Azalea Lane and turn L.

The 12-acre park has a children's playground, tennis courts, gardens, and brick treadway. On the trail are oaks, poplars, pines, dogwoods, and sweet gums. Azaleas, spirea, and other ornamental shrubs make this a park of springtime beauty.

Timrod Park

Timrod Park Trail

Length: 1 mi round-trip (1.6 km); **easy;** USGS Map: Florence W.; trailhead: South Coit Street.

Downtown at the jct of Cherokee Road and US 52-301, take Cherokee W for 1 block to jct of South Coit Street and turn R.

We started our walk from South Coit Street and followed upstream. The park has a children's playground, picnic area, and lighted tennis courts. Tall trees included poplar, sweet gum, magnolia, and oak. Azalea and dogwood were copious and colorful.

We entered the tea-rose garden and visited the one-room schoolhouse of Henry Timrod (1828–1867), poet laureate of the Confederacy. At this schoolhouse Timrod taught, among others, "Katie," who was later to become his wife. At 0.6 mi we reached the Florence Museum at Spruce and Graham Streets. It is open without charge daily, 10:00 A.M. to 5:00 P.M., except the last two weeks in August. We backtracked to our point of origin.

Greenville (Greenville County)

Greenville, incorporated in 1907, was Pleasantburg until 1821. It is a city with a population of more than 60,000 and is the county seat of Greenville County. It has more than 400 manufacturing plants and has been called the "Textile Center of the World," but recently chemical, plastic, and machinery products have become prominent. Its major institutions of higher education are Bob Jones University (1927), Furman University (1826), and Greenville Technical College (1962). The Art Museum at Bob Jones University has one of the nation's foremost collections of rare Biblical materials and sacred art. The city Parks and Recreational Services and the Greenville County Recreation Commission have established eight bicycle tours and loops comprising a total of more than 140 mi in the Greenville vicinity. One of these, the Reedy River Tour in the heart of the city, has a section in Cleveland Park that can be used as an excellent foot trail. The city is known for at least seven beautiful public gardens in which there are scenic walks. In addition, groups such as the South Carolina Chapter of the Sierra Club have constructed the 0.5-mi round-trip **Fernwood Nature Trail.** It has interpretive signs among tall trees, wildflowers, and carpets of ivy. The trail is at the corner of Fernwood Lane and Woodland Way.

Information: Greenville Park and Rec Services, Box 2207, Greenville, SC 29602; (864) 467–4350.

Reedy River Falls Historic Park and Greenway

The 24-acre Reedy River Falls Historic Park and Greenway was developed by the Carolina Foothills Garden Club on land given to the city by Furman University in 1969.

Access: In downtown Greenville at the jct of South Church St. (US Bus 29) and University Ridge, take University Ridge around the County Square Complex to the jct of Howe and Hitt Streets at the park entrance.

Reedy River Falls Trail

Length: 0.5 mi (0.8 km); **easy;** USGS Map: Greenville; trailhead: park driveway.

After reaching the access I parked by the driveway near the river. Among the azaleas was a sign installed by the Carolina Foothills Garden Club for an azalea planting. It read, "given to the glory of God and in loving memory of Sara Gossett Crigler and Betsy Highsmith Bruce by Frances Oates Beattie, 1972." From the sign I made a loop among the azaleas to the waterfalls. Large oak, sycamore, birch, elm, and ash spread a high canopy over the ornamental shrubs and wildflowers. The smell of ground ivy was prominent at the base of a huge sycamore with a 14.5-ft circumference. Behind it the water of Reedy River poured over tiers of rock ledges, a natural downtown waterfall.

Cleveland Park Trail

Length: 3.3 mi round-trip (5.3 km); **easy;** USGS Maps: Greenville, Greenville SE; trailhead: Reedy River Falls Park.

As I was parked at Reedy River Falls Park, I walked to the cul-de-sac and entered the Cleveland Park Trail downstream on an 8-ft-wide asphalt walkway for bicycling, jogging, and hiking. It is a well-designed trail, priceless for an intercity natural space. It is on this trail that the 10-km Reedy River Run is held each spring. At 0.1 mi I crossed a metal footbridge over the Reedy River. I passed by large birch, elm, and oak trees. Elderberry and trees of heaven were mixed with dogwood and redbud. At 0.3 mi I passed the Anderson Memorial and did a cloverleaf loop at the McDaniel Avenue bridge. At 0.6 mi I crossed a small stream in a meadow where false dandelion, dayflower, sorrel, lady fingers, and jewelweed grew. At 0.9 mi I passed twin cement footbridges. To my R was a large dogwood with a 3.9-ft circumference. At 1.2 mi I crossed the Woodland Way bridge over Reedy River, went upstream to a picnic area, and crossed Richland Way. At this point I entered a magnificent hardwood forest where for 0.5 mi I had to imagine that I was in the city and to my L was the state white poplar champ, over 11 ft in circumference. At 2 mi I turned L to visit the rose garden, which was at its height of blooming. I followed the trail to the rec center, visited the city zoo, and returned to continue my hike by the large playground. To my R were six lighted tennis courts. At 2.4 mi I crossed the cement footbridge over the Reedy River to rejoin the trail and then crossed McDaniel Avenue for a return to the cul-de-sac.

Greer (Greenville County)

Greer is named for J. Manning Greer, an early farmer who donated land for a Southern Railroad track from Greenville to the community. First called Greer's Station and incorporated in 1875, the community changed its name to Greer Depot in 1893, but changed it again in 1901 to Greer. There is a legend that farmer Greer's benevolence was on condition that no whiskey ever be sold in town. Today Greer is Greenville County's second largest city, "the heart of the piedmont," and growth is based on industry, commerce, and agriculture. Its parks and rec program has two rec centers and seven parks with lighted facilities.

Information: Parks and Rec, 226 Oakland Ave., Greer, SC 29651; (864) 877–9289.

Century B Park

Access: From jct of SC 14 and I-85, go N to Brushy Creek Rd., and turn W to Century B Park.

Century B Trail
Length: 0.5 mi (0.8 km); **easy;** USGS Map: Greer NW; trailhead: parking area.

The 25-acre park consists of lighted fields for sports, a nature area, and a trail through a hardwood forest. A footbridge is over Brushy Creek.

Tryon Park

Access: From the jct of US 29 and SC 14, go W to Tryon St. and turn L. Pass Tryon Street Elementary School to Oakland St. and turn L.

Tryon Park Trail
Length: 0.2 mi (0.3 km); **easy;** USGS Map: Greer NW; trailhead: parking area.

From the parking area on Oakland Street, I went past a picnic shelter and descended into the forest of oaks and pines. Two footbridges crossed a deep ravine. A spur trail led to the Tryon Street Elementary School, and I circled back to the origin of the walk. Facilities at the park include six lighted tennis courts, a children's playground, a miniature golf course, a recreational building, and the woods area for nature study.

Mauldin (Greenville County)

On the way into Mauldin on US 276, there is a sign that reads: THE CITY WITH A FUTURE. It is an apt slogan because of the city's rapid commercial and industrial growth and development since 1956— rapid enough to be on what local citizens call the "Golden Strip." Formerly called Butler's Crossroad, it was organized in 1910 and subsequently named in honor of Lt. Governor W. L. Mauldin.

Information: Parks and Rec Dept., P.O. Box 249, Mauldin, SC 29662; (864) 288–3354.

Mauldin City Park

One of two city parks, the 13-acre Mauldin City Park has a senior citizen's center, a children's playground, two lighted baseball fields, lighted softball and soccer fields, and a picnic area.

Access: From the center of town on US 276, turn on E. Butler Ave. and go 1.6 mi to jct with Corn St. Turn L to parking area on L.

Mauldin Park Trail

Length: 0.5 mi (0.8 km); **easy;** USGS Map: Greenville SE; trailhead: parking area.

From the parking area I walked on the paved 6-ft-wide trail in a loop around the recreational facilities. It is an excellent trail for walking or jogging.

Orangeburg (Orangeburg County)

Historic Orangeburg, "where living is a pleasure," is the county seat of Orangeburg County. It was named for William, the Prince of Orange, after a settlement of Swiss, Dutch, and German immigrants was established by the General Assembly in 1735. A prosperous small city, it has successfully combined area farming and industries of wood, textiles, and chemicals with its downtown commercial life. Its major educational institutions are South Carolina State College, which has the I. P. Stanback Museum and Planetarium (1896), Claflin College (1869), and Orangeburg-Calhoun Technical College (1968). Known as a city of roses, it has the year-round Edisto Memorial Gardens, at which the South Carolina Festival of Roses is held the first weekend in May. Among the city's parks and areas of recreation are Edisto Memorial Gardens and Summers Memorial Park.

Information: Orangeburg Parks and Rec Dept., 620 Middleton St., Orangeburg, SC 29115; (803) 534–6211.

Edisto Memorial Gardens

The 85-acre gardens are open all year and free to the public. Opened in 1927, the gardens are known for their magnificent display of more than 6,000 roses in 125 varieties, an attraction that operates in conjunction with the American Rose Society and the All American Rose Selection Committee. An additional 4,000 camellias, azaleas, and other flowering shrubs make this one of the state's most colorful and distinguished gardens. With daylilies, crepe myrtle, asters, and other summer flowers, there is a constant display of beauty. The park facilities include tennis courts, picnic areas, rest rooms, and hiking trails.

Access: From downtown jct of US 601 and 301, go W on John Calhoun Dr. to gardens on R at Riverside Dr.

Edisto Gardens Trails

Length: 1.5 mi (2.4 km); **easy;** USGS Map: Orangeburg; trailhead: parking area.

Debbie Cooper and Richard Galway of the American Rose Society had been telling me about the roses in Edisto Gardens long before they brought me here. It was a late May afternoon when we sauntered through avenue after avenue of color—pink, orange, scarlet, lavender, purple, white, mauve, burgundy—and sweet fragrance. "This is a Tropicana," Debbie said as she gently moved a large bud toward me to smell. "A rose is sweeter in the bud than in full bloom," she said, smiling, and quoting John Lyly. Blue-black pipevine butterflies were visiting rose after rose.

After a walk over the bridges to the lakes and swamp, we skirted the quiet Edisto, "the longest blackwater river in the world." We switched from one path to another, enjoying the tranquil scenery. Cypress, oak, sweet gum, and pine shaded the area. Spanish moss hung in streamers. We rested at the pavilion before crossing the street and returning through camellias and the daylily garden. (The following spring I returned to see the thousands of azaleas and camellias in full bloom.)

Summers Memorial Park

Access: From US 21 (Boulevard St. NE) jct with Carolina St.

(Mental Health Center sign), go 0.3 mi on Carolina St. to Wilson St. and turn L. Go 2 blocks to Park St., on R.

Webster Woods Trail

Length: 0.5 mi (0.8 km); **easy;** USGS Map: Orangeburg; trailhead: street parking.

I walked by a small stream in a park of tall pine, elm, ash, and oak draped with Spanish moss. Holly and dogwoods grew underneath in a generally open area between Park, Webster, and Summers Streets. On Summers Street a memorial park sign read: DONATED IN 1929 TO THE CITY IN MEMORY OF THOMAS RAYSOR SUMMERS, SON OF ABRAM WEST AND CAROLINE MOSS SUMMERS, WHO LOST HIS LIFE IN ACTION IN WWI, IN WATAU, BELGIUM.

Rock Hill (York County)

The City of Rock Hill Parks, Recreation and Tourism Department administers and maintains 27 parks with more than 263 acres. Its program is divided into five divisions: activities (cultural arts, Mayor's Teen Volunteers, neighborhood/community centers, swimming pools, special events, and senior citizens); community services (Cherry Park, youth sports, Confederate Park, Hargett Park, concessions, outdoor athletics); facilities/safety (greenways, maintenance, park planning, parks/playgrounds, risk management); therapeutics (Camp Arc, mentally handicapped, physically handicapped, Special Olympics); and administration (customer service, marketing/promotion, support services, tourism/hospitality).

The city has a population of more than 48,000 and was founded in 1852, taking its name from a nearby rock mound. It is also known for Winthrop University (1886), its textile and other industries, and Glencairn Garden, a 7.6-acre preserve featuring azaleas, dogwoods, wisteria, a goldfish pond, and fountains. Located at 725 Crest Street, Glencairn Garden was started by Dr. David A. Bigger in 1928, and his family deeded it to the city in 1958. Three of the city's parks have trails, which are described below. (The city is planning a citywide greenway system. Contact the facilities supervisor for a progress report about the 1.5-mi multi-use Northside Greenway; the 1.5-mi **Eagle Trail,** which connects to Cherry Park; and the 3-mi **River Park Trail** for walking.)

Information: Rock Hill Recreation and Park Department, P.O. Box 11706, Rock Hill, SC 29731; (803) 329–5260/5621.

Fewell Park

Fewell Park Trail

Length: 0.8 mi (1.3 km); **easy;** USGS Map: Rock Hill; trailhead: parking area at center.

From downtown at US 21 (Cherry Road) jct with SC 274, take SC 274 0.2 mi W to fork with India Hook Road; in the center of the fork is Alexander Road. Take Alexander to corner of Glendale. The day I visited this park, I began the 0.8-mi, 20-stop physical fitness trail in a pine forest from the park center. I enjoyed the forest of cedar, dogwood, oak, wild cherry, elderberry, and pine, but equally enjoyed what I found back at the center. It was one of those occasions when a local social club had left a table of refreshments for "those men running the exercise course." The park also has two lighted tennis courts and a picnic area.

Cherry Park

Cherry Park Trail

Length: 1.5 mi (2.4 km); **easy;** USGS Map: Rock Hill; trailhead: parking area.

From I-77 take Exit 82B to Cherry Road, proceed S for 2 mi and take a L into the park. The park is located on a 68-acre site with five softball and five soccer fields. The central tower has meeting rooms and scorekeepers' news media areas. A multiple-use lighted trail for bicyclists, joggers, and walkers winds around the beautifully land-scaped park. Shaded picnic and playground areas are also provided.

Simpsonville (Greenville County)

Information: Simpsonville Parks and Recreation, P.O. Box 668, Simpsonville, SC 29681; (864) 963–5958.

Simpsonville City Park

Simpsonville Nature Trail
Length: 0.5 mi (0.8 km); **easy;** USGS Map: Williamston NE; trailhead: parking area.

From Main Street and SR 417, Curtis Street, in downtown Simpsonville, turn on Curtis, pass City Hall, and turn L to the Simpsonville City Park. The 15-acre park has a children's playground, a picnic area, softball and baseball fields, lighted tennis courts, a basketball court, and a community center for civic and social events.

On an asphalt trail, I circled the park among oaks, pines, and cedars. The town is named after the "first real settler" in the area, Peter Simpson, and is on US 276, "The Golden Strip," 10 mi SE of downtown Greenville.

Spartanburg (Spartanburg County)

Spartanburg was founded in 1785, and both the city and county were named for the Spartan Regiment of the South Carolina militia, which distinguished itself during the Revolutionary War at the Battle of Cowpens. An industrialized city, two of its major products are textiles and peaches. The latter is emphasized with a picture of a ripe juicy peach on each of the city's street signs. The city is also known for its two outstanding colleges, Wofford (1854) and Converse (1889).

In addition, Spartanburg has set an excellent example of how a city and county can use their resources for a diversity of recreational services to their citizens. A joint park and recreation department has established more than 25 major parks, playgrounds, exhibit areas, and sports complexes. Six community centers serve the city and county, from Landrum near the state line to Pacolet on the SE side of the county.

Although it's not part of a park, there is a trail area near Spartanburg High School. It is the 0.5-mi **River Birch Trail,** constructed in cooperation with the Junior League, School District Seven, and the City of Spartanburg. The trail has a variety of hardwoods, shrubs, and wildflowers on a trail of asphalt and wood chips.

Access to the **River Birch Trail** is from US 29 on Fernwood Drive to Beechwood Street. Turn L and go to Sydnor Drive. The trail is behind the high school.

One of my favorite parks in Spartanburg is Cleveland, located on the N edge of the city, on US 176 and SC 56. Cleveland Park has lighted tennis courts, ball fields, picnic areas, an exercise station, a children's playground, a miniature train ride, and a lake with paddleboats.

But there is another special park in the city, Duncan Park, which has a trail. Duncan Park is described on the next page.

Information: Spartanburg City/County Parks and Rec Dept., 180 Daniel Morgan St., P.O. Box 5666, Spartanburg, SC 29304; (864) 596–3733.

Support Facilities: The closest public campground is Croft State Park, 4.2 mi E on SC 56. Open all year with excellent rec fac and full svc. Contact Superintendent, Croft State Park, Route 4, Box 28-A, Spartanburg, SC 29302; (864) 585–1283. A private campground is KOA, 2 mi N of Exit 69 on I-85, or 1 mi W of Exit 17 on I-26. Open all year with exceptional rec fac and full svc. Contact KOA, Route 7, Box 354D, Spartanburg, SC 29303; (864) 576–0970.

Duncan Park

Duncan Park baseball stadium is the home of the Spartanburg Spinners. It also has other lighted ballfields, tennis courts, a children's playground, a racquetball/handball court and a well-designed hiking/jogging trail near the lake.

Access: Downtown, at the jct of US 221 and SC 56 (S. Church and Henry Streets), take SC 56 on Henry and Union Streets, for 1.3 mi to the park on the R.

Duncan Park Trail

Length: 0.8 mi (1.3 km); **easy;** USGS Map: Spartanburg; trailhead: parking area.

From the parking area I followed the signs and completed the partial loop through a forest of oak, dogwood, poplar, maple, hickory, and scattered pine. Wildflowers grew near the footbridge and at the lakeside.

Sumter (Sumter County)

The city, the county, the fort in Charleston harbor, and the national forest are all named for distinguished Revolutionary War leader and senator Thomas Sumter (1734–1832), the "Gamecock General of the American Revolution."

Founded in 1788, the city has developed into an excellent example of an economically balanced commercial and agricultural area. Economic support from the nearby Shaw Air Force Base has also been a factor.

More than 13 parks and playgrounds are a credit to the city's progressive system of education, culture, and business. One of these parks is the outstanding Swan Lake Gardens.

Swan Lake Gardens

Founded in 1927 and developed by H. C. Bland, this 100-acre park with 45 acres of lakes is known for its tranquillity and beauty and for its millions of Japanese Iris blossoms; there are more here than at any other place in the nation. Facilities include a playground, a picnic area, tennis, and nature trails.

The annual Sumter Iris Festival is held here in late May, with the Fall Fiesta of Arts in late October. The Iris Festival had its beginning in 1940; and, except for a few years when it was not held, it has been an annual and much anticipated event of social, cultural, and educational activities. It is open daily, 8:00 A.M. to sundown, and is free.

Information: Swan Lake Gardens, P.O. Box 1449, Sumter, SC 29151; (803) 773–3371.

Access: In downtown Sumter at the jct of US 15/76/378, follow W. Liberty Street (SC 763) for 2 mi W to the park.

Swan Lake Trails

Length: 1.6 mi combined (2.6 km); **easy;** USGS Map: Sumter E; trailhead: parking area.

We first visited this enchanting park when the azaleas, dogwoods, jessamines, and camellias were in bloom, but when we returned to see the iris festival, it was difficult to describe its unique beauty. We walked around the lake S of Liberty Street, where more than 25 varieties of the huge flowering Kaempferi Iris were growing in every color of the rainbow. There was the gleeful sound of children feeding the ducks and the geese. Swan Lake has six varieties of swans, including the graceful White English and Australian swans. Cypresses were draped with Spanish moss, and lilies added more brilliance.

At 0.4 mi we crossed the dam to loop back to the parking lot at 0.7 mi. From here we crossed Liberty Street and looped around the N section of the lake to Haynsworth Street and back, for a total of 1.6 mi.

Union (Union County)

The town of Union, first known as Unionville, is the county seat of Union County, founded in 1785; both names were from the "Union Church," which served the early Episcopalians, Presbyterians, and Quakers who had immigrated from Virginia and Pennsylvania.

Information: Union County Rec Dept. (Union County Fairgrounds), P.O. Box 783, Union, SC 29379; (864) 429–1670.

Foster Park

FOSTER PARK IS TRULY A BEAUTIFUL SITE. LET'S KEEP IT THAT WAY, reads the sign near a parking area on Park Drive. It appears that this is exactly what the public is doing.

Formerly Veteran's Park, the area has a picnic area and children's playground on the E side of the lake, a fitness trail and handball/tennis court on the W side. Careful landscaping and the planting of trees and shrubs add to the beauty of Foster Park. On my visit to the park, a number of friendly ducks expected some bread crumbs, and an American egret stood watching for minnows.

Access: In Union go to the corner of N. Blvd. and Lakeside Dr. to the parking area.

Foster Park Trail

Length: 0.6 mi (1 km); **easy;** USGS Map: Union W, E; trailhead: parking area at handball/tennis court.

From the handball/tennis court we went R, circling the lake on a wide and well-maintained trail used for walking, jogging, and, in one section, physical-fitness stations. Vegetation along the trail included pines, dogwoods, domestic plants, and cattails at the upper edge of the lake.

Walterboro (Colleton County)

Walterboro is a historic city with a "proud tradition and confident future." It was first named Hickory Valley in 1784, when owners of rice plantations chose the area for summer homes. Named later for two of those original settlers, Paul and Jacob Walters, the town became the county seat in 1817. More than 45 historic buildings provide an outstanding display of architectural charm and beauty. Three buildings are on the National Register of Historic Places—the Colleton County Court House (1822), Old Colleton County Jail (1855), and Walterboro Library Society Building (1820).

Information: Walterboro-Colleton County Rec Center, 210 Recreation Rd., Walterboro, SC 29488; (843) 538–3031.

Support Facilities: Safari Green Acres Campground, jct of I-95 and SC 63 (Exit 53). Open all year, full svc, rec fac. Walterboro, SC 29488; (843) 538–3450.

Walterboro-Colleton Recreation Center

The Walterboro-Colleton Recreation Commission administers the area rec program. Among the parks is the 150-acre Walterboro-Colleton Recreation Center, which has seven baseball fields, a sheltered picnic area, outdoor basketball and volleyball courts, a 17,000-sq-ft community center, lighted tennis courts, and hiking trails.

Access: From downtown Walterboro go N on US 15 for 3.5 mi to SR 459 and turn R. Go 1.4 mi on SR 459 to SR 461 and turn R. Follow SR 461, Recold Rd., for 1 mi and turn R to park entrance.

Colleton Trail

Length: 2.6 mi (4.2 km); **easy;** USGS Map: Walterboro; trailhead: parking lot at community center.

Eric Tang hiked this loop trail with me. We began at the R corner of the parking lot in front of the community center and passed the tennis courts on the R. It appeared that an old physical-fitness course had once been near here. Following the trail markers, we crossed a small stream and reached a crosstrail at 0.6 mi. (To the R it is 0.1 mi to the high school grounds, and to the L it is 0.1 mi to the picnic shelters and gated service road.) We continued straight ahead through a mature forest of poplar, pine, and oak. Ostrich and sensitive ferns, wild ginger, sweet pepperbush, and myrtle were part of the low vegetation. At 1 mi we turned R in a more dense forest, but soon entered a timbered area. Orange milkweed and sumac were prominent. At 1.1 mi we crossed a paved road, entered a dense growth of berries, and came to a stream at 1.3 mi. We followed the trail downstream through a border of smilax and blackberry bushes. At 1.7 mi we recrossed the paved road and followed up another stream on a pleasant contour. We took the R fork at 1.9 mi. As the trail completed the loop, we saw false indigo, bristly locust, and sticky foxglove. After passing through a pine forest and then an oak forest, we returned to the picnic area and to the parking lot at 2.6 mi.

West Columbia and Cayce (Lexington County)

Across the Congaree River from downtown Columbia are West Columbia and Cayce. Two of the parks, Guignard and Granby Gardens, have trails. They are maintained and supervised by the City of Cayce Department of Parks and Recreation.

Information: Parks and Recreation, P.O. Box 2004, Cayce, SC 29171; (803) 796–9020.

Guignard Park

Facilities at Guignard Park include a picnic area, a children's playground, and an asphalt trail. The park was given to Cayce in 1961 by the heirs of John G. Guignard to be maintained as a public park in a state of natural beauty preserving the wildflowers, trees, and shrubs, and to provide a "place of quiet and restfulness." For access cross the Congaree River on SC 215 from Columbia and take the first L on Deliesseline Road.

Guignard Park Trail
Length: 0.3 mi (0.5 km); **easy;** USGS Map: Southwest Columbia; trailhead: parking area.

Follow the paved trail under large loblolly pine, gum, oak, beech, and maple. Landscaping consists of azaleas and ornamental shrubs. Near Axtell Street the trail loops back to the parking area.

Granby Gardens Park

The Granby Gardens Park facilities are a picnic shelter, a children's playground, and a nature trail. Access is at the jct of SC 2 and 12th Street. Turn N over the railroad, and go 0.2 mi to the Cayce Municipal Building driveway on the L. Park on the R.

Granby Gardens Nature Trail
Length: 0.8 mi (1.3 km); **easy;** USGS Map: Southwest Columbia; trailhead: parking area.

I followed the trail sign by a small stream on a wide trail that meandered through the forest of large poplar, loblolly pine, and oak and by the stream area where alder, bay, switchcane, and willow grew. Botanical gardens are being constructed, and a large multipurpose sports court was constructed in 1992.

Winnsboro (Fairfield County)

Winnsboro, chartered in 1785, is the county seat of Fairfield County and is named for Colonel Richard Winn, a distinguished Revolutionary War officer and early town leader. Lord Cornwallis had his headquarters here from October 1780 to January 1781. One outstanding feature in this town of rare architectural style is the oldest running town clock in the nation—since 1833. Among the town's parks is Fortune Springs Park with facilities for swimming, tennis, a playground, and formal gardens.

Information: Winnsboro Parks and Recreation, Congress St., Winnsboro, SC 29180; (803) 635–4041.

Fortune Springs Park

Fortune Springs Trail

Length: 0.3 mi (0.5 km); **easy;** USGS Map: Winnsboro; trailhead: parking area.

From US 321 and SC 200 jct, go 1 block W on SC 200 to Evans Street and turn L. Go 1 block on Evans Street and turn R on High Street, then continue 2 blocks to Park Street.

We parked at the Fairfield County Building and followed the trails, some of which were paved, around the beautiful reflection pool, lake, fountains, pavilion, and waterfalls. Large oaks, gums, willows, river birch, and pines partially shaded the many floral displays of azaleas and other flowering shrubbery. We were there early one morning near the swimming pool and the lake when the Peking and mallard ducks had not been fed. They followed us around until we shared some of our whole-wheat bread.

Chapter V
Private and College Trails

Beneath the pines' heroic crest,
Below the rapids in the glen . . .
Is a still place where waters rest.
                    Paul Hamilton Hayes
                    "Where Waters Rest"

SECTION 1
Private Trails

Asbury Hills United Methodist Camp
(Greenville County)

On a number of older maps, including some USGS maps, there is a little valley as beautiful as Eden called "The Youth Camp." That camp is no longer little or anonymous. It is a 1,800-acre historical preserve owned and maintained by the South Carolina United Methodist Conference. A few years ago it changed its name from Methodist Youth Camp to Asbury Hills, a more appropriate title because Francis Asbury, "the prophet of the long road," visited the area on his route from W North Carolina to Charleston. "We found a new road, lately cut, which brought me in at the head of Little River, at the old fording place, and within hearing of the falls (Raven Cliff Falls) a few miles off of the head of Matthews Creek . . . ," wrote Asbury in his *Journal* in 1803.

Before 1958, the conference had no camp of its own, so it borrowed or rented camping facilities. The dream of a campground to fulfill the programs of the Board of Education came closer to reality in 1962, when the conference purchased 312 acres and subsequently added another 1,688 acres. Today the camp has lodges, cabins, a dining hall, a swimming pool, an infirmary, a library, and other facilities. "This place has offered out-of-doors experiences for thousands of children and youth for 35 years," said C. Russell Davis, who succeeded Wes Voigt as camp director in 1997. The camp welcomes people of all faiths and traditions. Hikers must sign in at the Registration Building and indicate if they plan to camp.

Information: Asbury Hills United Methodist Camp, 150 Asbury Dr., Cleveland, SC 29635; (864) 836–3711.

Access: From the jct of SC 11 and US 276, go N on US 276 for 2 mi to the camp entrance on the L. After 0.7 mi reach the camp office building.

Blue Trail

Length: 0.8 mi (1.3 km); **easy;** USGS Map: Table Rock; trailhead: near base of dam.

From the dining hall I followed the road toward the dam and before the base of the dam turned L at the sign. The trail circled the lake by the canoe dock, crossed the **Asbury Trail** on a ridge, descended to a small cascade, and exited below the dam by a large hemlock. Vegetation along the trail was mountain laurel, false down foxglove, trailing arbutus, fetterbush, oaks, and pines.

Gold Trail

Length: 1 mi (1.6 km); **easy;** USGS Map: Table Rock; trailhead: parking area at dining hall.

From the dining hall near the bridge, I ascended on a slope in an open forest with scattered mountain laurel on a yellow-blazed loop trail, passing patches of trailing arbutus. I descended to Matthews Creek at 0.4 mi and rock-hopped across. I ascended on a steep slope in a mixture of rhododendron, fetterbush, fern, and galax. I turned R on an old road at 0.5 mi, passed the Tree House

Camp, a sheltered assembly platform, and rock-hopped Matthews Creek again. From here I returned to the dining hall at 1 mi.

Asbury Trail

Length: 5.4 mi round-trip (7.6 km); **moderate;** USGS Map: Table Rock; trailhead: E end of dam.

I began this unmarked trail, formerly called **The Loop,** with Ray Matthews and Sammy Gooding. We walked to the E end of the dam and followed the old wagon road on which Francis Asbury rode his horse early in the nineteenth century. "It wouldn't have taken Asbury long to get to Charleston if he had had a road like this all the way," Ray said as we ascended an easy contour. After 1 mi we crossed a stream, turned R, and had glimpses of Caesars Head through the tops of the trees. Yellow root and crested dwarf iris bordered the road. At 1.7 mi we reached a campsite on the R and a jct with an old road on the L. (The road on the L follows Matthews Creek for 1.3 mi up to Raven Cliff Falls area. It connects with the Mountain Bridge network of trails and the **Foothills Trail.** See Caesars Head State Park.) We continued ahead, rock-hopping across the cascading Matthews Creek. After passing a campsite on the L we ascended to a more recently used road. Here we turned R in our return to Asbury Hills. Numerous small streams trickled, bubbled, or splashed across the road each time we descended from the hillside. At one stream we saw bush honeysuckle (*Diervilla sessilifolia*), a yellow flowering shrub found only in high elevations of Greenville and Oconee Counties in South Carolina.

Erosion caused by trespassing four-wheel-drive vehicles at 3.4 mi was so severe that the creators of the ravines could no longer trespass. We continued to descend and reached US 276 at 4.3 mi. We entered a gate on the R and descended for 0.7 mi by the camp cabins to the jct with the camp entrance road. After turning R we hiked the paved road for another 0.4 mi to complete our loop of 5.4 mi.

Bethelwoods (York County)

Between York and Rock Hill, there is a retreat with 150 acres of clean woodland and a lake with wood ducks. It is Bethelwoods, where "childhood is given back to children, family life is returned to the family, and the pleasurable art of conversation is rediscovered" in rustic cabins, at pioneer wagon camps, in fields and meadows, in a swimming pool, in canoes, and on trails. Bethelwoods is a Christian Education Center and Joint Camping Venture of Charleston-Atlantic and Providence Presbyteries; it was formerly Piedmont Springs Bethel Presbytery, founded in 1936. It has programs for all ages and is open all year. Visitors are welcome but should request permission at the office to hike the trails. In addition to the trails described below, another is being developed around the perimeter of the camp.

Information: Bethelwoods, 922 West Mount Gallant Rd., York, SC 29745; (803) 366–3722.

Access: From the jct of SC 161 and SR 47 (6 mi E of downtown York and 9.5 mi W from I-77), turn on SR 47 and go 1.5 mi to SR 195. Turn L, and the camp entrance is on the L.

Bethelwoods Nature Trail and Wagon Camp Trail

Length: 1.6 mi round-trip, combined (2.6 km); **easy;** USGS Map: Rock Hill; trailhead: office parking area.

To hike the **Nature Trail,** I walked from the office across the dam and entered a young forest of Virginia pine, red and white oaks, dogwood, sweet gum, and poplar. The trail was wide and clean. At 0.2 mi there was a treehouse on the L. After entering a more mature forest, I curved L and reached the lake at 0.5 mi. Following the lakeshore I passed through wildflowers including milkweed, monkey flower, ironweed, lyre-leaf sage, everlasting, Solomon's seal, Maryland aster, and sericea.

Before beginning the next loop, I talked to Rebecca White, an administrative secretary who had been at the camp for more than 10 years. "I believe I love it here because of the program for all ages and the atmosphere," she said. From the office I followed the **Wagon Camp Trail** by the swimming pool to the Wagon Camp—a camp where campers sleep four to a wagon with built-in bunks and canvas covers—at 0.3 mi. I continued on a camp road to a field with scattered hickories and apple trees. At 0.5 mi I turned L on the wagon road by a large pen oak. At the wagon camp I turned R and backtracked to the office parking area at 0.8 mi.

Camp Thunderbird (York County)

Founded in 1936, Camp Thunderbird is one of the best summer camps in the state for boys and girls ages seven to 16. It features a fleet of sailboats, motorboats, and canoes; an excellent comprehensive program in aquatic sports, including whitewater; hiking, camping, and backpacking; golf; gymnastics; rappelling and rock climbing; tennis; equestrian sports; field sports; and nature study. Its objectives are to develop, through quality leadership, interpersonal relationships, spiritual growth, self-reliance, and self-confidence. The Environmental Education Center offers programs for school groups from September through May. The camp is owned and operated by the Young Men's Christian Association of Charlotte and Mecklenburg County (North Carolina). Visitors are welcome to hike the **nature trail,** but ask for permission at the camp office.

Information: Camp Thunderbird, Route 7, Box 50, Clover, SC 29710; (803) 831–2121.

Access: On SC 49 0.3 mi W of the Buster Boyd Bridge at Lake Wylie, turn off SC 49 at the River Hill Plantation to the camp entrance on the L.

Camp Thunderbird Nature Trail
Length: 1.2 mi (1.9 km); **easy;** USGS Map: Lake Wylie; trailhead: rear of the Environmental Education Center.

Ask the office staff for a trail guide. This guide covers 12 stations and twice that many piedmont trees, as well as explaining the rock formations, soil layers, forest succession, and ecology of the area. It is a walking, living, outdoor classroom for students of any age.

Francis Beidler Forest in Four Holes Swamp (Dorchester County)

The National Audubon Society, owner of the nation's oldest private sanctuary system, manages the more than 10,000-acre Francis Beidler Forest, one of the organization's 80 wildlife preserves in the United States. The forest is named in honor of the lumberman-conservationist who preserved the area from logging in the late nineteenth century. His decision allows the public to see the largest remaining stands of bald cypress and tupelo gum in the world. In a cathedral setting these 1,000-year-old giants and other trees such as water ash, water elm, water hickory, and water locust tower over a classic blackwater swamp. The longest boardwalk trail in the state, it is designed to accommodate the physically handicapped. It has a gift shop. A Visitor-Interpretive Center with all telephone and power lines underground welcomes the visitor from the individually designated parking spaces. No camping or pets are allowed. (A small fee is charged for a visit; the sanctuary is closed on Mondays.)

Information: Francis Beidler Forest, 336 Sanctuary Rd., Harleyville, SC 29448; (843) 462–2150.

Access: The forest is 40 miles NW of Charleston off I-26. Take Exit 187 to SC 27 and to US 78 following the signs. From I-95 jct with I-26, turn off I-26 at Exit 177 to Harleyville and follow the signs SE on US 178 to SR 28.

Four Holes Swamp Trail

Length: 1.6 mi (2.6 km); **easy;** USGS Map: Harleyville; trailhead: Visitor Center.

From the Visitor Center I followed the signs, and on the boardwalk I sensed that this hike would be different from any I had ever experienced. I felt suspended in a world changed only by the seasons—in the summer and fall, the swamp has low water or spaces with none at all, and in the winter and spring the water level is full. This fluctuation allows observation of more than 120 species of birds and 50 species of mammals and reptiles.

Halfway along the boardwalk were a rain shelter and a spur section that led to Lake Goodson for a view of a more open area of water. Water rippled around the shadowy base of the cypress knees, making them look like brown stones in a lake. The coiled supplejack hung through the Spanish moss, ominous, endless. I could easily spend a day on this trail, resting and observing the tranquil splendor of an ecosystem that is fast becoming extinct. Mike Dawson, a sanctuary naturalist transplanted from New York, said that the "forest grows on you; each walk is a new classroom." Emerson would likely agree. In one of his lectures he stated: "I would study, I would know, I would admire forever."

I have hiked the winding boardwalk in all seasons. On one of my last trips, when the water was low I saw a large cottonmouth moccasin with his broad head resting on a small branch in the water, waiting for an unfortunate lizard or frog. Growing nearby were flowering dragon head and lavender *justicia*.

Harbison Recreation Center (Richland and Lexington Counties)

Harbison has the state's longest cement trail, a lighted trail that weaves among the pines and rings with the laughter of children every day. Harbison is a model 2,000-acre development of beautiful residential areas, housing for senior citizens, shopping, offices, parks, greenways, schools, and recreation. The developers planned this community so that it would offer a parklike atmosphere, housing to suit people of all ages, lakes for boating, and trails for bicycling, jogging, and hiking—a community with energy and vision.

At the community recreation center, designed for year-round

fun and relaxation, is an indoor swimming pool, a gymnasium, racquet/handball courts, a weight room/exercise center, saunas, and facilities for art exhibits, recitals, and poetry readings. Although the development is private, the trails are open to the public without charge. Use of recreation center facilities are restricted to Harbison residents and to those with individual memberships.

Information: Harbison Community Association, 106 Hillpine Rd., Columbia, SC 29212; (803) 781–2281.

Support Facilities: (See Sesquicentennial State Park.)

Access: On US 176 NW of Columbia (4.3 mi from I-20 jct), turn at the entrance L (across from the Harbison State Forest). Follow Harbison Blvd. to Hillpine Rd., turn R, and turn L to the Recreation Center. From I-26 (exit 101) take US 176 SE 1.7 mi to enter on the R.

Harbison Trails

Length: 16 mi round-trip, combined (25.6 km); **easy;** USGS Map: Columbia N; trailhead: community recreation center.

From the community rec center, I followed the trail E on a main line of 8-ft-wide concrete (connector trails are 5 ft wide) to Creekside Place, curved R, and later entered a tunnel under Piney Woods Road. Other tunnels followed at Hillpine Road and Harbison Boulevard. I followed a labyrinth of routes, all well marked, to Lakeside, circled the lake, and returned to the community center. The center's manager said that the trail system has more than 3,100 cubic yards of cement and that it is part of a greenway system with additional miles that connects it to the second lake, across I-26.

Wild vegetation on the trail includes pine, oak, maple, hickory, sourwood, dogwood, ash, elm, and sumac. On one of my visits I saw ferns, false indigo, cattails, woodland sunflowers, and meadow pink near Lakeside. On a peninsula near a children's playground, Mark Austin and Jamie Scheuch were playing in the sand. We talked about the trails. They said what they liked best is that "the trails are lighted and we can walk after dark."

Hilton Head Island (Beaufort County)

Hilton Head Island contains some of the world's finest resorts, some of which have parklike natural areas or preserves. A few have private trails that may be open to the public, depending upon the stages of development. In the mid-1950s the Byrnes Bridge connected the island to the mainland, resulting in a rapid growth of resort paradises with year-round facilities.

The island has a history of at least 4,000 years of human habitation, beginning with the American Indians who lived on the island. From 1526, when it was sighted by the Spanish, to the early 1700s, Spanish, French, and English pirates fought for its control. In 1663 English captain William Hilton, for whom the island is named, sailed the *Adventure* into Port Royal Sound and described the area as the "best and frutefullest ile ever was seen."

In the early eighteenth century, English settlers established plantations and used West African "Gullah" slaves to raise rice, indigo, and Sea Island cotton.

In 1941 Josephine Pinchney wrote *Hilton Head*, a historical novel based on the life and times of Henry Woodward (c. 1646–1686), a surgeon befriended by the Indians in the Port Royal area. An early South Carolina hero, he has been called the "first English settler."

With the outbreak of the Civil War, approximately 25,000 Union troops and naval personnel occupied the island as a base for blockading Southern coastal cities, chiefly Charleston and Savannah. This occupation is covered in detail in Robert Carse's *Department of the South: Hilton Head Island in the Civil War*. After the war the island was left to the freed slaves, with the exception of a few large holdings of property retained by Northern investors as hunting areas. The former slaves developed their own culture—farming, fishing, education, religion, and dialect.

Nearly 6,000 Gullah dialect words have been identified among the Gullah of this island and other sea islands in South Carolina and Georgia. Some of them have been incorporated into standard

English usage: *goober* for peanuts, *juke* as in jukebox, and *gumbo* for okra. Their rapid speech did not carry a drawl. A folk art group, Bessie Jones and the Sea Island Singers, has been touring America for a number of years to illustrate the island heritage. (Between Beaufort and Hunting Island on US 21 is Penn Center, a museum of the heritage of the black people of the sea islands.)

Information: Chamber of Commerce, P.O. Box 5647, Hilton Head Island, SC 29928; (843) 785–3673.

Access: Hilton Head Island is 40 mi NE from Savannah and 95 miles SW from Charleston. From the jct of SC 170 and US 278, follow US 278.

Support Facilities: Outdoor resorts on Hilton Head Island may be restricted to motor homes or full hook-up units. The nearest state-park campground is Hunting Island State Park (see Chapter III).{x-ref} A commercial campground is KOA-Point South, from Exit 33 on I-95 and US 17, on US 17 behind Best Western Motel. Address: Route 1, Yemassee, SC 29945; (843) 726–5733/5728. Full svc, rec fac, including short hiking trails. Open all year.

Hitchcock Woods (Aiken County)

A 2,000-acre preserve, Hitchcock Woods has an extraordinary network of dirt roads for hikers, joggers, and equestrians. It is one of the last virgin forests in the area. The tract was originally owned by William C. Whitney and Thomas Hitchcock, who used it as a hunting preserve. After Whitney's death, Hitchcock purchased the estate and later he and his daughter, Helen Clark, gave it to the Hitchcock Foundation in 1939 to "never be sold to a private individual or firm."

Maintenance of the trails, bridges, and signs and management and protection of the natural resources in Hitchcock Woods are all directed by the trustees of the Hitchcock Foundation, a tax-exempt, nonprofit organization. The trustees request that users of the forest not litter, smoke, fish, hunt, build fires, or use motorized vehicles. (For more information contact the Hitchcock Foundation, P.O. Box 1702, Aiken, SC 29802.)

Information: Aiken Chamber of Commerce, 400 Laurens St. NW, Aiken, SC 29801; (803) 641–1111.

Access: From downtown Aiken at the jct of Richland Ave., US 78, SC 302, and Laurens St., take Laurens S for 6 blocks to S. Boundary Ave. and turn R. Park in the parking area at the gated road.

Hitchcock Woods Trails

Length: 20 mi (32 km); **easy** to **moderate;** USGS Map: Aiken; trailhead: end of South Boundary Street.

Each time I hike sections of this magnificent forest, I notice something new—a larger loblolly, or mulberry, or sweet gum or wildflower, or another cliff. Because the trails on the roads crisscross so frequently, and because spur trails require some backtracking, it was impossible to measure this network or describe how to hike it all. No camping is allowed, so I carried a day pack and carefully noted which direction I took at each intersection. In addition to all the roads, there are at least another 10 mi of dragline.

A linear gauge of distance from the trailhead to the memorial gate is 0.4 mi. Here is a sign that reads: THIS ENTRANCE IS CREATED IN MEMORY OF FRANCIS R. HITCHCOCK BY HIS FRIENDS, 1859–1926. From here it is 0.4 mi to the old Aiken Horse Show ring (a grassy field), but 0.6 mi if you ascend R on the road. From the ring it is another 1 mi to Barton's Lake and another 1.3 mi to Dibble Road.

Magnolia Plantation and Its Gardens (Charleston County)

All the superlatives you have heard or read about this historic garden with the seven bridges are true. John Galsworthy, distinguished author and garden specialist, has said it is the "most beautiful in the world . . . beyond anything I have ever seen." "Acres upon acres of rapturous beauty," according to *Readers Digest;* and "Artists and poets have labored in vain to convey their impressions of the loveliness," *National Geographic* has written. Internationally known as America's oldest major garden (c. 1685), this treasure house of beauty by the Ashley River is listed in the National Register of Historic Places. It is the 300-year-old ancestral home of the Drayton family, a family whose influence on colonial and early United States history is well documented.

The plantation was named "Magnolia" by Stephen Fox, the first owner, whose daughter Ann married Thomas Drayton, Jr., in the late seventeenth century. The gardens are now considered to be America's oldest man-made attraction. Originally a formal English garden designed by Thomas Drayton, Jr., it had expanded to ten acres by 1716. In 1825 John Grimke Drayton inherited the plantation and began to transform the gardens into a more informal and natural design. Since 1975 it has been owned by John Drayton Hastie (the ninth generation), who continues to develop and maintain its historic beauty through a nonprofit charitable foundation.

Open to the public since 1870, this garden of all seasons has more than 250 varieties of azaleas and 900 varieties of camellias. With these and all the outstanding displays of iris, tulips, jonquils, quince, hyacinths, and wisteria, it is obvious why some garden specialists say that springtime is its best season. Others say it is summer, with lilies, caladiums, canna, alliums, amaryllis, raphealepsis, oleander, pomegranate, hydrangeas, phlox, dahlias, roses, and mimosa. Summer blends into fall with roses, abelia, bougainvillea, hibiscus, cassia, lilies, and chrysanthemums. Horticulturists say that there are several million plants here and that something is blooming every month.

The 500 acres contain more than the original garden area. There is a canoe and hiking trail through the waterfowl refuge; an eighteenth-century herb garden; the plantation house filled with educational displays of plantation life; a biblical garden; an antebellum cabin; a rice barge; a picnic area; a gift shop; a petting zoo; a seventeenth-century horticultural maze made of more than 500 camellias; a topiary garden; the Audubon Swamp Garden; and the Carolina Woods Walk, which opened in 1988. The peak of azaleas is March 15 through April 30, and for camellias the peak is November 15 to March. The Nature Train tram accommodates those who are unable to stroll the plantation's nature trails. There are no camping facilities. The gardens are open daily from 8:00 A.M. to dark, and there is an admission charge.

Information: Magnolia Plantation and Its Gardens, Rt. 4, Hwy. 61, Charleston, SC 29414; (843) 571–1266; (800) 367–3517.

Access: On SC 61, Ashley River Rd., go 6.5 mi NW from jct of SC 61 and SC 7 in Charleston.

Support Facilities: One of the nearest campgrounds is Oak Plantation, a semiwooded campground on US 17, approximately 9 mi SW from the I-26 and US 17 jct. Full svc, rec fac. Open all year. Address: Rt. 2, Box 559, John's Island, SC 29455; (843) 766–5936.

Magnolia Gardens Trails

Length: 1.7 mi round-trip, combined (2.7 km); **easy;** USGS Maps: Ladson, John's Island; trailhead: parking area.

Although I had walked these combinations of courtly footpaths a number of times before, I set aside a day in June to walk and to measure them all and to hike the **Wildlife Trail.**

Walking among live oaks and peacocks, Eric Tang and I began the hike into the gardens in front of the main house at the sign. We followed the 30 interpretive points. The first stop was the biblical garden of 50 species. At 0.4 mi we reached the jct with the **Wildlife Trail** on the R. Then on the L was the historic site where Adam Bennett, chief slave to the Reverend John G. Drayton, was nearly hanged by General Sherman's pillagers in their efforts to force Bennett to reveal where the valuables of the plantation were buried. (It was Bennett who later hiked the 250 mi to Flat Rock, North Carolina, to inform Drayton that though the house had been burned to the ground, the "black roses," as Drayton af-

fectionately called his slaves, had not left and were continuing to take care of the plantation and gardens.)

At 0.5 mi we came to the Drayton family underground burial vault, which had been restored from the vandalism of General Sherman's troops. We crossed two arched bridges and reached the wildlife-observation tower, dedicated to George H. Burbage, at 0.7 mi. We returned to the main garden area and crossed another arched bridge at signpost #16. Another arched bridge followed, and a gazebo was on the R at 1.1 mi. The fragrance of roses came at 1.3 mi, shortly before we crossed another beautiful bridge. At the nucleus of the gardens, there were large camellia japonicas and decorative hedges of azaleas at signpost #20. After a few spur trails across the lawn, we reached signpost #24 at 1.7 mi.

Magnolia Wildlife Trail

Length: 3.4 mi (5.4 km); **easy;** USGS Maps: Ladson, John's Island; trailhead: parking area.

From the parking area we went back through the main gardens to the **Wildlife Trail** entrance by the river. We followed the sign along the top of a dike and saw wax myrtle, cedar, and small oak on each side. A boreal breeze came from across the marsh where we heard and saw egrets, herons, ibis, rails, and marsh wrens— only a few of the 200 species of birds found in the preserve. Jets, like huge birds from the marsh, lifted off from the International Airport nearby. A number of turtles had come up on the open trail, dug holes, and were laying eggs. One turtle had finished and was covering her nest to let the sun provide incubation. At 1.2 mi we passed a lake drainpipe and the jct of a trail (0.4 mi) on the L leading to the observation tower. At 1.6 mi we turned R on a service road, and at 2 mi reached the Indian Mound, the largest prehistoric Indian burial mound on the East Coast. (Its artifacts are now in the Smithsonian Institution.) We entered a pine and oak forest and passed a nursery where attendants were preparing new plantings. At 2.4 mi we crossed the entrance paved road, entered another nursery, and turned sharply L at 2.6 mi. At 2.7 mi we passed

the graves of Magnolia superintendent Adam Bennett; his wife
Hannah; and their two sons, John and Ezekiel. (After Adam's death
in 1910, his sons continued as superintendents until the 1940s.)
We passed over a dike between lakes, reached a paved road at 3 mi,
and turned R onto the road. We hiked back to the parking area at
3.4 mi. (A shorter route is to take the spur trail at 1.2 mi on the
Wildlife Trail, go 0.4 mi to the observation tower, and return
through the main gardens for a total of 2.3 mi.)

Middleton Place (Dorchester County)

We have J. J. Pringle Smith, a descendant of Henry Middleton, to
thank for Middleton Place. A National Historic Landmark and
America's oldest landscaped gardens, this majestic 110-acre rice
plantation by the Ashley River was restored by Smith and his wife,
Heningham, in the early 1900s. Its original beauty and elegance,
its "golden age," abruptly ended during the Civil War, when maintenance vanished and General Sherman's troops burned the main
plantation house in 1865. Only the S wing could be restored; it
served as a family residence until it was opened to the public.

The plantation's history begins with Henry Middleton in 1741.
He designed the magnificent terraces, *allées,* and ornamental lakes
to reflect the graceful designs of earlier French and English formal
gardens.

From 1741 to 1865 the plantation was the family seat of four
successive generations of Middletons—Henry, a president of the
First Continental Congress; Arthur, a signer of the Declaration of
Independence; the second Henry, governor of South Carolina and
U.S. Minister to Russia; and Williams, a signer of the Ordinance of
Secession in 1860.

The gardens and stableyards are open every day all year from
9:00 A.M. to 5:00 P.M.; the Middleton Place house is open from
10:00 A.M. to 4:30 P.M., but closed on Monday mornings. Admission is charged, and group rates are available by reservation. There

is a picnic area, but camping on the property is not permitted. Middleton Place Restaurant serves lunch daily, 9:00 A.M. to 3:00 P.M., to visitors in the garden. Dinner is available on Friday and Saturday from 6:00 to 9:00 P.M., and no gate admission is charged for those with dinner reservations. (Private parties and banquets can be arranged for groups.) Among the annual events are Camellia Walks (early February); Starlight Pops (May); Spoleto Festival Finale (June); Plantation Days (every Saturday in November); and Family Yuletide (December).

Information: Middleton Place, Ashley River Rd., Charleston, SC 29414; (843) 556–6020.

Access: From downtown Charleston go 14 mi NW on SC 61 to entrance on R, or from jct of SC 61 and SC 165 at Cooks Cross Rds. (S of Summerville), go 4.3 mi on SC 61 to entrance on L.

Middleton Place Garden Walk

Length: 1.8 mi (2.9 km); **easy;** USGS Map: Stallsville; trailhead: parking area.

From the parking area my wife and I followed the signs to the R of a reflection pool and along a border of ornamental shrubs to the ruins of the 1741 house and to the restored 1755 S wing. From here we walked to the spring house and then to the edge of the main parterres, where the original camellias given to the Middletons by André Michaux were planted. They were the first camellias planted in an American garden. The view of the terraces and the butterfly lakes is impressive from here. After we passed Arthur Middleton's tomb, we walked through a camellia *allée* and more formal gardens, passed huge crepe myrtles, and reached Cypress Lake. To our L was a path into the forest. Curving R, around a pool with azaleas, kalmia, palmettos, Spanish moss, and lilies, we admired the "wood nymph," a graceful marble statue that was buried for security during the Civil War.

Although we had heard of the 1,000-year-old Middleton Oak, it was not until we saw it that we understood its regal significance. We were told by a garden attendant that it was used "as an Indian

'Trail Tree,' a type of landmark or distance marker on the way to 'Whitepoint' or the Charleston peninsula."

From the sundial gardens we walked along the flooded rice fields to the butterfly lakes and the edge of the Ashley River. After turning R, through the azalea hillside, we crossed a bridge over an old rice millpond to visit the stableyards, an outdoor living museum with an active display of heritage crafts. At 1.8 mi we returned to the parking area.

Westvaco (Colleton County)

Westvaco Corporation has forest-management operations in South Carolina, Virginia, West Virginia, Tennessee, and Kentucky. Many of these lands are available for hunting, fishing, nature study, and other recreational and educational activities. The company has designated appropriate sites on its lands for biological study and protection of wildlife. One of its public use areas is the **Edisto Nature Trail** at Jacksonboro, described below.

A second trail, located at the jct of SR 66 and US 17A, S of Hendersonville, is designed for educational and environmental groups in cooperation with the South Carolina Department of Education and South Carolina Education Television. Emphasis is on the diversity of wildlife, fisheries, and wetland habitats. All visitors are accompanied on the trail by a forester or other resource professional, and advance reservations must be made through the Westvaco Walterboro office (843–538–8353).

Information: Westvaco Forest Resources Division, Southern Region, P.O. Box 1950, Summerville, SC 29484; (843) 871–5000.

Edisto Nature Trail

Length: 1 mi (1.6 km); **easy;** USGS Map: Jacksonboro; trailhead: parking area.

On US 17N in Jacksonboro at the trail parking area, we examined the trail design for information and then hiked counterclockwise by 51 numbered interpretive markers. (There is also a shortcut if you want to hike only half the distance.) Some of the vascular plants were wax myrtle, black cherry, black and sweet gums, devil's walking stick, Alabama supplejack, hackberry, switchcane, catalpa, yaupon, water hickory, sugarberry, and oak. At 0.4 mi we crossed two boardwalks over marsh near an old phosphate mine. At 0.5 mi we passed an old barge canal that once went to the Edisto River and, at 0.6 mi, an old railroad tram used at the former phosphate factory. After hiking through areas that once were rice fields, we returned to the parking area.

Champion International Corporation

Another paper company, the Champion International Corporation, has nearly 200,000 acres in South Carolina Wildlife Management lands "available for all reasonable public use." (See Wildlife Management Areas in Chapter III.) With nine regions in the nation, the company owns and manages forests throughout the South, the Lake States, the Rocky Mountains, and on the West Coast, as well as in Canada and Brazil. Its primary management objective on this and all tracts of fee lands is commercial timber production, but the corporation is also involved in numerous university research programs.

Although camping is not allowed, hikers will find many old logging roads suitable for nature study. On one nature study hike in the central part of the state, I found an extremely fragrant white wild azalea, a species that Doug Rayne, botanist of the South Carolina Heritage Program, thinks is *Rhododendron viscosum.* Growing near it by a stream was a climbing hydrangea, *Decumaria barbara,* an aerial rooted vine that is also extremely fragrant.

Information: Contact Champion International Corp., 37 Villa Rd., B-140, Suite 402, Greenville, SC 29615; (864) 271–8404.

Peachtree Rock Preserve (Lexington County)

Organized in 1951, the Nature Conservancy is an international nonprofit organization committed to protecting natural diversity. It maintains a system of more than 900 natural sanctuaries in the United States and has more than 500,000 members. Among those natural sanctuaries is the Peachtree Rock Preserve, a 306-acre natural area purchased by the South Carolina Nature Conservancy in 1980.

A concentration of more than 350 species of plants and more than 50 species of birds makes the preserve an extraordinary classroom for nature study, and it is only 16 mi from Columbia, the state capital. Other distinctive features in the preserve are the sandhills and sandstone outcrops.

The preserve contains typical pine and scrub oak sandhills, with stands of mature longleaf pine. There are also hardwood coves with meandering streams. With these abound smaller plant communities, such as 10 acres of evergreen shrub bogs and 15 acres of seepage slopes. In addition, the rock formations have numerous cryptogamic flora. Of the nine species of reptiles, only the Carolina pigmy rattlesnake is poisonous. During one of my early summer visits, I saw a flicker, downy woodpecker, Carolina wren, Carolina chickadee, vireo, towhee, and of course a noisy mockingbird—all in one location.

Information: South Carolina Nature Conservancy, P.O. Box 5475, Columbia, SC 29250; (803) 254–9049.

Access: From Columbia take SC 302/215 SW past the Metropolitan Airport to jct with SC 6 in Edmund. Follow SC 302 and SC 6 to a fork. Take SC 6 0.7 mi to second paved road on L, Bethel Church Rd. After 0.2 mi turn R at sign on dirt road and go 0.1 mi to parking area on L. (If from I-20, take SC 6, Exit 55, for 9.3 mi to Bethel Church Rd.)

Peachtree Rock Trail

Length: 3.6 mi combined (5.8 km); **moderate;** USGS Map: Pelion E; trailhead: parking area.

I followed the trail sign through young loblolly pines, turkey oak, bracken, and sparkleberry bushes until the trail divided at 0.1 mi. To the L was a delicate 15-ft waterfall. To the R was Peachtree Rock, a large sandstone rock balancing like a top, with mountain laurel scattered among the trees. The rock has marine fossils and intertidal deposits, evidence of its origin nearly 50 million years ago. Hard oxidized red sandstone, mottled red-yellow clay with a mixture of quartz pebbles, shell hash, kaolin sands, and silica gave a history of its creation. Indicative of an ancient maritime environment are the tubelike burrows of an aquatic animal called *Calianassa major.*

I chose to first follow the trails to the R of Peachtree Rock. On these I crossed small streams flowing (sometimes underground) to Hunt Creek. Titi, switchcane, and sensitive fern were prominent. On a more open area I saw sticky foxglove, a number of *vaccinium,* St. John's wort, and sandwort. Although the *Manual of the Vascular Flora of the Carolinas* does not list it in Lexington County, I am almost sure I saw *Silene caroliniana* along the trail. A spur trail led to an area of galax and woody goldenrod.

After 1 mi I hiked R at the fork of two old roads near a sawdust pile. At 1.6 mi I backtracked and turned R, up an incline to see an enormous white sand dune at 1.8 mi. Among the sparse vegetation were lichens such as cushion moss and spikemoss. Bits of red ferruginous rocks appeared more red than usual from the heavy dew. At 2 mi I faced a large, colorful rock formation. Tan pebbles, pin-purple kaolin, shining mica, and quartz grains shadowed, reflected, merged to remind me of a Boccioni painting and an observation of Alexander Pope in his *Essay on Man:* "All Nature is but art."

I ascended through a ground cover of evergreen sand myrtle, titi, and sweet pepperbush. A large cirque was to my L. At 2.4 mi I reached an old road, turned L, and passed the cemetery of the Bethel Methodist Church on the R. From here I descended to remnants of an old whiskey still and reached the waterfalls at 3.1 mi. After examining a number of spur trails, I returned to the parking area for a total of 3.6 mi. (This route can also be reversed to follow the conservancy's trail guide.)

Riverbanks Zoological Park and Botanical Garden (Lexington County)

Riverbanks Zoo opened in April 1974 and has since received international recognition and awards for its excellence in design, animal collections, and conservation programs. Some of its outstanding features include the state-of-the art Aquarium Reptile Complex and "Riverbanks Farm," showcasing common domestic animals. Riverbanks's animal exhibition philosophy arises from the zoo's commitment to conservation efforts. In well-maintained natural-habitat exhibits, groups of healthy animals can express themselves in appropriate and characteristic behaviors. Riverbanks has met the growing responsibility to propagate endangered animals by establishing breeding programs for 26 endangered species. On exhibit are more than 2,200 individual animals representing 50 mammal species, 120 bird species, 98 reptile and amphibian species, and 200 fish species.

In 1994 Riverbanks opened a new botanical garden, 70 acres of natural and formal botanical exhibits on the zoo's Lexington County property, across the Saluda River. Linked to the zoo by a small vehicular and pedestrian bridge, the site features theme gardens, walking trails, water features, and a visitor center with a gift shop and restaurant.

The Education Department offers a wide variety of programs for school groups, families, scout groups, and adults. These include the popular overnight Zoo Camp for students in grades 4 through 12. The camp offers the opportunity to study behind-the-scenes zoo husbandry and maintenance. These programs must be reserved in advance by calling (803) 256–4773.

Riverbanks, located off I-126 at the Greystone Boulevard exit, is open 9 A.M. to 4 P.M. daily except Thanksgiving and Christmas days.

Information: Riverbanks Zoological Park and Botanical Garden, P.O. Box 1060 (500 Wildlife Pkwy.), Columbia, SC 29202; (803) 779–8730 or 779–8717.

Stumphouse Tunnel Park (Oconee County)

During the 1830s commercial interests between the Midwest and the seaport at Charleston led to plans for a connecting railroad. South Carolina's John C. Calhoun was on the original surveying team, and it was his support that kept the idea alive after the first abandonment of plans. Two years after his death, the state legislature chartered the Blue Ridge Railroad Company and endorsed bonds for more than $1,250,000 for stockholders to raise contractual funds of $17,000,400. Doubt about the wisdom of a tunnel through Stumphouse Mountain led to a delay in plans until the company had assurance from H. B. Latrobe, an engineer specialist of the Baltimore & Ohio Railroad, that it was the best route. Construction began in January 1855.

The tracks would start in Belton, pass through Anderson, Pendleton, and Walhalla. From there they would gradually ascend around the SE slopes of Turnip Top Mountain and tunnel through Saddle Mountain, Middle Tunnel Ridge, and Stumphouse Mountain. Three other states, Georgia, North Carolina, and Tennessee, would have companies build the railroad to its W terminus in Knoxville. A total of 13 tunnels were planned, for a combined 13,820 ft; and the largest—5,863 ft—would be through Stumphouse Mountain.

The contractor for the Stumphouse tunnel was George Collyer, whose company began work in May 1856. To speed up the project, contractors had teams of workers at both ends of the tunnel. The laborers were mainly immigrants who worked 12 hours a day, six days a week, with only simple tools: sledgehammers, chisels, hand drills, and black powder for blasting. At the peak of construction, a community of about 1,500 men, women, and children lived in a village called Tunnel Hill. But three years and 4,363 ft into the tunnel, the contractor ran out of money, and the state refused to grant additional funds because of its pending secession from the United States. Tunnel Hill no longer had a purpose, and it died with the dream of the Blue Ridge Railroad.

Ownership of the area over the years has been a mixture of government and private owners. Today the park is owned by the Pendleton District Historical, Recreational, and Tourism Commission, a government agency, but the Blue Ridge Railroad Historical Trail is on private property. It is open (free) during daylight hours for picnicking, visiting the Isaqueena Falls and the entrance area to the sealed tunnel, and hiking.

Information: Pendleton District Historical, Recreational, and Tourism Commission, 125 East Queen St., P.O. Box 565, Pendleton, SC 29670; (864) 646–3782.

Access: From SC 28 turn on SR 226 (0.3 mi SE of Andrew Pickens Ranger District hq and 6 mi NW of Walhalla), and go 0.4 mi to parking area.

Isaqueena Falls Trail

Length: 0.2 mi round-trip (0.3 km); **moderate;** USGS Map: Walhalla; trailhead: top of falls area.

From the picnic area near the top of the falls, we followed the footbridge across the stream and descended on switchbacks on an exceptionally steep trail to the base of the 220-ft falls. We returned by the same route. The legend about the falls concerns a Cherokee maiden, Cateechee, who was called Isaqueena (also spelled Issaqueena) in Choctaw. Prior to the outbreak of the Cherokee War, Cateechee (meaning "Deer Head") had fallen in love with an English trader, Allan Francis. She overheard plans that the Cherokee were going to attack and massacre the inhabitants at Ninety Six. During the night she rode the distance to warn them. The village was saved, and Isaqueena married Francis. Later she was captured by the Cherokee, and in her escape she jumped off the top of the falls, landed on a ledge, and hid from her pursuers, who thought she was dead. Francis rescued her (probably having seen it happen), they canoed down Cane Creek, and lived happily ever after. (See Ninety Six National Historic Site in Chapter II.) For information on the Cateechee auto-trail, contact the DAR at 2003 Laurel Dr., Anderson, SC 29621.)

Blue Ridge Railroad Historical Trail

Length: 6.8 mi (10.9 km); **moderate** to **strenuous;** USGS Map: Walhalla; trailhead: sealed Stumphouse Mountain tunnel.

In 1983 we took our heavy-duty flashlights and walked 1,640 ft to the dead-end of the 25-ft-high and 17-ft-wide tunnel. We climbed up to the top tier of blue granite and cut out the lights to stand motionless and quiet. The temperature was 50 degrees, and the humidity was 90 percent. A stone and brick wall installed by Clemson University in the tunnel made light from the entrance appear as a pinpoint. Our reactions: "I could touch the dark, it was like velvet" . . . "I felt a vibration as if from the traffic overhead" . . . "I heard my heart" . . . "I heard a faint cathedral choir."

That was how Kevin Clarey, Taylor Watts, Les Parks, Dick Hunt, and I began our hike on the **Blue Ridge Railroad Historical Trail.** After 0.3 mi we walked back into daylight. (The tunnel is now sealed for safety reasons. Hiking is allowed on the remainder of the route.) From the tunnel area we followed the park road for 0.3 mi to cross a bridge over Cane Creek near the top of Isaqueena Falls. We took a sharp L up a steep path through rhododendron until we reached the old railroad bed.

The trail was devised and developed by Boy Scout Troop 219 and sponsored by the Baraccas Men's Class, Seneca Baptist Church in Seneca in 1976. Boy Scouts who hike the trail are eligible for the **Blue Ridge Railroad Trail** patch and medal. (Contact Executive Director, Blue Ridge Council, Boy Scouts of America, P.O. Box 6628, Station B, Greenville, SC 29606; (864) 233–8363.) The trail is listed in the National Register of Historic Railroad Trails.

We turned R and followed a red-arrow marker through a border of hardwoods, elderberry, grape, blackberry, and raspberry vines. We bypassed a caved-in cut at 0.5 mi. At 0.8 mi it was 90 yd L off the trail to a small opening of the 385-ft Middle Tunnel, which long ago filled with water. The trail skirted R on a slope with pine and oak and honeysuckle, where timber cutting has opened new roads. We reached the N end of the tunnel at 1.1 mi. Ahead we crossed a deep ravine on what is a good example of the contractor's plans to fill all ravines and hollows with earth and rock; an arched rock culvert is used for drainage without wooden trestles.

At 1.5 mi we entered a deep cut across the ridge and crossed a ravine. Logging roads altered the old railroad bed where we crossed small streams for a short distance. At 2.4 mi we reached the S end of the 616-ft Saddle Tunnel, of which only 200 ft were ever completed. It too is filled with water and fallen earth at the entrance. Les, a Boy Scout, was ahead of us, and we heard him scream, "It's a nickie! It's a nickie!" By the time we reached him, the rattlesnake had vanished.

We climbed steeply, following the logo signs, to a ridge with wildflowers and turned L at 2.5 mi. We detoured around a large hornets' nest and descended on a fresh dirt slide road made by a timber harvest of oaks, pines, and poplars. We reached the N end of Saddle Tunnel at 2.9 mi. Timber equipment had made the railroad bed wider as we passed through a deep cut at 3.1 mi. At 3.5 mi we turned off the lumber road and followed the logo signs onto the railroad bed for a section of undulating treadway. Cuts and ravines had not been completed at 3.5 mi, 3.7 mi, and 3.8 mi.

We reached graveled SR 174 at 3.9 mi, turned R, and followed SR 174 for 0.1 mi before turning R into a pine forest and the "white cliffs" exposed by the excavations. At 4.3 mi we went straight ahead at the fork and crossed a small stream at 4.4 mi. Back on the railroad bed, we crossed a timbered area where fallen pines covered the trail markers. After 0.1 mi we descended steeply again into a ravine, where mountain laurel, trailing arbutus, and gold star were prominent under the locust and poplar.

We climbed back to the railroad bed and noticed some mysterious rock shaped like a tombstone at 4.7 mi. Soon we ascended over the edge of a deep cut and descended steeply to reach a ravine at 4.9 mi. Twice we ascended steeply to the top of deep cuts, and we reached the top of the second at 5.2 mi. We descended and then ascended to an exceptionally deep cut where the trail was dangerously close to a precipice at 5.3 mi. At 5.5 mi we took a sharp L onto the railroad cut. After five more dips the trail leveled out, and we passed a private home on the L at 6.4 mi.

At 6.6 mi we came out in a clearing where large oaks were near the R border. (The NO TRESPASSING signs here do not apply to hikers.) At 6.8 mi we arrived at a dirt road near SR 181.

To reach this point, E terminus, from downtown Walhalla take SR 148, North Church Street, at jct with SC 28 for 1 mi to SC 174. Turn L on SC 174, and go 1.7 mi to SR 181. Turn L on SR 181 for 0.1 mi to R turn on dirt road. (For the complete **Blue Ridge Railroad Trail,** go to West Union on SC 28 and turn on SR 324, Torrington Street, at the S&W Grocery and Exxon Station. Cross the Southern railroad tracks toward the sawmill, and begin the foot trail on the L in the forest. It goes NW on the old railroad bed to Cane Creek, turns R, and comes back to Torrington Street to cross the bridge and return along the edge of a field to Brown's Lake at the dam. From here it follows the exit road to SC 183, North Catherine Street, and turns R. From SC 183 it turns L on SR 397 toward the Walhalla High School, where it takes a sharp R in the forest. After a L it crosses SR 397 again, passes the Walhalla Middle School, and follows the old railroad bed to a road. Here it turns R to SR 58, takes a L on SR 58 and goes to the jct of SR 181. At SR 181 it turns L, passes the grocery store and Exxon station on the R, crosses SR 174 and goes 0.1 mi to a dirt road on the R, referred to above at 6.8 mi. Total distance is approximately 5 mi. A shortcut on the trail from here is to take SR 174 N for 2.3 mi to the trail jct on the L.)

World of Energy (Oconee County)

Keowee-Toxaway Nature Trail

Length: 0.3 mi (0.5 km); **easy;** USGS Map: Old Pickens; trailhead: parking area.

For access to the trail from Pickens take SC 183 W, and from Walhalla take SC 183 N 10.5 mi to Lake Keowee. Follow signs to World of Energy. From Seneca take SC 130 N to SC 183 for 8 mi, and continue on SC 183-130 to the visitor center entrance on the R.

This trail is at the Duke Power Company's Keowee-Toxaway Complex, where the Oconee Nuclear Station began operation in 1973; the visitor center, the World of Energy, opened in 1969, and it offers an outstanding tour of seven exhibit areas explaining three energy sources: water, coal, and nuclear fission.

From the parking and picnic area, we descended on steps from the large entrance sign into the forest. Some plants were labeled; my team of hikers saw oak, dogwood, hickory, holly, sourwood, fern, bloodroot, wild hydrangea, squirrel cup, Hercules club, Oconee bell, Solomon's seal, sericea, wild azalea, five fingers, and Bowman's root. There were scenic views of Lake Keowee from the footbridges. The World of Energy is open Monday through Saturday, 9:00 A.M. to 5:00 P.M.; Sunday, 12:00 to 5:00 P.M.; it is closed on major holidays.

Information: World of Energy, 7812 Rochester Hwy., Seneca, SC 29678; (864) 885–4600 (800–777–1004 in N.C. and S.C. only).

SECTION 2
College Trails

Clemson University
(Oconee, Pickens, and Anderson Counties)

Information: College of Forest and Recreational Resources, Clemson University, Clemson, SC 29631; (864) 656–3215.

Indian Creek Forest Trail and Lawrence Trail

Length: 3.1 mi round-trip, combined (5 km); **easy;** USGS Map: Clemson; trailhead: parking area.

From the jct of US 76 and SC 122 in Clemson, I drove N on SC 133 for 3.8 mi to a Shell service station on the L (Lawrence Chapel was ahead on the L). I turned L, then R, into the 17,000-acre Clemson Experimental Forest. After 0.5 mi on a gravel road, I reached the **Indian Creek Forest Trail** parking and picnic area on the L.

I had a drink from the nearby springhouse and crossed Indian Creek into a hardwood forest, passed another spring by picnic tables, and followed a well-graded and clean trail. Mountain laurel and white pine were below the trail slope, Indian pipe and black cohosh were on the trail borders. At 0.4 mi I crossed a footbridge at a cove. A cemented stone resting bench was on the L. Twisted stalk and crested dwarf iris bloomed here. At 0.5 mi was a fork. To my L began the **Lawrence Trail,** and the **Indian Creek Forest Trail** continued on my R. I turned R, crossed a stone bridge at 0.6 mi, and passed through a small meadow to ascend on the ridge slope. At 0.9 mi I returned to the parking area.

I went back on the **Indian Creek Forest Trail** to the **Lawrence Trail** and followed upstream, crossed the stream in a cove with a mixed forest, and descended slightly to a L curve at 0.3 mi. Following the N side of the ridge, I saw signs of timber harvesting and an old logging road at 0.8 mi. Descending through a pine forest, I reached an old roadbed at 1.1 mi at a trail jct with the

Issaqueena Trail. (Straight ahead it is 2 mi one-way on the **Issaqueena Trail** to the dam.) I turned R to head 100 yards to Indian Creek and Willow Springs picnic area. I drank from the clean cement spring and walked up the road for 0.6 mi to the point of origin at Indian Creek parking area for a round-trip total of 2.2 mi. (From Willow Springs picnic area, it is 0.5 mi to the Lakeside area and another 0.5 mi to the Wildcat Creek rec area. After another 2 mi on the graveled road, there is a jct with SC 37-27; 0.5 mi farther is the falls area at the dam.)

Issaqueena Trail

Length: 4 mi round-trip (6.4 km); **easy;** USGS Map: Clemson; trailhead: Issaqueena Lake dam.

From the Indian Creek area I returned to the forest entrance and turned R toward the Issaqueena Lookout Tower on the R. After enjoying a panoramic view from the tower, I continued on the paved road for 0.4 mi to a gravel road on the R. From here to the dam it was 1.5 mi. I followed the well-designed trail up the E side of Lake Issaqueena through dense rhododendron and mountain laurel. At 0.4 mi I crossed a small stream, curved around from the cove, and saw a huge tulip poplar at 0.5 mi on the R, measuring 14 ft in circumference. The views of the lake from the trail were impressive. Maidenhair fern, crane-fly orchid, and crested dwarf iris grew in the damp coves. At 0.8 mi I crossed another small stream. By the edge of the lake a family of beaver had chiseled out a section of saplings to reroof their lodge. I turned R, toward the Indian Creek cove, at 1.6 mi. To my L were water lilies, and in the path were ladies tresses. Christmas ferns and wood betony grew on both sides of the trail. Wild azaleas and filberts were scattered in the open forest, and rose pink and bear's foot were prominent. At 1.9 mi I entered a stand of white pine and poplar to reach the jct with the **Lawrence Trail** at 2 mi. I backtracked.

On the way back the angle of the late afternoon sun made the lake look as if it were glazed with shimmering silver and pink flakes. It was an Emerson sunset, "the world through a prism."

Beaver Dam Trail and Firetower Trail

Length: 1.8 mi round-trip, combined (3.9 km); **easy;** USGS Map: Clemson; trailhead: Outdoor Lab parking area.

From US 76 Dick Hunt and I turned on SR 56 SW of Pendleton and drove 2.4 mi to the Clemson University Outdoor Lab. We met the lab director, Charlie White, who told us there are three campgrounds: Camp Sertoma, Jaycees Camp Hope, and Camp Logan. They all have dormitories or cottages, cafeterias, and recreational areas. "The facilities are open for rent to groups for overnight or day use," White said. Physical fitness and nature study are part of the lab's program.

From the parking area at the lab office, Kresge Hall, we entered a pine forest on a winding, graded, white-blazed trail. Common on the trail were dogwood, reindeer moss, hawthorn, and jessamine. At 0.3 mi we crossed a footbridge and at 0.4 mi reached a beaver dam. Growing in the area were switchcane, elderberry, papaw, devil's walking stick, fern, alder, cattail, joe-pye weed, trillium, cohosh, and wild azalea. At 0.6 mi we crossed a footbridge over a small stream and crossed another stream at 0.7 mi. Ascending we passed sassafras and goldenrod. At 0.8 mi we reached the paved entrance road, turned L, walked on the paved road for 0.25 mi, and turned R on the trail (not the old road). From here we ascended to the Clemson Lookout Tower at 1.1 mi. We could not climb the tower, but we tried our agility at rope swinging from a large red oak. We descended on a yellow-blazed trail, crossed a service road at 1.4 mi, entered Camp Logan at 1.5 mi, and returned to the parking area. The paved trails, which accommodate the handicapped, are between the camps and the lakeside.

Treaty Oak Trail

Length: 0.4 mi (0.6 km); **easy;** USGS Map: Clemson; trailhead: parking area.

From US 76 in Clemson, take SR 22 (0.5 mi W of the CN & W railroad track), go 1 mi to jct with SR 149 (SR 37 in Oconee County) and 0.7 mi to the parking area on the R, near the HOPEWELL sign. (If you visit from the Outdoor Lab on SR 65, go 0.6 mi to SR 122 on L. Follow SR 122 into Pickens County, where it becomes SR 155, and go 2 mi to SR 149, the CN & W railroad crossing. Turn L. The Treaty Oak parking area is on the R after 0.2 mi.)

Although the original treaty oak is dead and its location under Lake Hartwell, the DAR marker indicates that on November 28, 1785, the U.S. government signed its first treaty with the Cherokee Indian Nation under it (a treaty that was subsequently broken). Jess Grove of the College of Forest and Recreation Resources told me that the "signing was supposedly under a red oak."

Horticultural Gardens Trails

Length: 1.5 mi round-trip, combined (2.6 km); **easy;** USGS Map: Clemson; trailhead: parking area.

On US 76 in Clemson, slightly W of the National Guard Armory, turn S at the gardens sign on Perimeter Road.

We entered the garden at the parking area near the bright red caboose on the Southern Railroad. The list of what was in the gardens made us realize we would need at least half a day to see everything. (A full day would be better for a student of botany or horticulture.) We began on the trail to the R toward the picnic area, and read the labels along the way. We examined the new arboretum and continued on counterclockwise to the Garden of Meditation at 0.2 mi. We went upstream to the Spring House, Tea House, and Wildflower Collection. Backtracking, we chose to ascend on the **Nature Trail** through a hardwood forest. At 0.4 mi was a soil profile. Bird-watching stations followed. A sign read: THE FOREST IS THE POOR MAN'S OVERCOAT. At 0.6 mi we reached the Woody Ornamental Research Area and turned L to the Mini-Garden and Dwarf Vegetable Display. We lingered on the **Braille Trail,** amazed at the time and effort that must have gone into it. More than 80 Braille signs explained the cabin, gristmill, spring house, and plant life. At 0.9 mi we backtracked to the Hortitherapy Garden, circled the lake, and followed through the azalea and camellia trails to another arboretum at 1.3 mi. Ahead of us were floral displays for thousands of flowers. Continuing ahead we crossed a service road and entered the **Rhododendron Trail.** At 1.6 mi we returned to the parking area. The largest horticultural gardens in the South, the arboretums have at least 18 of the state's largest trees.

Coker College (Darlington County)

Kalmia Gardens Trail

Length: 1.6 mi (2.5 km); **easy;** USGS Map: Hartsville S; trailhead: parking area.

From the jct of SC 151 and US 15 (5th Street) in downtown Hartsville, go W on SC 151 (Carolina Avenue) for 2.5 mi to the entrance of the 30-acre Kalmia Gardens of Coker College on the R. The historic site was the home of Captain Thomas E. Hart, who settled in the area in 1817. A justice of the peace, educator, merchant, farmer, and postmaster, he died in 1842. Hartsville is named in his honor. The house and gardens are now owned and maintained by Coker College (1908), a small, private, coed, liberal arts, four-year institution. The Kalmia Gardens will be the gateway to the 700-acre Segacs-McKinnsy Heritage Preserve, owned by SCDNR Heritage Trust.

I followed the trail signs from the front of the house through thousands of azaleas and camellias under a magnificent canopy of mixed forest. At the first major fork I took the R, which led through a labyrinth of spur trails to the swamp at 0.4 mi. From this area I returned on a different trail to an observation deck. Banks of mountain laurel and galax were on the L. Cypress and gum were prominent on the R. After resting on one of the seats by a small pool in the center of the loop, observing the birds, and enjoying the tranquil scenery, I ascended to the lawn on the NE side of the house. An 89-step stairway at the edge of the flood plain to a ridge has been added to access a new trail. The gardens are open to the public daily during daylight hours without charge.

Information: Kalmia Gardens of Coker College, Coker College, 1624 W. Carolina Ave., Hartsville, SC 29550; (843) 383–8081.

Chapter VI
The Palmetto Trails

> The forest glimmers, mystic, mute,—
> A veiled enchantress...
>> Archibald Rutledge
>> "In a Forest," *Deep River*

This chapter has been added to provide you with a brief introduction to the state's longest dream trail, a mountains-to-sea trail, fast becoming a reality. Although I describe major passages already in existence in national forests, state parks, and a few private properties, I do not include the long passage currently under planning and development to connect the nearly 430-mi **Palmetto Trails.** General and updated information is available from Palmetto Trails, 1314 Lincoln St., Suite 213, Columbia, SC 29201-3154; (803) 771–0870; fax (803) 771–0590.

Named the **Palmetto Trails** (palmetto is the state tree), plans are to complete all passages by the year 2000. Its concept developed in 1994 within the private, nonprofit Palmetto Conservation Foundation, founded by Anne Springs Close of Fort Mill. She led in creating six land trusts and assisted the foundation in organizing the initial Palmetto Trails Committee. She serves on the Palmetto Trails board of directors. The trail will be "something that can unite us—the young, the old, children and families—walking together," she said to Maria Henson, editorial writer for the *Charlotte Observer.*

Unlike other border-to-border state trails, the **Palmetto Trails** has the advantage of more than $2.6 million seed money for the project. It has become "one of the few state trails in the country to be backed by the State Legislature and a spe-

317

cial proclamation of the Governor," said Thomas Dawson, the trail coordinator. In addition, there has been strong support by other conservationists, such as Senator Fritz Hollings; Congressman John Spratt; and South Carolina adjutant general Stan Spears. There has also been strong support from other government officials and departments such as the U.S. Forest Service; South Carolina Parks, Recreation and Tourism; and local county/city departments. Among some private organizations are Scouts and NCCC Americorp, the American Association of Retired Persons, and the Sierra Club. Large and small businesses are also supportive, with financial help or easements. Two examples are Santee Cooper and S.C. Electric and Gas Company. John S. Rainey of Santee Cooper has stated that the **Palmetto Trails** will "link two of our state's most valuable resources, our natural environment and our communities. This is community development in its finest form."

Except in the most NW part of the state, the trail's direction is NW to SE, the same as the state's major rivers. In the NW the trail connects with the state's famous and scenic **Foothills Trail** and the spectacular Mountain Bridge State Natural Area. From the **Foothills Trail** there is a connection to the **Bartram Trail,** which connects with the **Appalachian Trail** in Georgia (see Chapter I, Section 1). Ken Driggers, executive director of the foundation, has referred to the **Palmetto Trails** as "an extension to Maine."

The trail passes through 15 counties with sections designated as passages. Some areas of the proposed routing are Foothills Equestrian Nature Center, Cowpens National Battlefield, Pacolet Mills, Croft State Park, Sumter NF, Columbia (the capital city), Fort Jackson, Poinsett State Park, Manchester State Forest, Mill Creek Park, Santee NWR, Santee State Park, Lake Marian, Lake Moultrie, and Francis Marion NF. Examples of some of the first passages are 14-mi Sumter Passage in the Enoree Ranger District (see Chapter I, Section 3); the 15-mi Blue Wall Passage in Greenville County; the 14-mi Jackson Passage in

Richland County; the 16-mi High Hills of Santee Passage in Manchester State Forest and Poinsett State Park (see Chapter III, Section 3); the 27-mi Lake Moultrie Passage in Berkeley County; and the 47-mi Swamp Fox Passage in the Francis Marion Natural Forest, whose E edge is near the Atlantic Ocean (see Chapter I, section 4).

The **Palmetto Trails** provides general and specific precautions on hiking the passages. Among them are: be prepared with maps and directions; camp at only designated areas; notify someone of your plans with dates and locations; boil or purify natural water before drinking; determine the major hunting seasons (usually September through December, and April) and wear some blaze-orange clothing; stay on designated trails; take out all trash; be careful with campfires; and respect private property. Other precautions are to be aware of wet seasons, high temperature, areas with biting insects (particularly in swampy areas), and poisonous snakes and ivy.

It is also important that for you to know in advance if parts of the passage are for multiple use. (For example, the **Swamp Fox Trail** signage has considerable changes where bicycle and equestrian usage is restricted.)

I have hiked all the passages that were completed before February 1998 and will continue to hike the new ones as they develop. I found their diversity and potential recreational challenge an inspiration. I met others who shared my enthusiasm, and I was particularly impressed with the assistance provided by the staff of Palmetto Trails, specifically Thomas Dawson; and of Jim Schmid of Parks, Recreation and Tourism. I learned early to appreciate the teams of workers constructing the trail. During the fall of 1997 I met workers on the **Swamp Fox Trail** with muddy clothes and wet feet constructing logwalks, boardwalks, and bridges in swamps and mushy soil—all for the purpose that hikers to follow would have dry feet. Their muddy shoeprints and muddy handprints on new boardwalks were symbols of skill and hard work. My most unforgettable experience was the

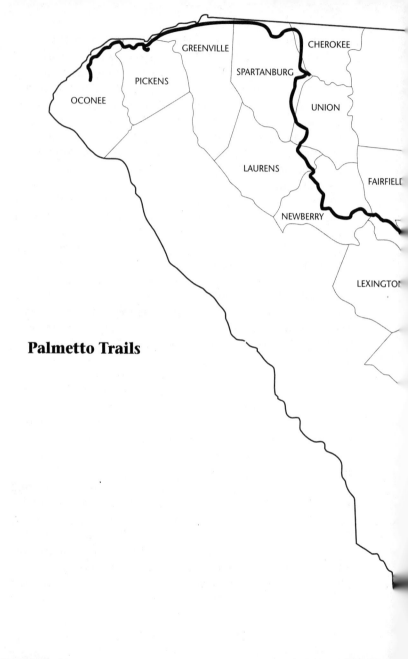

Palmetto Trails

crossing of Wadboo Creek Swamp. Think of the construction crew when you pass through.

Expect constant changes on the **Palmetto Trails.** There may be a need for some rerouting; seasons and weather alter the scenery; and new services will develop along the route. An example is that during my first hike of the Lake Moultrie Passage I did not stop at the Russellville Convenience Store (1.2 mi off the trail) in the hopes that a store would be open in Bonneau Beach. With an unexpected loss of supplies, I had to hike more than 2 mi N to Bonneau after arriving at the Canal Recreation Area. But what a surprise on my second hike in December 1997, when Bonneau Beach had a Handy Mart that included fried chicken and ice cream. Enjoy it while you can, because it is about 50 mi before you reach Awendaw.

Although I describe some of the established trails that existed before the **Palmetto Trails** (such as the **Swamp Fox Trail** E to W), the new and developing passages are not described here. **Palmetto Trails** will be publishing information on each passage and eventually a complete guidebook. From one brochure: "Imagine . . . the camaraderie of the trail with family and friends, travelling by foot, horseback or bicycle in sweet harmony with the elements."

Appendix

National and Regional Organizations and Clubs

American Birding Association
P.O. Box 6599
Colorado Springs, CO 80934
(800) 850–2473

American Camping Association, Inc.
5000 State Rd., 67 N
Martinsville, IN 46151
(317) 342–8456

American Hiking Society
P.O. Box 20160
Washington, DC 20041
(703) 255–9304

American Trails Inc.
1400 Sixteenth St., NW
#300
Washington, DC 20036
(202) 483–5611

Appalachian Trail Conference, Inc.
P.O. Box 807
Harpers Ferry, WV 25425
(304) 535–6331

Center for Marine Conservation, Inc.
1725 Desales St., NW
Suite 500
Washington, DC 20036
(202) 429–5609

Clean Water Fund
1320 Eighteenth St., NW
Washington, DC 20036
(202) 457–0336

Defenders of Wildlife
1101 14th St., NW
Washington, DC 20005
(202) 682–9400

Friends of the Earth
1025 Vermont Ave., NW
Washington, DC 20005
(202) 783–7400

National Audubon Society
700 Broadway
New York, NY 10003
(212) 977–3000

National Geographic Society
1145 17th St., NW
Washington, DC 20036
(202) 857–7000

National Parks and Conservation Association
1776 Massachusetts Ave., NW
Washington, DC 20036
(202) 223–6722

National Wildlife Federation
1400 Sixteenth St., NW
Washington, DC 20036
(202) 797–6800

Rails-to-Trails Conservancy
1400 Sixteenth St., NW
Suite 300
Washington, DC 20036
(202) 797–5400

The Nature Conservancy
1815 North Lynn St.
Arlington, VA 22209
(703) 841–5300

The Sierra Club
85 Second St., 2nd Floor
San Francisco, CA 94105
(415) 977–5500

The Wilderness Society
900 Seventeenth St., NW
Washington, DC 20006
(202) 833–2300

Wildlife Action, Inc.
P.O. Box 866
Mullins, SC 29574
(843) 464–8473

State and Nearby Area Citizens' Groups

Bartram Trail Society (Georgia)
Highway 106, Box 803
Scaly Mountain, NC 28755

Bartram Trail Society (North Carolina)
Route 3, Box 406
Sylva, NC 28723
(828) 293–9661

Boy Scouts of America
715 Betsy Dr.
(P.O. Box 144)
Columbia, SC 29210
(803) 750–9868

Foothills Trail Conference, Inc.
P.O. Box 3041
Greenville, SC 29602
(864) 467–9537

Georgia Appalachian Trail Club
P.O. Box 654
Atlanta, GA 30301
(404) 636–6495

Greenville Natural History
Association
P.O. Box 8164
Greenville, SC 29604

Girl Scouts of America
3920 Forest Dr.
Columbia, SC 29202
(803) 782–5133

Nantahala Appalachian Trail
Club
15 White Oak St., Apt. 3
Franklin, NC 28734
(828) 524–8759

Sierra Club Chapter
(South Carolina)
1314 Lincoln St.
Suite 211
P.O. Box 2388
Columbia, SC 29201
(803) 256–8487
Contact the chapter for ad-
dresses and telephone numbers
of the following groups:
Bachman (Columbia/Sumter
area)
Bartram (Greenville/Spartan-
burg area)
Cathcart (Hilton Head area)
Foothills (Northwest and Pick-
ins area)
Knob (Chester/Rock Hill area)

Lunz (Charleston area)
Pee Dee (Florence area)
Savannah River (North Augusta
area)
Winyah (Myrtle Beach area)

South Carolina Forestry
Association
4901 Broad River Rd.
Columbia, SC 21303
(803) 798–4170

South Carolina Wildlife
Federation
715 Woodrow
Columbia, SC 29205
(803) 771–4417

United States Govern-
ment Departments

Department of Agriculture
Forest Service
P.O. Box 96090
Washington, DC 20090
(202) 205–0957

Department of Agriculture
Regional Forester, Southern
Suite 800
1720 Peachtree Rd., NW
Atlanta, GA 30367
(404) 347–4177

Department of Commerce
National Marine Fisheries
Service, Regional Office
9721 Exec Center Dr.
St. Petersburg, FL 33702
(813) 570–5301

Department of the Interior
National Park Service
Interior Bldg.
P.O. Box 37127
Washington, DC 20013
(202) 208–4747

Department of the Interior
National Park Regional Director
75 Spring St., SW
Atlanta, GA 30303
(404) 331–5185

Department of the Interior
Fish and Wildlife Service, SE
Region
1875 Century Blvd.
Atlanta, GA 30345
(404) 679–4000

United States Congressional Committees

Committee on Agriculture, Nutrition and Forestry (Senate)
Room 328-A, Russell Bldg.
Washington, DC 20510
(202) 224–2035

Committee on Energy and
Natural Resources (Senate)
SD-364, Dirksen Bldg.
Washington, DC 20510
(202) 224–4971

Committee on Environment
and Public Works (Senate)
SD-410, Dirksen Bldg.
Washington, DC 20510
(202) 224–6176

Committee on Agriculture
(House)
Room 1301, Longworth House
Office Bldg.
Washington, DC 20515
(202) 225–2171

Committee on Interior and
Insular Resources (House)
Room 1324, Longworth House
Office Bldg.
Washington, DC 20515
(202) 225–2761

State Government Agencies

Appalachian Council of
Governments
50 Grand Ave.
Drawer 6668
Greenville, SC 29607
(864) 242–9733

Department of Agriculture
Wade Hampton Office Bldg.
Box 11280
Columbia, SC 29211
(803) 734–2210

Department of Health and
    Environmental Control
Marion Sims Bldg.
2600 Bull St.
Columbia, SC 29201
(803) 734–4880

Department of Parks, Recreation
    and Tourism
Edgar Brown Bldg.
1205 Pendleton St.
Columbia, SC 29201
(803) 734–0122

Forestry Commission
Box 21707
Columbia, SC 29221
(803) 896–8800

Ocean & Coastal Resource
    Management
1362 McMillan Ave.
Suite 400
Charleston, SC 29405
(843) 744–5838

Land, Water, and Conservation
    Division, DNR
2221 Devine St.
Suite 222
Columbia, SC 29205
(803) 734–9100

Wildlife and Marine Resources
    Department, DNR
Dennis Bldg.
P.O. Box 167
Columbia, SC 29202
(803) 734–3888

State and Adjoining
National Forests

Supervisor's Office (Marion and
    Sumter NFs)
4931 Broad River Rd.
Columbia, SC 29210
(803) 561–4000

Francis Marion National Forest
    Wambaw District
South Pinckney St.
P.O. Box 788
McClellanville, SC 29458
(843) 887–3257

Witherbee District
2421 Witherbee Rd.
Cordesville, SC 29434
(843) 336–3248

Sumter National Forest
Andrew Pickens District
112 Andrew Pickens Circle
Mountain Rest, SC 29664
(864) 638–9568

Enoree District
Route 1, Box 179
Whitmire, SC 29178
(803) 276–4810

Long Cane District
810 Buncombe St.
Edgefield, SC 29824
(803) 637–5396

Chattahoochee National Forest
Tallulah Ranger District
1755 Cleveland Highway
Gainesville, GA 30501
(770) 536–0541

Nantahala National Forest
Highlands Ranger District
2010 Flat Mountain Rd.
Highlands, NC 28741
(828) 526–3765

River Recreation Teams

The following white-water outfitters provide rafting and canoeing on the Chattooga River.
For other information contact

America Outdoors, P.O. Box
10847, Knoxville, TN 37939;
(423) 558–3597.

Chattooga Rent-A-Raft
50 Executive Park S
Suite 5010
Atlanta, GA 30329
(404) 325–7155

Chattooga River Adventures
14546-B Long Creek Hwy.
Mt. Rest, SC 29664
(800) UGO–RAFT

Nantahala Oudoor Center, Inc.
13077 Highway 19W
Bryson City, NC 23713
(828) 488–2175
Rafting: (800) 232–7238
Catalog: (800) 367–3521
Instruction: (888) 662-1662,
    ext. 6000

Southeastern Expeditions
50 Executive Park S
Suite 5016
Atlanta, GA 30329
(800) 868–7238

Wildwater Ltd.
P.O. Box 309
Long Creek, SC 29658
(800) 451–9972

Trail Guide Sales

For a list of bookstores or trail-supply stores that sell *Hiking South Carolina Trails,* write or call The Globe Pequot Press, P.O. Box 833, Old Saybrook, CT 06475; (800) 243–0495 or (800) 962–0973

Canoe and Kayak Trails

The following outfitters provide canoe and kayak adventures in the coastal area.

Blackwater Adventures (Pinopolis); (843) 761–1850

Carolina Heritage Outfitters (Canadys); (843) 563–5051

Cassina Point Outfitters (Edisto Island (843) 869–2535

Outside Hilton Heat (Shelter Cove); (843) 686–6996

Outside Program (Middleton Place); (843) 556–0500

The Kayak Farm (St. Helena Island); (843) 838–2008

Tullifinny Joe's (Coosawatchi); (843) 726–4545

W3 Outfitters (Charleston); (843) 577–2633

Black River Expeditions (Georgetown); (843) 546–4840

Coastal Expeditions (Sullivan's Island); (843) 884–7684

Tidewater Trails (Georgetown); (843) 546–2481

General Index

Abbeville County, 67, 185
Aiken County, 197, 204, 245, 292
Aiken State Park, 197
Anderson County, 142, 178, 204, 292, 311
Andrew Jackson State Park, 182
Andrew Pickens Ranger District, 17, 19
Asbury Hills United Methodist Camp, 283

Baker Creek State Park, 184
Bamberg County, 205
Barnwell County, 198
Barnwell State Park, 198
Beaufort County, 217, 291
Berkeley County, 93, 223
Bethelwoods Camp, 286
Big Bend Trail, 33
Bluff Unit, 136
Brickhouse Campground, 83
Buck Hall Recreation Area, 13, 98
Bull Sluice, 18, 28
Bull's Island, 128
Burrells Ford Campground, 17, 32, 33

Caesars Head State Park, 146, 159

Calhoun Falls State Park, 185
Camden, 246
Campobello-Gramling School Outdoor Laboratory, 242
Camp Thunderbird, 287
Canal Recreation Area, 98
Cape Romain National Wildlife Refuge, 127
Carolina Sandhills National Wildlife Refuge, 133
Cassidy Bridge Hunt Camp, 17
Cayce, 279
Century B Park, 267
Champion International Corp., 301
Charleston, 121, 211, 253
Charleston County, 93, 121, 127, 211, 226, 237, 253, 293
Charles Towne Landing State Park, 211
Chattahoochee National Forest, 20
Chattooga River, 17, 19
Chattooga River Information Station, 18
Chau Ram Park, 242
Cheraw State Park, 143
Cherokee County, 119, 122, 152
Cherry Hill Recreation Area, 23
Cherry Park, 272

330

Chester, 183, 253
Chester County, 186, 193, 256
Chesterfield County, 133, 224
Chester State Park, 186
Civilian Conservation Corps
    (CCC), 169, 171, 174, 179,
    191
Clarendon County, 135, 208,
    239
Clemson University, 311
Cleveland Park, 265
Coker College, 315
Colleton County, 213, 215,
    278, 300
Colleton State Park, 213
Columbia, 257
Columbia Canal and Riverfront
    Park, 259
Commissioners Rock, 22
Congaree Swamp National
    Monument, 117
Cowpens National Battlefield,
    119
Croft State Park, 146

Darlington, 260
Darlington County, 224, 260,
    315
Devils Fork State Park, 148
Dillon County, 220
Dingle Pond Unit, 137
Dorchester County, 215, 288,
    298
Drawbar Cliffs, 29, 45

Dreher Island State Park, 182,
    187
Duke Power Company, 148,
    193, 310
Duncan Park, 275

Earlwood Park, 258
Eastatoe Gorge Natural Area, 42
Edgefield County, 67
Edgefield Ranger District, 67
Edisto Beach State Park,
    143–45, 213
Edisto Memorial Gardens, 269
Ellicott Rock Wilderness Area,
    13, 17, 24, 171
Enoree Ranger District, 83
Eutaw Springs Battlefield Site,
    207

Fairfield County, 83, 192, 280
Fell Hunt Camp, 79
Fewell Park, 272
Florence, 261
Florence County, 201, 208, 261
Foothills Trail Conference, 29,
    30
Fort Sumter National Monu-
    ment, 121
Fortune Springs Park, 281
Fort Watson, 136, 207
Foster Park, 277
Francis Beidler Forest, 288
Francis Marion National Forest,
    11, 93

Georgetown County, 219
Givhans Ferry State Park, 143, 215
Granby Gardens Park, 280
Greenville, 171, 176, 265
Greenville County, 29, 159, 231, 240, 265, 267, 283
Greenwood County, 67, 126, 191
Greer, 267
Guignard Park, 279
Guilliard Lake Scenic Area, 114

Hampton County, 234
Hanging Rock Battle Monument, 224
Harbison Recreation Center, 289
Hartwell Lake (Lake Hartwell), 142
Hell Hole Bay Wilderness Area, 93
Hickory Knob State Resort Park, 179, 189
Hilton Head Island, 291
Historic Camden Visitor Center, 248
Hitchcock Woods, 245, 292
Hopeland Gardens, 245
Horry County, 221, 299
Horsepasture River Gorge (N.C.), 29, 39
Hunting Island State Park, 217
Huntington Beach State Park, 219

Isaqueena Falls, 171

Jackson County (N.C.), 29
Jasper County, 138, 236
Jeffries Creek Park, 262
Jones Gap State Park, 29, 159

Keowee-Toxaway State Park, 149
Kershaw County, 246
King Creek Falls, 33
Kings Mountain National Military Park, 122
Kings Mountain State Park, 152

Lake Greenwood State Park, 191
Lake Hartwell State Park, 158
Lake Jocassee, 17, 29, 39, 148, 171
Lake Keowee, 45, 149
Lake Murray, 188
Lake Wateree State Park, 192
Lancaster County, 179, 224
Landsford Canal State Park, 193
Laurel Fork Creek Falls, 31
Laurens County, 83, 230, 241
Laurens County Park, 241
Lee County, 199
Lee State Park, 143, 145, 199
Lexington County, 257, 279, 289, 302, 304
Lick Fork Lake Recreation Area, 67
Little Pee Dee State Park, 220

Long Cane Ranger District, 67
Long Cane Scenic Area, 67, 78
Lucas Park, 263
Lynches River State Park, 201

Magnolia Plantation and
    Gardens, 293
Mauldin City Park, 268
Maxcy Gregg Park, 258
McCormick County, 67, 139,
    180, 189
Middleton Place, 298
Midway Hunt Camp, 78
Modoc Campground, 141
Molly's Rock Picnic Area, 91
Mountain Bridge Recreation and
    Wilderness Area, 29
Museum of York County, 243
Myrtle Beach State Park, 152,
    221

Nantahala National Forest, 20,
    29, 35
Nature Conservancy, 12
Newberry County, 83, 187
Ninety Six National Historic
    Site, 126

Oconee County, 17, 19, 142,
    148, 158, 171, 242, 305,
    310, 311
Oconee State Park, 28, 29, 30,
    145, 171
Old Santee Canal State Park,
    223

Orangeburg, 269
Orangeburg County, 206, 269

Palmetto Islands County Park,
    237
Paris Mountain State Park, 143,
    174
Parsons Mountain Lake
    Recreation Area, 75
Peachtree Rock Preserve, 302
Pickens County, 19, 142, 149,
    179, 311
Pleasant Ridge County Park,
    240
Pocotaligo Swamp Park, 239
Poinsett State Park, 143, 146,
    202

Raven Cliff Falls, 29, 48
Redcliffe State Historic Site, 204
Reedy River Falls Historic Park,
    265
Richland County, 117, 195,
    257, 289
Riverbanks Zoological Park, 304
Rivers' Bridge State Park, 146,
    205
Rock Hill, 271
Rose Bud Picnic Area, 17
Rose Hill Plantation State Park,
    146, 177

Sadlers Creek State Park, 178
Saluda County, 67
Sand Hills State Forest, 224

Santee Coastal Reserve, 226
Santee National Wildlife
    Refuge, 135, 207
Santee State Resort Park, 206
Sassafras Mountain, 45
Savannah Coastal Refuges, 138
Sesquicentennial State Park,
    143, 195
Sewee Shell Mound, 93
Sidney Park, 260
Simpsonville City Park, 273
Sloan Bridge Picnic Area, 18,
    24
South Carolina Nature
    Conservancy, 302
Spartanburg, 273
Spartanburg County, 146, 242,
    273
Stumphouse Mountain Tunnel
    Park, 172, 305
Sugar Loaf Recreation Area, 225
Summers Memorial Park, 270
Sumter, 275
Sumter County, 202, 208, 275
Sumter National Forest, 11, 21,
    171
Swan Lake Gardens, 276

Table Rock State Park, 29, 45,
    145, 179
Tallulah Ranger District Office,
    19
The Battery, 94
Thurmond Lake, 20, 139, 184
Tillman Sand Ridge WMA, 235

Timrod Park, 260, 263
Transylvania County (N.C.), 29
Treaty Oak Area, 313
Tryon Park, 268
Tyger Ranger District, 83
Union, 173, 277
Union County, 83, 177, 277
Upper and Lower Summer-
    house Ponds, 132
Upper Whitewater Falls (N.C.),
    171

Virginia Acres Park, 246

Walhalla National Fish Hatch-
    ery, 17, 25, 34, 171
Walterboro, 278
Walterboro-Colleton
    Recreation Center, 278
Wambaw Creek Wilderness
    Area, 93
Wambaw Ranger District, 13,
    95
Wambaw Swamp and Little
    Wambaw Swamp Wilder-
    ness Areas, 93
Webb Wildlife Center, 234
Westvaco, 300
West Columbia, 279
Whetstone Road Base Camp, 18
Whitten Center, 230
Wildcat Wayside State Park, 231
Wildlife Management Areas,
    231
Willis Knob Horse Camp, 18

Winnsboro, 280
Witherbee Ranger District, 94,
    95
Woodall Shoals, 17
Woods Bay State Park, 208
Woods Ferry Recreation Area,
    92
World of Energy, 310
Wylie Park, 256

Yellow Branch Picnic Area, 18,
    29
York County, 122, 152, 243,
    271, 286, 287
Young Adults Conservation
    Corps (YACC), 12
Youth Conservation Corps
    (YCC), 12

Trail Index

Trails labeled with a (B) are bi-cycle trails, (E) equestrian trails, (P) for the physically handi-capped, (R) river trails, and (V) vehicular trails. All other trails are (H) for hiking, walking, or jogging. Some trails are multi-ple use. All (B)(E) and (P) trails are (H) trails also. The highway bicycle trails would be an ex-ception.

Andrew Jackson Nature Trail,
    183
Animal Forest Trail, 212 (P)
Artesian Nature Trail, 199
Asbury Trail, 285
Ashepoo River Trail, 3 (R)

Bad Creek Trail, 22
Baker Creek Walking Trail, 185
Barnwell Lake Trail, 198
Bartram Trail, 19
Battery Warren Trail, 94
Bearcamp Creek Trail, 28
Beaver Dam Trail, 313
Beaver Pond Nature Trail, 221
Beaver Run Nature Trail, 189
Bethelwoods Nature Trail, 286
Beech Ridge Trail, 159
Big Bend Trail, 23
Bill Kimball Trail, 167
Billy Dreher Nature Trail, 188
Black River Trail, 3 (R)
Blue Ridge Railroad Historical
    Trail, 307
Blue Trail, 284

Bluff Trail, 118
Boardwalk Trail, 118 (P), 220
Brissy Ridge Trail, 175
Bull's Island Wildlife Trail, 131
Bull Sluice Trail, 28
Buncombe Trail, 83 (E and H)

Caesars Head Trail, 161
Campobello-Gramling Trail, 243
Camp Thunderbird Nature Trail, 287
Caney Fork Falls Trail, 186
Carolina Connector Trail, 1 (B)
Carolina Woods Walk, 295
Carrick Creek Trail, 182
Cedar Bluff Trail, 186
Cedar Spring Cycle Trail, 75 (B)
Central Trail, 2 (B)
Century B Trail, 267
Charles Towne Garden Trails, 212
Chattooga Trail, 19, 20
Chauga Nature Trail, 242
Cherokee Interpretive Trail, 150
Cherry Hill Nature Trail, 23
Cherry Park Trail, 272 (B)
Cistern Trail, 138
Clarks Hill Trail, 140
Cleveland Park Trail, 266 (B)
Coastal Trail, 2
Colleton Trail, 278
Columbia Canal Trail, 259 (B)
Congaree and Cooper Rivers Trail, 3 (R)

Coquina Nature Trail, 209
Cowpens Battlefield Trail, 120 (P)
Creek Trail, 230
Croft Jogging Trail, 147
Cypress Swamp Nature Trail, 213

Despartes Island Nature Trail, 192
Dingle Pond Trail, 137
Duncan Park Trail, 275

Earlwood Park Trail, 258
Eastatoe Gorge Trail, 42
East Fork Trail, 25
Edisto Gardens Trails, 270
Edisto Nature Trail, 300
Edisto River Canoe and Kayak Trail, 3 (R)
Ellicott Rock Trail, 22, 26
Enoree River Trail, 3 (R)
Explorer Trail, 230

Fairforest Creek Trail, 146
Fewell Park Trail, 272
Firetower Trail, 313
Florence Beauty Trail, 262 (V and H)
Foothills Trail, 29, 174
Fork Mountain Trail, 26
Fortune Springs Trail, 281
Fosters Mill Trail, 146
Foster Park Trail, 277
Four Holes Swamp Trail, 288 (P)

Gold Nugget Trail, 153
Gold Trail, 284
Granby Gardens Nature Trail, 280
Greenwood Lake Nature Trail, 192
Guignard Park Trail, 280
Guilliard Lake Trail, 114

Hanging Rock Battle Trail, 224
Harbison Trails, 290 (B and P)
Hartwell Lake Beaver Trail, 142
Hilliard Falls Spur Trail, 38
Hilltop Trail, 203
Historic Camden Trail, 249
Hitchcock Woods Trails, 293 (E and H)
Hopeland Gardens Trail, 246 (P)
Horn Creek Trail, 68
Horticultural Gardens Trails, 314 (P)
Hospital Rock Trail, 170
Huger Loop Trail, 93
Indian Creek Forest Trail, 311
Indian Mound Trail, 214
Ion Swamp Trail, 93
Isaqueena Falls Trail, 306
Issaqueena Trail, 312

Jeffries Creek Trail, 262
Jericho Trail, 93 (E and H), 111
Jungle Trail, 197

Kalmia Gardens Trail, 315

Keowee-Toxaway Nature Trail, 310
Kerrigan Nature Trail, 220
King Creek Falls Trail, 27
Kings Mountain Battlefield Trail, 123 (P)
Kings Mountain Hiking Trail, 124, 153
Kingsnake Trail, 118

Lake Johnson Loop Trail, 147 (E and H)
Lake Placid Trail, 176
Landsford Canal and Nature Trail, 194
Laurel Group Trail, 203
Laurel Hill Wildlife Trail, 138 (V and H)
Laurens County Park Nature Trail, 241
Lawrence Trail, 311
Lick Fork Lake Trail, 68
Lighthouse Nature Trail, 218
Limestone Nature Trail, 207
Little Pee Dee River Trail, 3 (R)
Living on the Land Trail, 76
Long Cane Horse and Hiking Trail, 76 (E and H)
Lucas Park Trail, 263
Lupine Nature Trail, 206

Magnolia Garden Trails, 295 (P)
Magnolia Wildlife Trail, 297
Marsh Boardwalk Trail (Hunting Island), 218

Marsh Trail, 239
Marshland Trail, 229
Mauldin Park Trail, 269 (P)
Maxcy Gregg Park Trail, 258
Middleton Place Garden Walk,
    299 (P)
Mill Creek Pass Trail, 176
Mill Pond Nature Trail, 209
Modoc Nature Trail, 141
Modoc Walking Trail, 141
Molly's Rock Trail, 91

Natural Bridge Nature Trail, 151
Naturaland Trust Trail, 48
Nature Island Trail, 239
Ninety Six History Trail, 126 (P)
Northern Crescent Trail, 2 (B)

Oakpinolly Nature Trail, 208
Oak Ridge Trail, 118
Oconee Bells Nature Trail, 149
Oconee Trail, 172
Old Fort Loop Trail, 132
Old Santee Canal Trail, 223 (P)
Old Walled City Trail, 254 (B
    and P)
Old Waterwheel Trail, 172
Osprey Trail, 239
Overmountain Victory Trail, 124

Palmetto Trails, 317
Parsons Mountain Cycle Trail,
    75 (B)
Parsons Mountain Trails, 76

Peachtree Rock Trail, 302
Pine Grove Trail, 179
Pine Tree Hill Trail, 249
Pinnacle Mountain Trail, 181
Pleasant Ridge Nature Trail,
    240
Pocotaligo Swamp Trail, 240

Raven Cliff Falls Trail, 48
Raven Rock Hiking Trail, 151
Redcliffe Trail, 204
Reedy River Falls Trail, 266
Rhododendron Trail, 315
Rim of the Gap Trail, 159
River Birch Trail, 274
River Bluff Nature Trail, 216
River Trail, 118
Rocky Gap Trail, 18
Rocky Ridge Trail, 146
Rose Hill Nature Trail, 178

Saluda River Trail, 3 (R)
Sandhill Nature Trail (Lee State
    Park), 201
Sandhill Nature Trail
    (Sesquicentennial State
    Park), 195
Sandpiper Pond Nature Trail,
    220
Santee and Wambaw Rivers
    Trails, 3 (R)
Santee Coastal Reserve Nature
    Trails, 229
Santee River Trail, 3 (R)

Santee Wildlife Trail, 136
Savannah River Run Trail, 2 (B)
Savannah River Swamp Trail,
    236
Savannah River Trail, 3 (R)
Sculptured Oak Nature Trail,
    222
Sesqui Physical Fitness Trail,
    196
Sewee Shell Mound Interpretive
    Trail, 93
Sheepshead Ridge Loop Trail,
    132
Sidney Park Trail, 260
Simpsonville Nature Trail, 273
    (P)
Spoon Auger Trail, 27
Stagecoach Trail, 202
Sugar Loaf Mountain Trail, 225
Sulphur Springs Loop Trail, 175
Swamp Fox Trail (Francis Mar-
    ion National Forest), 93, 95
Swan Lake Trails, 276

Table Rock Trail, 180
Tamassee Knob Trail, 28

Tate's Trail, 134
Timrod Park Trail, 263
Treaty Oak Trail, 313
Turkey Creek Trail (North), 70
Turkey Creek Trail (South), 71
Turkey Ridge Trail, 189
Tryon Park Trail, 268
Tyger River Trail, 3 (R)

Wagon Camp Trail, 286
Walter Ezell Trail, 2 (B)
Washo Boardwalk Trail, 229
Webster Woods Trail, 271
Weston Lake Trail, 118
Wildcat Nature Trail, 231
Wild Mint Trail, 184
Williams Park Trail, 260
Willis Knob Trail, 18
Winding Stairs Trail, 24
Woodland Pond Trail, 134
Woods Ferry Trail, 92
Wrights Bluff Nature Trail, 136
Wylie Park Trail, 256

Yellow Branch Nature Trail, 28
York County Nature Trail, 244

About the Author

Allen de Hart has been hiking, designing, and constructing and writing about trails since he was a teenager. In his home state of Virginia, news reporters call him the hiker's guru. He has hiked more than 12,500 different trails and over 33,000 miles in forty-six states and eighteen foreign countries. He completed the Appalachian Trail in 1978, the Buckeye Trail in 1981, and the Florida Trail in 1988. A graduate of the Adjutant General's Corps of the U.S. Army and with graduate degrees in history from the University of Virginia, he is an emeritus professor of history in the Social and Behavioral Science Department at Louisburg College in North Carolina, and advisor to the College president in Cultural Affairs. He also teaches courses in hiking and backpacking and conducts nationwide hiking tours. He is founder of two botanical gardens, one in Virginia and one in North Carolina.

Books he has authored include *Hiking and Backpacking; North Carolina Hiking Trails; Hiking the Old Dominion: The Trails of Virginia; Hiking and Backpacking Basics; Hiking the Mountain State: The Trails of West Virginia; South Carolina Trails; Monongahela National Forest Hiking Guide* (with Bruce Sundquist); *Adventuring in Florida, the Georgia Sea Islands and the Okefenokee Swamp, Trails of the Triangle,* and *Trails of the Triad.* He has also written numerous articles on specific trails and prepared special features on the Appalachian Trail hut system, hiking and rafting in the Grand Canyon, canoeing in the Okefenokee Swamp, and climbing the peaks of Colorado and California. He served for fourteen years on the board of directors of the North Carolina Trails Committee in the Division of Parks and Recreation.

In the early 1940s, while living in Greenville, he hiked the trails in he Chattooga River area. He hiked the 875-mile North Carolina Mountains to Sea Trail with Alan Householder in 1997. From this journey across the state, he is preparing a guidebook to be published in the spring of 1999.